EIXAMPLE
Pages 66–75
Street Finder maps 3,4

0 metres 750

0 yards 750

CATALONIA
Pages 90–111

FURTHER AFIELD
Pages 84–89

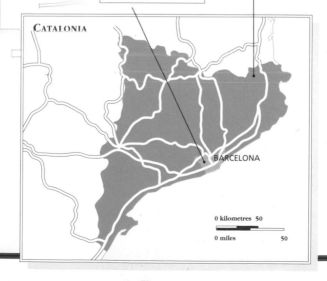

CATALONIA

Eixample

BARCELONA

0 kilometres 50

0 miles 50

DK TRAVEL GUIDES

BARCELONA
& CATALONIA

DORLING KINDERSLEY *TRAVEL GUIDES*

BARCELONA
& CATALONIA

Main contributor: ROGER WILLIAMS

DORLING KINDERSLEY, INC.
LONDON • NEW YORK • SYDNEY • MOSCOW • DELHI
www.dk.com

DORLING KINDERSLEY, INC.

www.dk.com

PROJECT EDITOR Catherine Day
ART EDITORS Carolyn Hewitson, Marisa Renzullo
EDITORS Elizabeth Atherton, Felicity Crowe
DESIGNER Suzanne Metcalfe-Megginson
MAP CO-ORDINATOR David Pugh

MAIN CONTRIBUTOR
Roger Williams

MAPS
Jane Hanson, Phil Rose, Jennifer Skelley (Lovell Jones Ltd),
Gary Bowes, Richard Toomey (ERA-Maptec Ltd)

PHOTOGRAPHERS
Max Alexander, Mike Dunning, Heidi Grassley, Alan Keohane

ILLUSTRATORS
Stephen Conlin, Claire Littlejohn, Maltings Partnership,
John Woodcock

Reproduced by Colourscan, Singapore
Printed and bound by L. Rex Printing Company Limited, China

First America n Edition, 1999
2 4 6 8 10 9 7 5 3

Published in the United States by DK Publishing, Inc.,
95 Madison Avenue, New York, New York 10016

Reprinted with revisions 2000

Library of Congress Cataloging-in-Publication Data

Barcelona, -- 1st American ed.
p. cm. -- (Dorling Kindersley Travel Guide)
ISBN 0-7894-4620-0
.1. Barcelona & Catalonia (Spain) Guidebooks. I. DK Publishing, Inc.
II. Series.
DP402.B24B253 1999
914.6'720483 -- dc21   99-23491
                                                            CIP

**The information in every
Dorling Kindersley Travel Guide is checked annually**.
Every effort has been made to ensure that this book is as up-to-date as
possible at the time of going to press. Some details, however, such as
telephone numbers, opening hours, prices, gallery hanging arrangements
and travel information are liable to change. The publishers cannot accept
responsibility for any consequences arising from the use of this book.
We value the views of our readers very highly. Please write to: Senior
Managing Editor, Dorling Kindersley Travel Guides, Dorling Kindersley,
9 Henrietta Street, London WC2E 8PS.

THROUGHOUT THIS BOOK, FLOORS ARE NUMBERED IN ACCORDANCE
WITH LOCAL CATALAN USAGE.

◁ **Previous pages: Bench, Parc Güell, Barcelona; Miravet on the Riu Ebre, southern Catalonia**

CONTENTS

INTRODUCING BARCELONA AND CATALONIA

**Jaume I, "El Conquistador",
ruler of Catalonia 1213–76**

**One of the many popular cafés in
Barcelona's redeveloped Old Port**

BARCELONA AREA BY AREA

The small, whitewashed town of Cadaqués on the Costa Brava

Pa amb tomàquet – bread rubbed with tomato, garlic and olive oil

Spectacular stained-glass roof of the Palau de la Música Catalana

CATALONIA

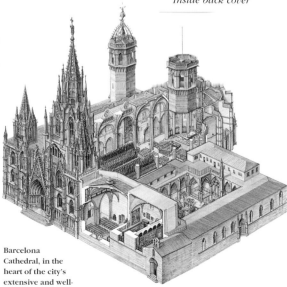

Barcelona Cathedral, in the heart of the city's extensive and well-

HOW TO USE THIS GUIDE

HIS GUIDE has expert recommen-
dations and detailed practical
information to enrich any visit to
Barcelona and Catalonia. *Introducing
Barcelona and Catalonia* puts the area
in geographical, historical and cultural
context. *Barcelona and Catalonia* is
a six-chapter guide to important sights:
Barcelona at a Glance highlights the
city's top attractions; *Old Town,
Eixample* and *Montjuïc* explore Barcelona's central districts in more detail;
Further Afield views sights outside the
city centre; and *Catalonia* delves into
the region's four provinces. *Travellers'
Needs* covers hotels, restaurants and
entertainment. The *Survival Guide*
provides vital practical information.

BARCELONA AND CATALONIA

The region is divided into
five sightseeing areas – the
central districts of Barcelona,
sights outside the centre,
and those beyond the city.
Each area chapter opens
with an introduction and a
list of sights covered. Central
districts have a Street-by-
Street map of a particularly
interesting part of the area.
The sights further afield
have a regional map.

Sights at a Glance lists
the area's key sights
(great buildings, art
galleries, museums and
churches) by category.

Each chapter of *Barcelona
and Catalonia* has a different
colour-coded thumb tab.

Locator maps show where
you are in relation to other
parts of Barcelona or Spain.

1 Area Map of the city
*Sights are numbered
and located on a map, with
Metro stations where help-
ful. The sights are also
shown on the* Barcelona
Street Finder *on pp156–65.*

2 Street-by-Street map
*The area shaded pink
on the* Area Map *is shown
here in greater detail with
accurate drawings of all
the buildings.*

A suggested route for
a walk covers the more
interesting streets in the area.

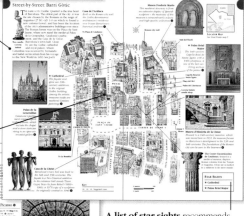

A list of star sights recommends
places no visitor should miss.

**3 Detailed information
on each sight**
*The sights listed at the start
of the section are described
individually and follow the
numbering on the* Area Map.
*A key to symbols summariz-
ing practical information is
shown on the back flap.*

4 Introduction to Catalonia

The chapter on Catalonia has its own introduction, providing an overview of the history and character of the region. The area covered is highlighted on the map of Spain shown on page 91. The chapter explores Catalonia's rich historical, cultural and natural heritage, from the monasteries of Montserrat and Poblet to Tarragona's casteller *festivals, from the sandy beaches of the Costa Daurada to the snowy peaks of the Pyrenees.*

5 Pictorial Map

This gives an illustrated overview of the whole region. All the sights covered in this chapter are numbered, and the network of major roads is marked. There are also useful tips on getting around the region by bus and train.

6 Detailed information on each sight

All the important cities, towns and other places to visit are described individually. They are listed in order following the numbering given on the Pictorial Map. Within each town or city there is detailed information on important buildings and other sights.

Stars indicate the best features and works of art.

The Visitors' Checklist provides a summary of the practical information you will need to plan your visit.

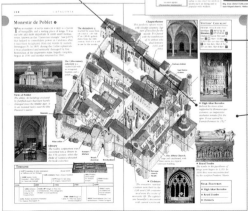

7 The top sights

These are given two or more full pages. Historic buildings are dissected to reveal their interiors. For larger historic sites, all the important buildings are labelled to help you locate those that most interest you.

INTRODUCING
BARCELONA
AND CATALONIA

Putting Barcelona and Catalonia on the Map

C ATALONIA LIES in the northeastern corner of the
Iberian Peninsula and occupies six per cent of Spain.
Barcelona, its capital, lies almost exactly halfway along
its coastline, which in turn stretches a quarter of the
way down Spain's Mediterranean seaboard. Barcelona
is the main bridging point to
the Catalan-speaking
Balearic Islands.

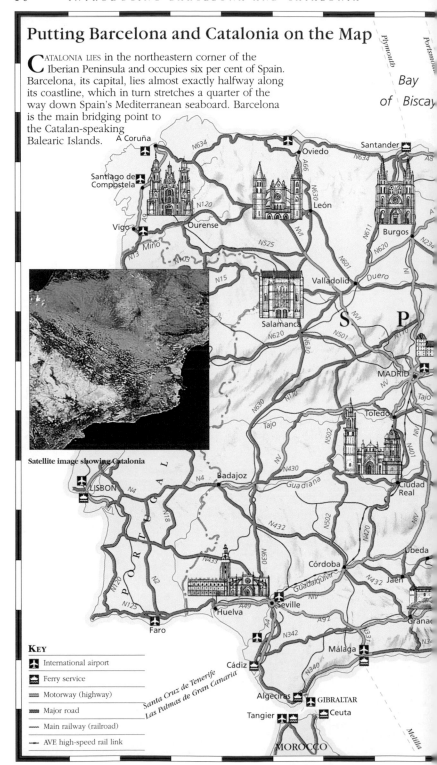

Satellite image showing Catalonia

KEY

✈	International airport
⛴	Ferry service
▬	Motorway (highway)
▬	Major road
—	Main railway (railroad)
➤	AVE high-speed rail link

◁ *Paral·lel any 1930*, a portrait of one of Barcelona's main avenues in 1930 by Emili Bosch Roger (1894–1980)

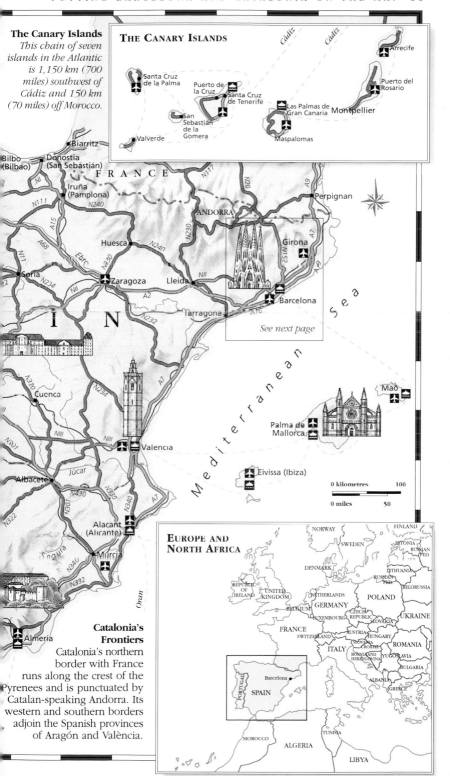

The Canary Islands
This chain of seven islands in the Atlantic is 1,150 km (700 miles) southwest of Cádiz and 150 km (70 miles) off Morocco.

THE CANARY ISLANDS

Santa Cruz de la Palma

Puerto de la Cruz

Santa Cruz de Tenerife

San Sebastián de la Gomera

Valverde

Las Palmas de Gran Canaria

Maspalomas

Arrecife

Puerto del Rosario

Cádiz

Cádiz

Montpellier

Biarritz

Bilbo (Bilbao)

Donostia (San Sebastián)

F R A N C E

Iruña (Pamplona)

N240

N117

N20N

A9

Perpignan

ANDORRA

N230

Huesca

N240

Girona

A7

N152

Soria

N111

A15

A68

N320

Ebro

Zaragoza

Lleida

NII

Barcelona

A2

N232

Tarragona

A16

See next page

Cuenca

N234

Mediterranean Sea

Maó

Palma de Mallorca

Valencia

Júcar

Eivissa (Ibiza)

Albacete

N430

N330

N340

A7

0 kilometres   100

0 miles   50

Alacant (Alicante)

Murcia

N322

N301

N340

N332

Oran

Almería

Segura

Catalonia's Frontiers
Catalonia's northern border with France runs along the crest of the Pyrenees and is punctuated by Catalan-speaking Andorra. Its western and southern borders adjoin the Spanish provinces of Aragón and València.

EUROPE AND NORTH AFRICA

NORWAY

FINLAND

SWEDEN

ESTONIA

RUSSIAN FED.

DENMARK

LITHUANIA

RUSSIAN FED.

BELORUSSIA

REPUBLIC OF IRELAND

UNITED KINGDOM

NETHERLANDS

POLAND

BELGIUM

GERMANY

LUXEMBOURG

CZECH REPUBLIC

UKRAINE

SLOVAKIA

FRANCE

SWITZERLAND

AUSTRIA

HUNGARY

SLOVENIA

CROATIA

ITALY

BOSNIA AND HERZEGOVINA

YUGOSLAVIA

ROMANIA

BULGARIA

ALBANIA

GREECE

PORTUGAL

SPAIN

Barcelona

MOROCCO

ALGERIA

TUNISIA

LIBYA

Barcelona City Centre

Set between the mountains and the sea, which still play an integral part in city life, Barcelona is a rare city, a patchwork of distinctive districts telling the story of its growth from a medieval core to the 19th-century expansion and today's ultra-modern showpieces. The three main sightseeing areas described in this guide illustrate this startling diversity. The hill of Montjuïc, abutting the sea, forms the southwestern end of an arc of steep hills that almost completely encloses the city. It is a district of monumental buildings and open spaces. The Old Town has a superb Gothic heart with a myriad of narrow streets twisting among ancient houses. The densely populated Eixample, in contrast, is a district of immensely long, straight streets and superb Modernista architecture.

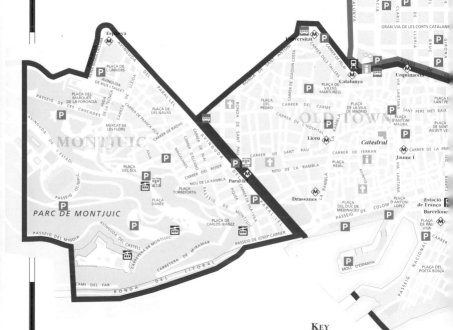

Montjuïc
There are wonderful views from the top of this large hill. Several of Barcelona's best museums are here, including the Archaeological Museum (see p80) which displays this Roman mosaic excavated in the city.

0 kilometres   1

0 miles   0.5

KEY

▢	Major sight
Ⓜ	Metro station
▤	Train station
▤	Bus stop
▤	Boat boarding point
▥	Cable car
▥	Funicular
▤	Police station
P	Parking
ⓘ	Tourist information
✝	Church

Eixample

This area covers the most interesting part of the city's 19th-century expansion. Walks along its streets will reveal countless details of the Modernista style, such as this ornate doorway of Casa Comalat (see p49) in Avinguda Diagonal

Old Town

This area includes all the oldest districts of Barcelona and its port, the 18th-century fishing "village" of Barceloneta and the new waterside developments. This new swing bridge is in the Old Port (see p64).

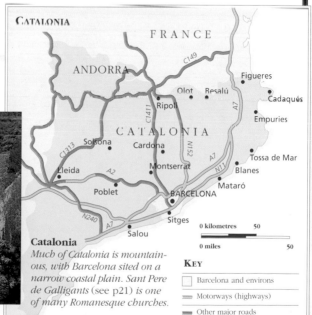

Catalonia

Much of Catalonia is mountainous, with Barcelona sited on a narrow coastal plain. Sant Pere de Galligants (see p21) is one of many Romanesque churches.

KEY

☐ Barcelona and environs

▬ Motorways (highways)

▬ Other major roads

0 kilometres   50
0 miles   50

A PORTRAIT OF CATALONIA

BARCELONA IS ONE OF THE GREAT *Mediterranean cities. Few places are so redolent with history, few so boldly modern. Animated and inspired, it is a city that sparkles as much at night-time as in the full light of day. It is famous for its main avenue, La Rambla, for its bars, its museums and its enthusiasm for life.*

Barcelona is the capital of the autonomous region of Catalonia, the most northeasterly corner of Spain, bordering France. The region is divided into four provinces, named after their provincial capitals: Barcelona, Girona, Lleida and Tarragona.

The city of Barcelona lies between two rivers, the Llobregat and the Besòs, and is backed by the Collserola hills which rise to a 512-m (1,680-ft) peak at the Tibidabo amusement park. The city grew up as the industrial sweatshop of Spain, though the shunting yards and seaside warehouses have now gone. Around four million people live in Barcelona and its suburbs – about half the population of Catalonia. It is Spain's second city after its old rival, Madrid.

La dama del
paraigua

POLITICS AND SOCIETY

Catalonia is governed by the Generalitat, housed in the Palau de la Generalitat in the heart of the Old Town and on the site of the Roman forum. The region's parliament, in the Parc de la Ciutadella, shares a building with the Museu d'Art Modern. The city of Barcelona has a separate administration, and its town hall, the Casa de la Ciutat, faces the Generalitat across the Plaça de Sant Jaume.

Catalonia is developing its own police force, which has now taken over from Spain's national police in most of Catalonia.

Catalans are conservative and, as in many other countries, people in rural areas are more conservative than those in the cities. For the more than 20 years

Strollers and shoppers on La Rambla enjoying Barcelona's plentiful winter sunshine

◁ Stunning floral mosaic pillars at the Palau de la Música Catalana in Barcelona

St George's Day in April – the day for giving books

Catalans are not burdened with self doubt. The vigour with which they have rebuilt parts of their capital since the early 1980s shows flair and a firm hand. Places of great sentimental value, such as Barceloneta's beach-side restaurant shacks and the Cafè Zurich, a famous rendezvous for writers, artists and intellectuals at the top of La Rambla, were torn down. Stunning new buildings such as the Museu d'Art Contemporani were put up in the middle of the Old Town, but restoration work on old buildings is also carried out without hesitation.

since Franco's death, the Generalitat has been run by the conservative Convergència i Unió under the charismatic presidency of Jordi Pujol. During the same period the city council has been run by a socialist party.

Catalans, who have no taste for bull-fighting and whose sedate national dance, the *sardana*, is unruffled by passion, are a serious, hardworking people. Some would rather be associated with northern Europeans than with other Spaniards, whom they regard as indolent. Part of their complaint against Madrid has been that, as one of the richest regions of Spain, they put more into the national coffers than they take out.

Two emotions are said to guide Catalans: *seny*, which means solid common sense, and *rauxa*, a creative chaos. A bourgeois, conservative element of Barcelona society can be seen at concerts and in pastry shops, but a certain surreal air is often evident, on La Rambla, for instance, where sometimes it seems that anything goes. The two elements are mixed in each person, and even the most staid may have the occasional *cop de rauxa*, or moment of chaotic ecstasy. Such outbursts are used to explain the more incendiary moments of Catalonia's history.

Street performer on La Rambla

LANGUAGE AND CULTURE

A Romance language similar to the old Langue d'Oc, or Provençal, once used in France, Catalan is Catalonia's official language, spoken by some eight million people. It has always been a living language and it continued to be spoken in the home even when it was banned by Franco. Catalans do not think it rude to talk to each other in Catalan in front of

Poster for a Pedro Almodóvar film

Strand bei Tossa de Mar an der Costa Brava

ren überall volle Opernhäuser. Die Katalanen lesen mehr Bücher als andere Spanier. Seit den 70er Jahren blüht die katalanische Literatur: Vielen Schriftstellern wurden Preise verliehen, doch nur wenige Werke ins Deutsche übersetzt.

ARBEIT UND FREIZEIT

Die Katalanen sind sehr traditions- und familienbewußt. Sonntags trifft sich die Familie zum Essen, und auch wochentags kommt man, wenn möglich, zum Mittagessen nach Hause. Dadurch gibt es viermal täglich Stoßzeiten. Die Geschäfte schließen gegen 20 Uhr, und zwischen 18 und 20 Uhr sind die Straßen voll. Gegen 22 Uhr ißt man zu Abend oder geht aus. Heute gibt es zunehmenden Druck, die Geschäftszeiten dem übrigen Europa anzugleichen.

Der Fußballmannschaft FC Barcelona die Treue zu halten ist eine Frage des Nationalstolzes. Beliebt sind auch Restaurant-, Konzert- und Kinobesuche. Die Woche beginnt in Barcelona stets ruhig, doch am Wochenende füllen sich des Nachts die Straßen.

talanisch zu sprechen. Alle Schilder und offiziellen Dokumente sind in Spanisch und Katalanisch gehalten

Wenn *rauxa* tatsächlich für die Kreativität verantwortlich ist, dann ist Katalonien reichlich damit gesegnet. Der Modernisme, angeführt von Antoni Gaudí, stellt Kataloniens Beitrag zur Weltarchitektur dar. Maler wie Joan Miró, Salvador Dalí und Antoni Tàpies wurden hier geboren, und Pablo Picasso verbrachte seine prägenden Jahre in Barcelona. Entwürfe von Javier Mariscal, Schöpfer der olympischen Motive von 1992, Möbel von Oliver Tusquets und Mode von Toni Miró verleihen der Stadt ein besonderes Flair. Regisseure wie Pedro Almodóvar *(Frauen am Rande des Nervenzusammenbruchs)* und Bigas Luna *(Jamón Jamón)* genießen internationales Ansehen.

Montserrat Caballé

In den letzten 150 Jahren hat Katalonien einige ausgezeichnete Musiker hervorgebracht. Die Komponisten Isaac Albéniz (1860–1909), Enrique Granados (1867–1916) und Federico Mompou (1893–1987) bereicherten die klassische Hauptströmung um iberische Elemente. Pablo Casals (1876–1973) gilt als einer der größten Cellisten aller Zeiten, und Montserrat Caballé sowie José Carreras garantie-

Demonstration für Kataloniens Unabhängigkeit

Blumen des Matorral

Bienen-ragwurz

DER MATORRAL IST die charakteristische Landschaft an Spaniens östlicher Mittelmeerküste. Das Macchia-Gebiet voller Wildblumen entstand als Folge jahrhundertelanger Rodungen. Denn die Steineiche wurde als Bauholz gebraucht, Weide- und Ackerland entstand. Viele Pflanzen haben sich an die extremen klimatischen Bedingungen angepaßt. Im Frühjahr überziehen gelbe Ginsterbüsche sowie rosafarbene und weiße Zistrosen die Hügel, und der Duft von Rosmarin, Lavendel und Thymian sowie das Summen der Insekten, die sich an Nektar und Pollen laben, erfüllen die Luft.

Der Spanische Ginster *trägt gelbe Blüten. Die schwarzen Samenkapseln platzen bei Trockenheit auf, und die Samen fallen auf den Boden.*

Die Mexikanische Agave kann bis zu zehn Meter hoch werden.

Das Brandkraut, *ein hübscher, oft in Gärten angepflanzter Strauch, hat lange, von Büscheln leuchtend gelber Blüten umgebene Äste. Seine Blätter sind grau-weiß.*

Aleppo-Kiefer   **Rosmarin**

Beim Rosen-knoblauch *krönen violette oder rosafarbene Blütendolden einen Stengel. Er überlebt den Sommer als die bekannte Zwiebel.*

EXOTISCHE EINWANDERER

Einigen Pflanzen aus der Neuen Welt ist es gelungen, sich auf dem kargen Boden des Matorral anzusiedeln. Der Feigenkaktus, den Christoph Kolumbus eingeführt haben soll, trägt köstliche Früchte, die man nur mit dicken Handschuhen pflücken kann. Die schnell wachsende Mexikanische Agave mit den stacheligen Blättern entwickelt ihren kräftigen Blütenstand erst nach 10 bis 15 Jahren und stirbt dann.

Blühender Feigenkaktus

Blütenstand der Mexikanischen Agave

Der Gartenthymian, *ein niedriges, aromatisches Kraut, wird vor allem für die Küche angebaut.*

Der Spiegelragwurz, *eine kleine Orchidee, die auf Grasflächen wächst, unterscheidet sich von anderen Orchideen durch den glänzenden blauen Fleck auf seiner Lippe.*

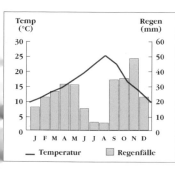

Temp (°C)		Regen (mm)

Temperatur — Regenfälle

KLIMA

Die meisten Pflanzen des Matorral blühen im warmen, feuchten Frühjahr. Im trockenen, heißen Sommer schützen sie sich durch dicke Blätter und wachsartige Ausscheidungen vor Feuchtigkeitsverlust oder speichern Wasser in ihren Knollen.

Steineichen sind in Ostspanien weit verbreitet. Ihre gummiartigen Blätter speichern Feuchtigkeit.

Der Erdbeerbaum ist ein immergrüner Strauch mit glänzenden, gezackten Blättern. Seine ungenießbare Frucht wird rot, wenn sie reif ist.

Baumheide

Graublättrige Zistrosen wachsen an sonnigen Plätzen, haben faltige Blüten und gelbe Staubbeutel.
Schmalblättrige Zistrosen sondern ein aromatisches Harz ab, das für Parfüm verwendet wird.

Der Sternklee ist eine niedrige Pflanze, deren Frucht zu einer sternförmigen Samenkapsel wird. Die Blüten sind rosa.

TIERWELT DES MATORRAL

Die Tiere, die im Matorral leben, sieht man am ehesten frühmorgens, bevor es heiß wird. Unzählige, von Blume zu Blume fliegende Insekten stellen eine gute Futterquelle für die Vögel dar. Kleinere Säugetiere wie Wühlmäuse sind nur bei Nacht aktiv, wenn es kühler ist und nur wenige Raubtiere in der Nähe sind.

Treppennattern fressen kleine Säugetiere, Vögel und Insekten. Junge Nattern erkennt man an der schwarzen, leiterartigen Musterung, ältere an zwei einfachen Streifen.

Skorpione verstecken sich am Tag. Werden sie erschreckt, heben sie den Schwanz zu einer Drohgebärde über den Körper. Ihr für kleine Tiere tödlicher Stich kann bei Menschen Reizungen hervorrufen.

Die Grasmücke, ein scheuer Vogel mit dunklem Gefieder und hohem Schwanz, singt während der Balz Melodien. Die Männchen sind bunter als die Weibchen.

Der Schwalbenschwanz ist einer der auffälligsten Schmetterlinge des Matorral. Weit verbreitete Insekten sind auch Bienen, Ameisen und Heuschrecken.

Romanische Kunst und Architektur

KATALONIEN HAT EINE FÜLLE mittelalterlicher Gebäude im unverwechselbaren regionalen romanischen Stil aus dem 11. bis 13. Jahrhundert. Die meisten der über 2000 Bauten sind Kirchen. Besonders gut erhalten sind die in den Pyrenäen, die weitgehend von Angriffen und Modernisierung verschont blieben. Die Kirchen hatten hohe Glockentürme, Mittelschiffe mit Tonnengewölbe, Rundbogen, phantasievolle Skulpturen und bemerkenswerte Wandgemälde. Einige Fresken und Möbel sind nun im Museu Nacional d'Art de Catalunya *(siehe S. 80)* in Barcelona zu sehen, das über die weltweit größte Sammlung romanischer Kunst verfügt.

Sant Jaume de Frontanyà (siehe S. 96) *ist eine ehemalige Augustinerkirche mit typischen lombardischen Bandrippen (11. Jh.) unterhalb der Dächer der drei Apsiden. Ungewöhnlich ist der achteckige Dachaufsatz.*

Vielha •

Pont de Suert •

• Andorra la Vella

Puigcerdà •

• Sort

• La Seu d'Urgell

Berga •

Sant Climent de Taüll, eine großartige Kirche im Vall de Boí (siehe S. 95), *wurde 1123 geweiht. Die Fresken, darunter ein Christus als Pantokrator* (siehe S. 80), *sind Repliken. Die Originale, die nun in Barcelona sind, gehören zu den schönsten Kataloniens.*

0 Kilometer   30

MONESTIR DE SANTA MARIA DE RIPOLL

Heilige

Geschichte Salomos

Altes Testament

David und seine Musikanten

Geschichte Mose

Christus mit historischen Figuren

Visionen des Daniel

Sockel mit Mustern

Das Portal der Kirche des ehemaligen Benediktinerklosters in Ripoll ist wegen seiner allegorischen Schnitzereien als »Ripoll-Bibel« bekannt. Die Kirche wurde 879 gegründet und 1032 unter Abt Oliva umgebaut, das Portal aber erst im späten 12. Jahrhundert hinzugefügt. Christus sitzt über dem Eingang inmitten der Tiere, die die Apostel symbolisieren, und die monatlich zu verrichtenden landwirtschaftlichen Tätigkeiten sind auf den Eingangssäulen dargestellt. Entlang der Wand gibt es sieben biblische Friese. Der oberste *(siehe S. 96)* über dem Tympanon stellt die alten Männer in der Apokalypse dar, die anderen sind oben genannt.

Sant Pere de Camprodon (siehe S. 97), 1169 geweiht, ist eine Klosterkirche im spätromanischen Stil. Das leicht zugespitzte Tonnengewölbe über dem Mittelschiff kündigt den gotischen Stil an.

Sant Cristòfol de Beget (siehe S. 97) ist eine wunderschöne Kirche in einem malerischen Weiler. Zur einzigartig erhaltenen Innenausstattung gehören ein romanischer Taufstein und dieses berühmte Kruzifix (12. Jh.).

GEBIET MIT ROMANISCHEN SEHENSWÜRDIGKEITEN

Sant Pere de Rodes, 600 Meter über dem Meeresspiegel gelegen, war ein Benediktinerkloster. Im Mittelschiff seiner Kirche sind die Pfeiler eines ehemaligen römischen Tempels zu sehen.

Figueres

Roses

Ripoll

Olot

Girona

Vic

Sant Pere de Besalú (siehe S. 97) ist die Kirche (12. Jh.) eines früheren Benediktinerklosters. Steinlöwen bewachen dieses Fenster über dem Portal. Der Chorumgang hat fein geschnitzte Kapitelle.

Sant Feliu de Guixols

Das Museu Episcopal de Vic (siehe S. 106) neben der Kathedrale besitzt eine erstklassige Sammlung romanischer Kunst, wie diese farbenprächtige und anrührende Darstellung von Mariä Heimsuchung, die früher den Altar im Kloster Lluçà schmückte.

Sant Pere de Galligants (siehe S. 98), eine ehemalige Benediktiner-abtei und Paradebeispiel für den romanischen Stil, hat ein Portal (11. Jh.) mit Fensterrosette und einen achteckigen Glockenturm. Biblische Szenen schmücken die Kapitelle des Klosters, heute Gironas archäologisches Museum.

Gaudí und der Modernisme

Kamin der Casa Vicens

Gᴇɢᴇɴ Eɴᴅᴇ des 19. Jahrhunderts entstand in Barcelona der Modernisme, ein neuer Stil in Kunst und Architektur, eng verwandt mit dem Jugendstil. In ihm drückte sich das katalanische Nationalbewußtsein aus. Seine Hauptvertreter waren Josep Puig i Cadafalch, Lluís Domènech i Montaner und vor allem Antoni Gaudí i Cornet *(siehe S. 72)*. In Eixample *(siehe S. 66ff)* entstanden – für reiche Kunden – viele dieser originellen Bauten.

Jeder Aspekt eines Modernisme-Baus, auch die Inneneinrichtung, wurde vom Architekten entworfen. Hier Tür und Kachelrahmen von Gaudís Casa Batlló von 1906 (siehe S. 72).

Eine spektakuläre Kuppel schließt den drei Stockwerke hohen Salon ab. Die kleinen runden Löcher, ein arabisches Element, wirken wie Sterne.

Die Obergalerien sind mit Täfelung und Kassetten reich geschmückt.

Die spiralförmige Auffahrt zeigt früh von Gaudís Vorliebe für Kurven. In der gewellten Fassade der Casa Milà wird dieses Charakteristikum später besonders deutlich (siehe S. 73).

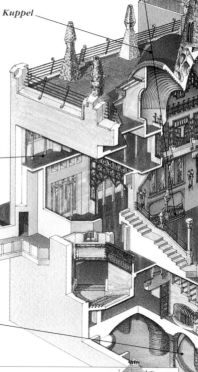

DIE ENTWICKLUNG DES MODERNISME

1859 Bauingenieur Ildefons Cerdà i Sunyer macht Vorschläge zur Stadterweiterung

1900 Josep Puig i Cadafalch baut die Casa Amatller *(siehe S. 72)*

1878 Gaudi beendet sein Studium

1903 Lluís Domènech i Montaner baut das Hospital de la Santa Creu i de Sant Pau *(S. 73)*

Hospital, Detail

1850	1865	1880	1895	1910	1925

1883 Gaudi übernimmt die Konstruktion der neogotischen Sagrada Familia *(siehe S. 74f)*

Detail der Sagrada Familia

1888 Die Weltausstellung gibt dem Modernisme Auftrieb

1910 Casa Milà vollendet

1905 Domènech i Montaner baut die Casa Lleó Morera *(siehe S. 72)*, Puig i Cadafalch die Casa Terrades *(siehe S. 73)*

1926 Gaudi stirbt

Bizarr geformte Kamine wurden ein Markenzeichen Gaudís, wie hier auf dem schimmernden Satteldach der Casa Batlló zu sehen ist.

Schmiede-eiserne Lampen erhellen den Hauptsaal.

Keramikfliesen zieren die Kamine.

GAUDÍS MATERIALIEN

Gaudí entwarf oder arbeitete mit fast jedem Material. Er verband reine, unbearbeitete Stoffe wie Holz, roh behauenen Stein, Bruchstein und Ziegel mit Meisterwerken aus Schmiedeeisen und Buntglas. Keramikfliesen bedecken seine fließenden, unebenen Formen.

Buntglasfenster in der Sagrada Família

Fliesenmosaik, Parc Güell *(siehe S. 88f)*

Detail eines Eisentors, Casa Vicens *(siehe S. 48)*

Keramikfliesen an El Capricho

Spitzbogen, die Gaudí schon im Palau Güell ausgiebig verwendet hat, zeigen sein Interesse an gotischer Architektur. Hier ein Gang im Col·legi de les Teresianes von 1890, einer Klosterschule im Westen Barcelonas.

Der Zierschmuck spielt auf das katalanische Wappen an.

PALAU GÜELL

Gaudís erster Großbau in der Stadtmitte *(siehe S. 59)* begründete seinen Ruf als herausragender Architekt. Das für seinen Gönner Eusebi Güell im Jahr 1889 erbaute Wohnhaus liegt eingezwängt in einer engen Straße, so daß die Fassade kaum zur Geltung kommt. Im Inneren strukturierte Gaudí mit Lettnern, Galerien und Nischen den Raum. Zu sehen ist auch sein einzigartiges Mobiliar.

Organische Formen inspirierten die schmiedeeiserne Arbeit an den Toren des Palastes. Gaudí bezieht sich oft auf Tiere, wie bei diesem bunt gekachelten Drachen, der die Stufen im Parc Güell bewacht.

Katalanische Malerei

KATALONIENS MALEREI HAT EINE SCHÖNE, wenn auch qualitativ unausgeglichene Tradition, die ihren Ausgang in den Pyrenäen nahm, wo phantasievolle Fresken romanische Kirchen schmücken *(siehe S. 20 f)*. Dem Zeitalter der Gotik, in dem Katalonien auf der Höhe seiner Macht stand, folgte eine künstlerisch weniger bedeutende Periode. Doch der Wohlstand des 19. Jahrhunderts förderte eine neue Kreativität. Im 20. Jahrhundert brachte die Region einige der größten Maler Europas hervor, die sich stark zu Kataloniens unvergleichlicher romanischer Kunst hingezogen fühlten.

ihrer Werke zeigt das Museu Nacional d'Art de Catalunya neben Kataloniens einzigen nennenswerten Künstlern dieser Epoche – Francesc Pla und Antoni Viladomat.

Prozession vor Santa Maria del Mar **(um 1898) von Ramon Casas**

Der hl. Georg und die Prinzessin **(Ende 15. Jh.) von Jaume Huguet**

GOTIK

EINER DER ERSTEN namentlich bekannten Künstler Kataloniens war Ferrer Bassa (1285–1348), Hofmaler von Jaume II. Bassas Werke in der Kapelle des Klosters von Pedralbes *(siehe S. 87)* sind die ersten bekannten Beispiele der Öl-Wandmalerei, zweifellos beeinflußt von der damaligen italienischen Kunst.

Die frühesten Skulpturen der katalanischen Gotik stammen vom Meister Bartomeu (1250–1300), dessen orientalisch wirkender *Kalvarienberg* im Museu d'Art von Girona *(siehe S. 99)* zu sehen ist. Auch in Vic und Solsona gibt es gotische Sammlungen *(siehe S. 106)*, doch Barcelonas Museu Nacional d'Art de Catalunya *(siehe S. 80)* hat die beeindruckendste. Erwähnenswert sind die Werke

von Lluís Borrassà (1365–1425), der das Altarbild in Tarragonas Kathedrale malte, sowie von Lluís Dalmau (gest. 1463), der in Brügge bei Jan van Eyck studierte. Ein Merkmal der katalanischen Gotik ist *esgrafiat*, das Vergolden von Heiligenscheinen, Stoffen und anderem. Ein Beispiel ist *Der heilige Georg und die Prinzessin* von Jaume Huguet (1415–92), einem der größten Künstler der katalanischen Gotik.

RENAISSANCE BIS KLASSIZISMUS

ZWISCHEN DEM 16. UND 18. Jahrhundert verblaßte Kataloniens Kunst. Im Vordergrund standen nun andere große spanische Meister: El Greco in Toledo, Murillo und Zurbarán in Sevilla, Ribera in València sowie Velázquez und später Goya in Madrid. Einige

19. JAHRHUNDERT

BARCELONAS KUNSTSCHULE eröffnete 1849 über der Börse *(siehe S. 60)*, gefördert von neuen Kunstmäzenen, die ihren Reichtum der industriellen Revolution verdankten. Die Industrie bildete jedoch bereits ihre eigenen Künstler aus. 1783 hatte man in Olot *(siehe S. 97)* eine Schule für Textildesign gegründet, deren Hauptvertreter, Josep Berga i Boix (1837–1914) und Joaquim Vayreda i Vila (1843–94), auch die Werkstätten der Art Cristià ins Leben riefen, die bis heute Kirchenstatuen anfertigen.

Den Grün- und Brauntönen der Olot-Landschaftsmaler stand das blasse Blau und

Die Gärten von Aranjuez **(1907) von Santiago Rusiñol**

Warten auf die Suppe (1899) von Isidre Nonell

Rosa der Sitges-Luministen – Arcadi Mas i Fontdevila (1852–1943) und Joan Roig i Soler (1852–1909) gegenüber. Sie waren beeinflußt von Marià Fortuny, der 1838 in Reus geboren wurde und in Rom und Paris lebte. Barcelonas Stadtrat beauftragte ihn mit einem Gemälde vom Sieg der Spanier bei Tetuán in Spanisch-Marokko, an dem 500 katalanische Freiwillige beteiligt waren. Das Gemälde hängt nun im Museu d'Art Modern *(siehe S. 63)*.

1892, 18 Jahre nach der ersten Impressionistenausstellung in Paris, brachte Mas i Fontdevila in Sitges die Schule von Olot und die Luministen zusammen. Die Ausstellung galt als das erste Modernisme-Ereignis, das auch Werke wie von Santiago Rusiñol (1861–1931) und dem herausragenden Ramon Casas (1866–1932) zeigte. Rusiñol, der Sohn eines Textilmagnaten, kaufte ein Haus in Sitges, Cau Ferrat *(siehe S. 110)*, das zum Treffpunkt der Modernisten wurde. Bei Casas, der erste Einwohner Barcelonas, der ein Auto besaß, trafen sich alle damaligen Berühmtheiten *(siehe S. 63)*. Rusiñol und Casas gründeten auch das Café Els Quatre Gats *(siehe S. 63)* nach dem Vorbild des Cafés Le Chat Noir in Paris.

Die Kathedrale der Armen (1897) von Joaquim Mir

20. JAHRHUNDERT

PABLO RUIZ PICASSO (1881–1973) lebte zwar nur acht Jahre in Barcelona *(siehe S. 60)*, doch diese waren ausgesprochen prägend. Sein Frühwerk war, wie im Museu Picasso *(siehe S. 61)* zu sehen, von der Stadt und ihrer Umgebung wie auch den führenden katalanischen Künstlern – dem Landschaftsmaler Isidre Nonell (1873–1911) sowie von Joaquim Mir (1873–1940), Rusiñol und Casas – beeinflußt. Schon bald übersiedelte Picasso jedoch nach Paris. Während der Franco-Zeit ging er freiwillig ins Exil, verlor aber nie den Kontakt zu Katalonien.

Auch Joan Miró (1893–1983) besuchte die Kunstschule. Wegen mangelnden Könnens hinausgeworfen, wurde er mit seinen verspielten abstrakten Gemälden zu einem der originellsten Maler des 20. Jahrhunderts.

Spielerisches war auch Salvador Dalí *(siehe S. 99)* eigen, den Miró genauso förderte, wie Picasso ihn gefördert hatte. Dalí folgte ihnen nach Paris, wo Miró ihn mit den Surrealisten bekannt machte. Nach dem Bürgerkrieg blieb Dalí in Katalonien; sein Haus in Port Lligat *(siehe S. 102)* ist sein schönstes Werk.

Auch Josep-Maria Sert (1876–1945) blieb in Katalonien. Er ist vor allem für seine Wandgemälde in Barcelonas Casa de la Ciutat *(siehe S. 55)* sowie im Rockefeller Center und im Speisesaal des Waldorf Astoria in New York bekannt. Sein Werk in der Kathedrale von Vic *(siehe S. 106)* wurde im Bürgerkrieg zerstört, doch gelang es ihm, es noch einmal anzufertigen, bevor er starb.

Der bekannteste katalanische Maler der Gegenwart ist Antoni Tàpies. Wie viele vor ihm, ist er tief in seiner eigenen Kultur verwurzelt. Er malt zwar abstrakt, verwendet aber oft die Farben der katalanischen Flagge und ist von der romanischen Kunst beeinflußt. Wie Picasso und Miró hat er sein eigenes Museum *(siehe S. 72)*. Werke anderer lebender Katalanen sind in Barcelonas Museu d'Art Contemporani *(siehe S. 58)* zu sehen.

Lithographie (1948) in den katalanischen Farben von Antoni Tàpies

Die katalanische Küche

Nyora-Paprika

D**IE KATALANISCHE KÜCHE** wurde erstmals Anfang des 14. Jahrhunderts im *Llibre de Sent Sovè* beschrieben. Sie vereint in sich *mar i muntanya* (Meer und Berg) – Fleisch, Wurst und Wild aus dem Hinterland sowie Meeresfrüchte und Fisch von der Küste –, was zu Kombinationen wie Hühnchen mit Hummer führt. Der von den Arabern eingeführte Safran wird für Paella verwendet, Schokolade aus Amerika für pikante und süße Speisen. Klassische Gerichte basieren auf Saucen: *allioli* (Knoblauchmayonnaise), *picada* (Knoblauch, Nüsse, Toastbrot, Petersilie, Gewürze), *romesco* (geröstete Nüsse, Knoblauch, Tomaten, Paprika, Brot), *samfaina* (Zwiebel, Paprika, Tomaten, Knoblauch, Zucchini, Auberginen) und *sofregit* (Zwiebel, Knoblauch, Tomaten, Paprika).

Amanida catalana *ist ein Salat aus Gemüse und geräuchertem Fleisch oder Käse, Fisch oder Meeresfrüchten.*

Petersilie   Muscheln

Tintenfisch   Riesengarnelen

Tomate   Engelbarsch

Graellada de marisc *ist ein Teller mit gegrillten Meeresfrüchten, serviert mit* allioli *(Knoblauchmayonnaise).*

Arròs negre *(«schwarzer Reis») ist Kataloniens berühmtestes Reisgericht. Es stammt von der Costa Brava und wird zubereitet aus Reis, Tintenfisch, Engelbarsch, Meeresfrüchten, Zwiebeln, Knoblauch, Tomaten, Fischbrühe, Olivenöl und der Tinte des Tintenfischs, die dem Gericht seinen Geschmack und seine Farbe verleiht.*

Avellanes *(Haselnüsse) sind eine wichtige katalanische Frucht. Die Bewohner der Provinz Tarragona behaupten, ihre seien die besten. Sie werden als Zutat zu Kuchen und Süßigkeiten verwendet, vor allem aber zusammen mit Mandeln in der* romesco- *und* picada-*Sauce.*

Suquet, *ein Eintopf aus Fisch und Meeresfrüchten, oft mit Safran, Wein, Tomaten und Kartoffeln zubereitet.*

Canelons a la barcelonesa *sind eine in Barcelona beliebte Art Cannelloni, gefüllt mit Hühnerleber und Schwein.*

Paella, *traditionell über offenem Feuer mit Reis aus dem Ebrodelta gekocht, wird mit Meeresfrüchten oder Wild zubereitet.*

Fideus a la cassola *ist eine Art Nudelgericht mit roter Paprika, Schweinekoteletts oder Schweinefilet und Würstchen.*

Botifarra amb mongetes, *ein traditionelles Gericht aus gegrillter schwarzer Wurst und weißen Bohnen.*

Esqueixada *ist ein kräftig gewürztes, beliebtes katalanisches Gericht: ein Salat aus Kabeljau, Zwiebeln und Paprika.*

Llagosta i pollastre *ist eine katalanische Kombination aus Hummer und Huhn in einer Tomaten-Haselnuß-Sauce.*

Pollastre rostit amb samfaina *heißt die Kombination aus Brathuhn und samfaina, einem katalanischen Gemüsemix.*

Crema catalana *ist eine Eiercreme mit einer Schicht karamelisierten Zuckers, der sehr kalt serviert wird.*

Coca de Sant Joan – *Hefekuchen mit kandierten Früchten und Pinienkernen, serviert am Fest des hl. Johannes* (siehe S. 31).

Birne

Apfel

Kirsche

Orange

Kürbis

Fruites confitades *(kandierte Früchte): eine beliebte Methode, die Produkte der Region zu konservieren; sie werden gerne für Kuchen oder als Süßigkeit verwendet*

Ametlles garrapinyades

Torró d'Agramunt

Süße Nüsse
wie ametlles garrapinyades *(mit Zucker überzogene Mandeln) wurden in Spanien von den Mauren eingeführt. Torró (turrón) wird auf zweierlei Weise hergestellt: aus einer weichen Paste gemahlener Mandeln oder wie der Haselnuß-torró aus Agramunt in der Provinz Lleida aus ganzen Nüssen.*

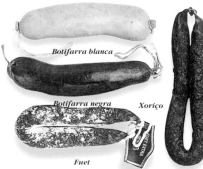

Botifarra blanca

Botifarra negra

Xoriço

Fuet

WÜRSTE

Katalanische Würstchen, *embotits*, vor allem die aus der Stadt Vic, sind berühmt. Die weiße *botifarra* enthält Schweinefleisch, Kutteln und Pinienkerne, die schwarze Sorte Blut, Schweinebauch und Gewürze. *Bulls* (von *bullit* – gekocht) bestehen aus mehreren in Schweinedarm gefüllte Fleischsorten. Geräucherte Würstchen sind die *llonganisseta* und der lange, trockene *fuet*. *Pernil* ist ein luftgetrockneter Schinken, *salsitxa* eine dünne, rohe Wurst. Der rote *xoriço* (*chorizo*) ist mit Paprika gewürzt und wird zu Brot gegessen oder in Eintöpfen gekocht.

Die Sektregion

Codorníus welt-
berühmtes Etikett

Cava ist einer von Kataloniens ge-schätztesten Exporten. Der relativ preisgünstige Sekt wird hergestellt wie französischer Champagner, mit einer zweiten Fermentierung in der Flasche, in der man ihn verkauft. Von der Mitte des 19. Jahrhunderts an wurde er vermarktet, und 1872 be-gann Josep Raventós, der Chef der berühmten Weinkelle-rei Codorníu, mit der Produktion in großem Stil. Codorníu wird noch immer von seinen Nachfahren in Sant Sadurní d'Anoia, der *cava*-Hauptstadt des Weinbaugebiets Pene-dès, geleitet. Auch heutzutage werden für *cava* regionale Traubensorten verwendet – Macabeo, Xarel·lo und Parel-lada. Die wörtliche Übersetzung von *cava* ist »Keller«.

Codorníu, der erste mit der méthode champenoise her-gestellte Sekt, verhalf cava zu internationalem Ansehen.

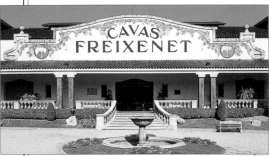

Freixenet wurde 1914 von der Familie Sala gegründet und gehört nun zu den führenden cava-Sorten. Das Anwesen liegt in Sant Sadurní d'Anoia, dem Herzen der cava-Region. Die unverkennbare schwarze Freixenet-Flasche ist weltweit bekannt.

Raïmat, von der Familie Raventós aus der Chardon-nay-Traube hergestellt, halten viele Weinkenner für den besten cava. Das 3000 Hektar große Raïmat-Anwesen, ein ehemaliges Ödland westlich von Lleida, hat seinen eigenen Bahnhof und ein Arbeiterdorf und wurde von der spanischen Regierung zum »landwirtschaftlichen Modellbetrieb« erklärt.

DIE WEINE KATALONIENS

Die katalanischen Weinsorten sind *negre* (rot), *rosat* (rosé) und *blanc* (weiß). *Garnatxa* ist ein Dessertwein, *ranci* ein ausgereifter Weißwein. Eine Tradition bei lokalen Festen oder in Bars alten Stils ist die, Wein aus einem *porró* (Krug mit langem Schnabel) in den Mund zu gießen. Es gibt sieben offizielle *Denominació-de-Origen*-Regionen:

EMPORDÀ-COSTA BRAVA: leichte Weine aus dem Nordosten wie *vi de l'any*, im Produktionsjahr getrunken, und *cava*, hergestellt in Peralada.

ALELLA: winzige Region nördlich von Barcelona mit guten Weißweinen.

PENEDÈS: gute Rot- und Weißweine mit Namen wie Torres und Codorníu. Besuchen Sie das Weinmuseum in Vilafranca del Penedès *(siehe S. 107)*.

CONCA DE BARBERÀ: kleine Mengen Rot- und Weißwein.

COSTERS DEL SEGRE: die köstlichen Rotweine des Raïmat-Anwesens.

PRIORAT: schwere Rot- und Weißweine (Falset) aus einer hübschen Region mit kleinen Dörfern westlich von Tarragona.

Ein *porró* zum Weintrinken

TARRAGONA UND TERRA ALTA: traditionell schwere Weine.

Die Jugendstilkellerei in Sant Sadurní d'Anoia ist Codornías modernistisches Paradestück, 1906 von Josep Puig i Cadafalch entworfen. Die Keller erstrecken sich über 26 Kilometer. Besucher werden mit einem kleinen Zug herumgefahren.

Codorníu wurde bereits 1888 für seinen *cava* mit Goldmedaillen ausgezeichnet. Ab 1897 wurde er statt Champagner bei Staatsanlässen serviert.

LEGENDE

☐ Wichtige *cava*-Regionen

0 Kilometer 20

Manresa

D È S

rrega

N11

Igualada

Terrassa

Sabadell

ERS DEL GRÀ

Masquefa

⑥

② ①

③ Sant Sadurní d'Anoia

④

Montblanc

Vilafranca del Penedès

BARCELONA

GUTE ERZEUGER

Codorníu
  Sant Sadurní d'Anoia ①
Freixenet
  Sant Sadurní d'Anoia ②
Gramona
  Sant Sadurní d'Anoia ③
Mascaró
  Vilafranca del Penedès ④
Raïmat
  Costers del Segre ⑤
Raventós Rosell
  Masquefa ⑥

Valls

A2

El Vendrell

Vilanova I la Geltrú

Castelldefels

us Tarragona

HINWEISE

Einkaufen

Je trockener der Wein, desto teurer ist er. Die trockensten *cavas* sind *brut de brut* und *brut nature. Brut* und *sec* sind nicht ganz so trocken. Halbtrockene *semiseco*- und süße *dulce*-Weine schmecken am besten zum Dessert. Die Weine sind günstiger als die französischen, doch einige kleine Hersteller verlangen hohe Preise.

Besuch einer Kellerei

Viele *cava*-Kellereien sind während der Geschäftszeiten geöffnet (aber im August geschlossen). Sant Sadurní d'Anoia mit den Kellereien Freixenet und Codorníu liegt 45 Zugminuten von Barcelonas Bahnhof Sants entfernt. Das Touristenbüro in Vilafranca del Penedès (*siehe S. 107*) informiert über alle *cava*-Kellereien.

Lohnenswert ist der Besuch der Freixenet-Keller. Das Unternehmen setzt jährlich mehr Flaschen cava um, als Champagner verkauft wird.

DAS JAHR IN KATALONIEN

IN ALLEN STADTVIERTELN Barcelonas sowie in den Städten und Dörfern Kataloniens begeht man mit einer *festa major* den Namenstag des Schutzpatrons. Die Sardana *(siehe S. 111)* wird getanzt, und an der Costa Brava singt man *havaneres* (Habaneras). Bei allen Feiern spielt das Essen – besonders Gebäck und Kuchen – eine zentrale Rolle. In vielen Städten gibt es

Am Tag des hl. Georg schenkt man sich Rosen

Umzüge der Riesen *(gegants)*, »Großköpfe« *(capgrosses)* und Zwerge *(nans)* – Pappmachékarikaturen einst mit den Handelsgilden verbundener Menschen. Die Katalanen lieben die Pyrotechnik, und zur Sommersonnenwende feiert man überall im Land die Revetlla de Sant Joan mit riesigen Feuerwerken. Viele Feiern beginnen am Vorabend des Festtags.

Bücherstände in Barcelona zum Tag des hl. Georg, *el dia del llibre*

FRÜHLING

WENN DIE ERDE sich erwärmt, weicht die Mandelblüte der Kirsch- und Apfelblüte. Ende März beginnt man Forellen und andere Süßwasserfische zu angeln. Ostern ist ein Familienfest. Man verläßt die Stadt und besucht Verwandte oder macht ein Picknick und sucht nach wildem Spargel. Der Mai ist die beste Zeit, um Wildblumen zu sehen, die besonders prächtig in den Pyrenäen wachsen.

MÄRZ

Sant Medir *(3. März).* In Barcelona werden bei Umzügen im Stadtteil Gràcia Süßigkeiten verteilt, in Sants etwas später.
Sant Josep *(19. März).* Viele Katalanen heißen Josep (oft Pepe abgekürzt), und dies ist ein regionaler Feiertag. Die Menschen feiern ihren Namenstag – den Tag des Heiligen, nach dem sie benannt sind – mehr als ihren Geburtstag.

Terrassa-Jazzfestival *(gesamter März).* Konzerte von Musikern aus aller Welt, an Wochenenden im Freien (kein Eintritt).

APRIL

Setmana Santa *(Karwoche).* Die Woche vor Ostern, mit vielen Veranstaltungen.
Diumenge de Rams *(Palmsonntag).* In den Kirchen, vor allem in der Sagrada Família in Barcelona, werden Palmzweige gesegnet. In Girona gibt es Prozessionen »römischer Soldaten« und an mehreren Orten, wie dem Kurort Sant Hilari Sacalm in der Provinz Girona, Passionsspiele.
Dijous Sant *(Gründonnerstag),* Verges, Provinz Girona. Als Skelette verkleidete Männer führen einen Totentanz *(dansa de la mort)* auf, der auf das 14. Jahrhundert zurückgehen soll.
Pasqua *(Ostern).* Am Karfreitag *(Divendres Sant)* werden Kreuze, dem Kreuzweg Jesu folgend, durch die Straßen getragen. Am Ostermontag *(Dilluns*

de Pasqua) kaufen Paten ihren Patenkindern *mona* (Schokoladenkuchen), und die Bäcker wetteifern um das ausgefallenste Konfekt.
Sant Jordi *(23. April).* Fest des heiligen Georg, des Schutzpatrons Kataloniens, und Todestag von Cervantes *(siehe S. 39),* der 1616 starb. Männer und Jungen schenken ihrer Mutter, Frau oder Freundin eine Rose und bekommen ein Buch geschenkt. Das Fest ist auch als *el dia del llibre* (Tag des Buches) bekannt.

MAI

Fira de Sant Ponç *(11. Mai).* Traditionelles Fest rund um die Carrer de l'Hospital in Barcelona, an der einst das Stadtkrankenhaus stand. Verkauf von medizinischen Kräutern und Honig.
Fronleichnam *(Mai/Juni).* Blumenteppiche auf den Straßen von Sitges, und in Berga tanzt ein Monsterdrachen *(la Patum)* durch die Stadt.

An Fronleichnam bedecken Blumenteppiche die Straßen

DURCHSCHNITTLICHE TÄGLICHE SONNENSCHEINDAUER

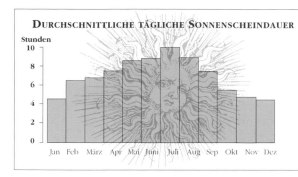

Stunden

Sonnenschein
Barcelona ist eine sonnige Stadt. Einen Großteil des Jahres ist der Himmel blau, und im Sommer scheint die Sonne oft bis zu zehn Stunden. Im Winter kann es im Schatten kalt sein, doch die Sonne steht noch immer so hoch, daß man auf einer geschützten Terrasse im Freien sitzen kann.

SOMMER

DIE MEISTEN Bewohner Barcelonas leben in Apartments und verlassen an Wochenenden oft die Stadt in Richtung Küste oder Berge. Freitag nachmittags und Sonntag abends sollte man deswegen die Autobahnen tunlichst meiden. Die Schulferien dauern lange. Sie beginnen Anfang Juni, wenn das Meer zum Schwimmen warm genug ist. In den Jachthäfen drängen sich die Boote, der Duft gegrillter Muscheln erfüllt die Luft, und der Besucher hat eine riesige Auswahl an Veranstaltungen. Viele Geschäfte in Barcelona schließen im August.

JUNI

Festival del Grec *(Juni/Juli).* Kunstfestival mit Künstlern aus dem In- und Ausland über ganz Barcelona verteilt. Hauptveranstaltungsorte sind das Teatre Grec, der Mercat de les Flors und der Poble Espanyol.
Revetlla de Sant Joan *(23. Juni).* Die Sommersonnwende feiert man mit einem Feuerwerk vor allem auf dem Montjuïc in Barcelona. In ganz Katalonien werden Freudenfeuer entzündet, und vom Gipfel des Mont Canigó bringt man Fackeln nach Frankreich hinunter. Man trinkt *cava* – Sekt *(siehe S. 28 f)* – zu einem speziellen *coca* (Kuchen), bestreut mit Pinienkernen und kandierten Früchten *(siehe S. 27).*
Castellers *(24. Juni).* In Tarragona, einer für ihre *casteller*-Feste berühmten Provinz, wetteifern Männer darum, auf ihren Schultern den höchsten Menschenturm zu bauen *(siehe S. 107).*

Urlauber in Platja d'Aro, einem Urlaubsort an der Costa Brava

Konzertsaison *(Juni/Juli).* Das Institut Municipal de Parcs i Jardins organisiert in verschiedenen Parks Barcelonas Konzerte klassischer Musik.

JULI

Cantada d'havaneres *(1. So im Juli).* Cremat (Kaffee mit Rum) trinkende Musiker- und Sängergruppen schmettern *havaneres* (Habaneras) am Strand von Calella de Palafrugell an der Costa Brava.

Ein *casteller*-Team in Aktion

Virgen del Carmen *(16. Juli).* Ein maritimes Festival in Barcelonas Hafen mit Umzügen und *havaneres* spielenden Kapellen.
Santa Cristina *(24. Juli).* Das größte Festival in Lloret de Mar an der Costa Brava, eine geschmückte Flottille bringt eine Statue der Jungfrau an Land.

AUGUST

Festa major de Gràcia *(eine Woche etwa ab 15. August).* Jeder Stadtteil Barcelonas veranstaltet seine eigene *festa*, bei der man um die phantasievollste Dekoration der Straßen wetteifert. Die *festa* im alten Stadtteil Gràcia ist die größte und spektakulärste. Sie umfaßt Konzerte, Bälle, Konzerte, Wettbewerbe und Straßenspiele.
Festa major de Sants *(um den 24. August).* Die jährliche *festa* in Barcelonas Stadtteil Sants.
Festa major de Vilafranca del Penedès *(Mitte August).* Dieses Fest ist eine der besten Gelegenheiten, um *casteller*-Wettbewerbe zu erleben *(siehe S. 107).*

DURCHSCHNITTLICHE MONATLICHE NIEDERSCHLÄGE

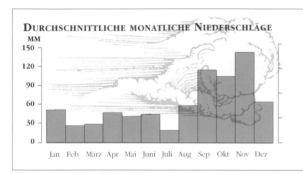

MM
150
120
90
60
30
0

Jan Feb März Apr Mai Juni Juli Aug Sep Okt Nov Dez

Niederschläge
In Barcelona regnet es wenig – gerade genug, daß die Grünflächen der Stadt nicht vertrocknen. Der Regen kommt jedoch meist plötzlich und wolkenbruchartig herunter und ist in den Sommermonaten von heftigen Gewitterstürmen begleitet. Tagelang anhaltender Nieselregen ist äußerst selten.

HERBST

Viehtrieb aus den Pyrenäen am Ende des Sommers

DIE TRAUBENERNTE *(verema)* ist ein Glanzpunkt des Herbstes, direkt bevor sich die Weinreben rot und golden färben. Es ist die Zeit, in der ein reiches Pilzangebot vorhanden ist. Ab Oktober gehen die Jäger auf die Jagd nach Rothühnern, Zugenten und Wildschweinen. Die ganz Abgehärteten kann man noch bis November im Meer schwimmen sehen.

SEPTEMBER

Diada de Catalunya *(11. September).* Kataloniens Nationalfeiertag gedenkt des Verlustes der Autonomie 1714 *(siehe S. 41).* Politische Demonstrationen zeugen von einem starken Separatismusgefühl. Überall weht die katalanische Flagge.
La Mercè *(24. September),* Barcelona. Fest zu Ehren von Nostra Senyora de la Mercè (der Gnädigen Jungfrau) mit Konzerten, Messen und Tänzen. Versäumen Sie nicht den *carrefoc* – einen Umzug feuerspeien-

Winzer bei der Traubenernte im Herbst

der Drachen und Monster – oder *piro musical* – Musik mit Feuerwerk.
Sant Miquel *(29. September).* Das Fest zu Ehren von Barcelonas Schutzpatron erinnert an Napoléons Besatzung Spaniens *(siehe S. 41).* Bum Bum, ein napoleonischer General, marschiert zu Gewehrsalven durch die Straßen. Am Strand wird getanzt.

OKTOBER

Festes de Sarrià i de Les Corts *(1. So im Oktober).* Jeder Stadtteil Barcelonas feiert ein Fest zu Ehren seines Schutzpatrons.
Dia de la Hispanitat *(12. Oktober).* Nationalfeiertag zum Gedenken an die Entdeckung Amerikas 1492 *(siehe S. 40).*

NOVEMBER

Tots Sants *(1. November).* An Allerheiligen ißt man Röstkastanien und Süßkartoffeln und besucht am darauffolgenden Tag, dem *Dia dels difunts* (Allerseelen), die Gräber verstorbener Verwandter.

FEIERTAGE

Any Nou *(Neujahr)* 1. Jan
Reis Mags *(Heilige Drei Könige)* 6. Jan
Sant Josep 19. März
Divendres Sant *(Karfreitag)* März/Apr
Dilluns de Pasqua *(Ostermontag)* März/Apr
Festa del Treball *(Tag der Arbeit)* 1. Mai
Sant Joan *(Johannistag)* 24. Juni
Assumpció *(Mariä Himmelfahrt)* 15. Aug
Diada de Catalunya *(Nationalfeiertag)* 11. Sep
La Mercè 24. Sep
Dia de la Hispanitat *(Spanischer Nationalfeiertag)* 12. Okt
Tots Sants *(Allerheiligen)* 1. Nov
Dia de la Constitució *(Verfassungstag)* 6. Dez
Immaculada Concepció *(Unbefleckte Empfängnis)* 8. Dez
Nadal *(Weihnachten)* 25. u. 26. Dez

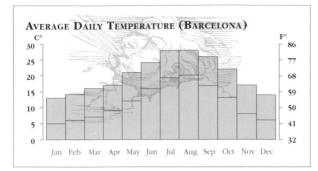

AVERAGE DAILY TEMPERATURE (BARCELONA)

Temperature Chart
This chart shows the average minimum and maximum daily temperatures record-ed in Barcelona. The sunshine in winter can be deceptive, as daytime temperatures can occasionally dip to near freezing. Summer days are consistently hot. Hats and a high-factor sun screen are essential.

WINTER

Ski resorts in the Pyrenees are a popular destination at weekends. Though days can be sunny and lunches still taken alfresco, the weather is unpredictable and the nights can be chilly. Christmas is a particularly delightful time to be in Barcelona, when the city vibrates with the spirit of celebration and sharing. Crafts and decorations are on sale in the Feria de Santa Llúcia in front of the Cathedral.

DECEMBER

Nadal *(25 & 26 Dec).* The two days of Christmas are a time for people to come together. Traditional Christmas lunch consists of an *escudella* (meat stew) followed by turkey stuffed with apples, apricots, prunes, pine nuts and raisins.
Revellón *(31 Dec).* All over Spain on New Year's Eve it has become a custom for people to eat a grape between

A ski resort in the Pyrenees, a popular destination for weekenders

each chime of the midnight bell. To manage the feat brings good luck all year.

JANUARY

Reis Mags *(6 Jan).* On the eve of the Epiphany the three kings arrive in various guises throughout Catalonia giving sweets to children. The main cavalcade in Barcelona is down by the port.
Santa Eulàlia *(12 Jan).* The feast of the ancient patron saint of Barcelona is celebra-ted in the old town. There is

dancing and many people dress up as giants.
Els Tres Tombs *(17 Jan).* Horsemen in top hats and tails ride three times through the city to honour St Anthony, patron saint of animals.
Pelegrí de Tossa *(20 & 21 Jan),* Tossa de Mar. A 40-km (25-mile) pilgrimage marking the end of the plague; this town's biggest annual event.

FEBRUARY

Carnestoltes (Carnival) *(Feb/ Mar).* King Carnival presides over the pre-Lent celebrations, children wear fancy dress and every *barri* (district) in Barcelona puts on a party. Sausage omelettes are eaten on Shrove Tuesday *(Dijous gras),* and on Ash Wednesday *(Dimecres de cendra)* a sardine is ceremoniously buried *(Enterrament de la sardina).* There are big celebrations in Platja d'Aro on the Costa Brava and Vilanova on the Costa Daurada. Sitges is the place to go to see the full transvestite indulgence of the feast.
Internacional de Cotxes d'Època *(first Sun in Lent).* A popular veteran car rally that runs from Barcelona to Sitges.

The winter festival of Els Tres Tombs in Vilanova i la Geltrú

Procession of *gegants* (giants) during the September festival of La Mercé in Barcelona ▷

THE HISTORY OF CATALONIA

The Catalans have always been great seafarers, merchants and industrialists. Since they were united under the House of Barcelona, their nationhood has been threatened by marriages, alliances and conflicts with Madrid, and the road to their present status as a semi-autonomous region within Spain has been marked by times of power and wealth and troughs of weakness and despair.

Barcelona was not a natural site for human settlement. Its port was negligible and its heights, Montjuïc, had no water. The oldest evidence of man in Catalonia comes rather from other sites scattered across the region, notably the dolmens of the Alt (high) Empordà and passage graves of the Baix (low) Empordà and Alt Urgell.

In the first millennium BC the lands around Barcelona were settled by the agrarian Laeitani, while other parts of Catalonia were simultaneously colonized by the Iberians. The latter were great builders in stone and remains of one of their settlements are still visible at Ullastret on the Costa Brava. Greek traders arrived on the coast around 550 BC, founding their first trading post at Empúries (Emporion, *see p102*) near Ullastret. It was the Carthaginians from New Carthage in southern Spain who put Barcelona on the map. They named the city after Hamil Barca, father of Hannibal who led his army of elephants from Catalonia over the Pyrenees and Alps to attack Rome.

Roman mosaic floor excavated in Barcelona depicting the Three Graces

In reprisal, the Romans arrived at Empúries and began the subjugation of the whole Iberian peninsula. They wiped out the Carthaginians as well as the Laeitani and established Tarraco (Tarragona, *see p110*) in the south of Catalonia as the imperial capital of Tarraconensis, one of the three administrative regions of the peninsula.

Roman Barcelona can be seen in the city gate beside the cathedral, while the 3rd-century walls that once encircled the town lie by the medieval Royal Palace (*see p54*). Foundations of the Roman city have been excavated in the basement of the Museu d'Història de la Ciutat (*see p55*), and pillars from the Temple of Augustus can be glimpsed inside the Centre Excursionista de Catalunya (*see p53*) behind the cathedral.

When the Roman empire collapsed, Visigoths based in Toulouse moved in to fill the vacuum. They had been vassals of Rome, practised Roman law, spoke a similar language and in 587 their Aryan king, Reccared, converted to the Christianity of Rome.

◁ **Troops fraternizing with local militia in the Baixada de la Llibreteria, Barcelona, during the 1833–9 Carlist War**

THE MOORS AND CHARLEMAGNE

The Visigoths established their capital at Toledo, just south of modern Madrid. When King Wirtzia died in 710, his son, Akhila, is said to have called on the Saracens from north Africa for help in claiming the throne. In 711, with astonishing speed, Muslim and Berber tribes began to drive up through the Iberian peninsula, reaching Barcelona in 717, then Poitiers in France in 732, where they were finally stopped by the Frankish leader, Charles Martel.

Page from a 15th-century manuscript of the *Llibre del Consolat de Mar*

The Muslims made their capital in Córdoba in southern Spain, while the Visigothic nobles found hiding places in the Pyrenees, from which they conducted sorties against the invaders. They were aided by Charles Martel's grandson, Charles the Great (Charlemagne). In 801 Barcelona was retaken by the Franks, only to be lost and taken again. The shortness of the Muslim occupation left Catalonia, unlike the rest of Spain, unmarked by the culture and language of Islam.

Ramon Berenguer I of Barcelona (1035–76)

THE COUNTS OF BARCELONA

Charlemagne created the Spanish March, a buffer state along the Pyrenees, which he entrusted to local lords. The most powerful figure in the east was Guifré el Pelós (Wilfred the Hairy), who consolidated the counties of Barcelona, Cerdanya, Conflent, Osona Urgell and Girona and founded the monastery of Ripoll *(see p96)* – *el bressol de Catalunya* (the cradle of Catalonia). Guifré died in battle against the Moors in 897, but he had started a dynasty of Counts of Barcelona which was to last, unbroken, for 500 years.

Before the end of the 11th century, under Ramon Berenguer I, Catalonia had established the first constitutional government in Europe with a bill of rights, the *Usatges*. By the early 12th century, under Ramon Berenguer III, Catalonia's boundaries had pushed south past Tarragona. Catalan influence also spread north and east when he married Dolça of Provence, linking the two regions and, more lastingly, the principality of Barcelona was united with its neighbour Aragon in 1137 by the marriage of Ramon Berenguer IV and Petronila of Aragon. In 1196 the great monastery of Poblet *(see pp108–9)* in Tarragona province took the place of Ripoll as the pantheon of Catalan royalty.

717 Catalonia occupied by Muslims

801 Moors ejected. Charlemagne sets up buffer state

Charlemagne (742–814)

1060 Constitution, *Usatges*, is drawn up around the time that the word Catalan is first recorded

AD 700	800	900	1000

711 North African Muslims invade Spanish mainland

Moorish sword

778 Charlemagne, leader of the Franks, begins campaign to drive Moors from Spain

878 Guifré el Pelós (Wilfred the Hairy), Count of Cerdanya-Urgell, consolidates eastern Pyrenees and gains virtual autonomy. He starts 500-year dynasty of Counts of Barcelona

1008–46 Abbot Oliva builds church at Ripoll and oversees Benedicti building including Vic and Monserrat

MARITIME EXPANSION

Under Jaume I the Conqueror (1213–76), Catalonia began a period of prosperity and expansion. By the end of the 13th century the Balearic islands and Sicily had been conquered; many of the ships used in the enterprise were built at the vast Drassanes shipyards in Barcelona (see p65). Catalonia now ruled the seas and the *Llibre del Consolat de Mar* was a code of trading practice that held sway throughout the Mediterranean. Swashbuckling admirals included Roger de Llúria, who won a definitive victory over the French fleet in the Bay of Roses in 1285, and Roger de Flor, leader of a bunch of fierce Catalan and Aragonese mercenaries, the Almogàvers. These won battles for both the King of Sicily and the Byzantine emperor before Roger de Flor was murdered in 1305.

During Jaume I's long reign the *Corts* (parliament) was established, the city walls were rebuilt to enclose an area ten times larger than that enclosed by the old Roman walls, and noble houses arose down the new Carrer Montcada

(see pp 60–61). La Llotja (the stock exchange) was sited by what was then the main port, and the church of Santa Maria del Mar (see p60) was built by grateful merchants. Under Pere IV (1336–87) two great halls were built: the Royal Palace's Saló del

Ex voto in the form of a 15th-century ship

Tinell and the Casa de la Ciutat's Saló de Cent (see pp 54–5).

Prosperity brought a flowering of Catalan literature. Jaume I wrote his own *Llibre dels Feits (Book of Deeds)*, and Pere el Gran's conquest of Sicily in 1282 was described in glowing terms in a chronicle of Catalan history written by Bernat Desclot around 1285. The great Catalan poet Ramon Lull (1232–1315), born in Mallorca, was the first to use a vernacular language in religious writing. From 1395 an annual poetry competition, the Jocs Florals, was held in the city, attracting the region's troubadours. In 1450, Joanot Martorell began writing his Catalan chivalric epic narrative *Tirant lo Blanc*, though he died in 1468, 22 years before it was published. Miguel de Cervantes, author of *Don Quijote*, described it as simply "the best book in the world".

Wall painting showing Jaume I during his campaign to conquer Mallorca

1137 Barcelona united to neighbouring Aragon by royal marriage	1258–72 *Consolat de Mar*, a code of trading practice, holds sway throughout the Mediterranean	1282 Pere el Gran takes Sicily. His exploits are recorded in Desclot's *Chronicles*	1347–8 Black death kills a quarter of the population		
				1359 Generalitat founded	1423 Conquest of Naples
1100	**1200**		**1300**	**1400**	
1148 Frontier with Moors pushed back to Riu Ebre	1213–35 Jaume I (The Conqueror) takes Mallorca, Ibiza and Formentera		1324 Sardinia captured		
			1302–5 Catalan mercenaries under Admiral Roger de Flor aid Byzantium against the Turks		
	Jaume I (1213–76)	1287 Conquest of Mallorca under Alfons III			

FERNANDO AND ISABEL OF CASTILE

Catholic Spain was united in 1479 when Fernando II of Catalonia-Aragon married Isabel of Castile, a region which by then had absorbed the rest of northern Spain. In 1492 they drove the last of the Moors from the peninsula, then, in a fever of righteousness, also drove out the Jews, who

Baptizing Jews during the era of the Catholic Monarchs

had large and commercially important populations in Barcelona *(see p54)* and Girona. This was the same year that Columbus had set foot in America, returning in triumph to Barcelona with six Carib Indians *(see p56).* However, the city lost out when the monopoly on New World trade was given to Seville and Cádiz. Though it still had great moments, such as its involvement in the victory over the Turks at Lepanto in 1571 *(see p65),* Barcelona went into a period of decline.

REVOLTS AND SEIGES

During the Thirty Years War with France (1618–59), Felipe IV forced Barcelona's *Corts* to raise an army to fight the French, towards whom the Catalans bore no grudge. A viceroy was imposed on the city and unruly Spanish troops were billeted throughout the region. In June 1640 the population arose, and harvesters *(segadors)* murdered the viceroy. The *Song of the Harvesters* is still sung at Catalan gatherings *(see p32).* Barcelona then allied itself with France, but was besieged and defeated by Felipe. The peace of 1659 ceded Catalan lands north of the Pyrenees to France.

Wall tile for a Catalan trade guild

A second confrontation with Madrid arose during the War of the Spanish Succession when Europe's two dominant royal houses, the Habsburgs and Bourbons, both laid claim to the throne. Barcelona, with England as an ally, found itself on the losing side, supporting the Habsburgs. As a result, it was heavily

The great siege of Barcelona in 1714 during the War of the Spanish Succession

TIMELINE

1492 Columbus discovers Americas. Barcelona barred from trade with the New World. Jews expelled	**1494** Supreme Council of Aragon brings Catalonia under Castilian control	*The Spanish Inquisition, active from 1478*	**1619** Spanish capital established in Madrid	**1659** Treaty of the Pyrenees at end of Thirty Years War draws new border with France; Roussillon ceded to France
AD 1450	**AD 1500**	**AD 1550**	**AD 1600**	**AD 1650**
1479 Fernando II of Catalonia-Aragon marries Isabel of Castile, uniting all the houses of Spain	**1490** *Tirant lo Blanc,* epic tale of chivalry by Martorell *(see p39),* published in Catalan	**1571** Vast fleet sets sail from Barcelona to defeat the Ottomans at sea at Lepanto	**1640** Revolt of the harvesters *(segadors)* against Spanish exploitation of Catalan resources during Thirty Years War with France

Women joining in the defence of Girona against
the Napoleonic French in 1809

besieged by troops of the incoming
Bourbon king, Felipe V. The city fell
on 11 September 1714, today celebrated
as National Day (see p32). Felipe then
proceeded to annul all of Catalonia's
privileges. Its language was banned,
its universities closed and Lleida's
Gothic cathedral became a barracks.
Felipe tore down the Ribera district of
Barcelona and, in what is now Ciutadella Park (see p62), built a citadel to
keep an eye on the population.

With the lifting of trade restric-
tions with the Americas, Catalonia
began to recover economically.
Progress, however, was inter-
rupted by the 1793–95 war with
France and then by the 1808–14
Peninsular War (known in Spain
as the War of Independence) when
Napoleon put his brother Joseph
on the Spanish throne. Barcelona
fell in early 1808, but Girona
withstood a seven-month siege.
Monasteries, including Montserrat

(see pp104–5) were sacked and pillaged.
They suffered further in 1835 under a
republican government when many
were seen as too rich and powerful
and were dissolved. This was a polit-
ically vigorous time, when a minority
of largely rural reactionaries fought a
rearguard action against the liberal
spirit of the century in the Carlist Wars.

THE CATALAN RENAIXENÇA

Barcelona was the first city in Spain to
industrialize, mainly around cotton
manufacture, from imported raw material from the Americas. It brought
immigrant workers and a burgeoning
population, and in 1854 the city burst
out of its medieval walls (see p67).
Inland, industrial centres such as
Terrassa and Sabadell flourished and
colònies industrials (industrial work-
houses) grew up along the rivers
where mills were powered by water.

Just as the wealth of the 14th century
inspired Catalonia's first flowering, so
the wealth from industry inspired the
Renaixença, a renaissance of Catalan
culture. Its literary rallying points were
Bonaventura Aribau's Oda a la patria
and the poems of a young monk, Jacint
Verdaguer, who won poetry prizes in
the revived Jocs Florals (see p39).

Well-to-do barcelonins selecting from a wide range of
locally produced calico in the early 19th century

|
Felipe V
(1700–24)	1808–14 Peninsular War (War of Independence): Girona besieged, Barcelona occupied, Monastery of Montserrat sacked	1823–6 French occupy Catalonia	1835 Monasteries dissolved	
			1833–9 First Carlist War	1859 Revival of Jocs Florals poetry competition feeds Renaissance of Catalan culture.
AD 1700	**AD 1750**	**AD 1800**	**AD 1850**	
	1714 Barcelona sacked by Felipe V, first Bourbon king. Catalan univer- sities closed. Catalan language banned			1849 Spain's first railway built to link Barcelona and Martorell
	1778 Catalonia allowed to trade with the Americas, bringing new wealth		1833 Aribau's Oda a la patria published Poet Bonaventura Carles Aribau i Farriols	

A hall of Spanish goods at the 1888 Universal Exhibition

CATALANISM AND MODERNISME

The *Renaixença* produced a new pride in Catalonia, and "Catalanism" was at the heart of the region's accelerating move towards autonomy, a move echoed in Galicia and the Basque Country. Interruptions by the Carlist Wars came to an end in 1876 and resulted in the restoration of the Bourbon monarchy.

The first home-rule party, the *Lliga de Catalunya*, was founded in 1887, and disputes with the central government continued. It was blamed for the loss of the American colonies, and therefore lucrative transatlantic trade, and for involving Spain in unnecessary conflict in Morocco. *La setmana tràgica* (tragic week) of 1909 saw the worst of the violent protests: 116 people died and 300 were injured.

Meanwhile, on a more cultural and artistic level and to show off its increasing wealth, Barcelona held in 1888 a

Poster for 1929 Exhibition

Universal Exhibition in the Parc de la Ciutadella where Felipe V's citadel had recently been torn down. The urban expansion *(eixample)* inland was carefully ordered under a plan by Ildefons Cerdà *(see p67)* and industrial barons employed imaginative architects to show off their wealth, most successfully Eusebi Güell and Antoni Gaudí *(see pp22–3)*. The destruction of the monasteries had left spaces for sumptuous buildings such as the Palau de la Música Catalana *(see p61)*, the Liceu opera house and La Boqueria market *(see p135)*.

Spain's non-involvement in World War I meant that Catalonia's Modernista architecture was unscathed. Barcelona's place as a showcase city was confirmed with the 1929 International

Antoni Gaudí, Modernisme's most creative architect

Exhibition on Montjuïc, many of whose buildings still remain.

CIVIL WAR

The *Mancomunitat*, a local council established in 1914, disappeared on the arrival in 1923 of the dictator Primo de Rivera, Barcelona's military governor. In 1931 Francesc Macià declared himself President of the Catalan Republic, which lasted three days. Three years later Lluís Companys was arrested and sentenced to 30 years' imprisonment for repeating the experiment.

TIMELINE

1872–6 Third and last Carlist War	**1888** Universal Exhibition held in Parc de la Ciutadella, showing off the new Modernista style		*Primo de Rivera (1870–1930)*	
		1909 *Setmana tràgica:* violent protest against Moroccan Wars		

AD 1875		AD 1900		AD 192

| | **1893** Anarchist bombs in Liceu opera house kill 14 | **1901** *Lliga Regionalista,* new Catalan party, wins elections | **1929** International Exhibition on Montjuïc | |
| | *Carlist soldiers* | | **1931** Francesc Macià declares independence for Catalonia | |

Refugees on the march in 1939, fleeing towards the Pyrenees to seek asylum in France

Finally, on 16 July 1936, General Francisco Franco led an army revolt against the Republican government and the fledgling autonomous states. The government fled Madrid to Valencia, then Barcelona. City and coast were bombed by German aircraft, and shelled by Italian warships. When Barcelona fell three years later, thousands escaped to camps in France and thousands, including Companys, were executed in Franco's reprisals. Catalonia lost all it had gained, and its language was outlawed once more.

The *noche negra*, the dark night that followed Franco's victory, left Barcelona short of resources and largely neglected by Madrid. The 1960s, however, brought new economic opportunities, and between 1960 and 1975 two million Spaniards came to work in the city. The arrival of the first tourists to the coast during that time, to the Costa Brava and Costa Daurada, changed the face of Spain for ever.

LIFE AFTER FRANCO

Champagne flowed freely in Barcelona's streets on the news of Franco's death in 1975. Democracy and the monarchy, under the Bourbon Juan Carlos, were restored and Jordi Pujol of the conservative *Convergència i Unió* party was elected leader of the Generalitat, Catalonia's regional government. Catalonia has since won a large degree of autonomy, including tax-raising powers.

Barcelona's socialist mayor Pasqual Maragall, a town planner, steered through the radical shake-up of the city for the 1992 Olympic Games. In less than a decade, in what seems like a second *Renaixença*, Barcelona changed dramatically, with a bold new waterfront, inspired urban spaces, new access roads, and state-of-the-art museums and galleries.

Opening ceremony, 1992 Barcelona Olympic Games

1939 50,000 go into exile in France. Catalan President Companys executed	**1975** Franco dies. King Juan Carlos restores Bourbon line	
1947 Spain declared a monarchy with Franco as regent	**1979** Partial autonomy granted to Catalonia	**1992** Olympic Games held in Barcelona
AD 1950	AD 1975	AD 2000
1953 US bases welcomed	**1960s** Costa Brava leads package holiday boom	**1985** Medes Islands become Spain's first marine nature reserve
1936–9 Spanish Civil War. Republican government retreats from Madrid to Valencia, then Barcelona		**1986** Spain enters European Union

Cobi, the Olympic mascot

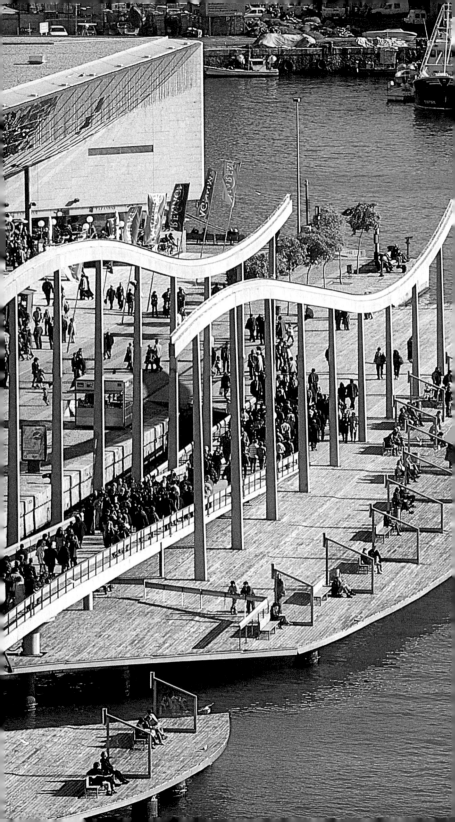

BARCELONA
AND CATALONIA

Introducing Barcelona

BARCELONA, one of the Mediterranean's busiest ports, is more than the capital of Catalonia. In culture, commerce and sports it not only rivals Madrid, but also considers itself on a par with the greatest European cities. The success of the 1992 Olympic Games, staged in the Parc de Montjuïc, confirmed this to the world. Although there are plenty of historical monuments in the Ciutat Vella (Old Town), Barcelona is best known for the scores of buildings in the Eixample left by the artistic explosion of Modernisme (see pp22–3) in the decades around 1900. Always open to outside influences because of its location on the coast, not too far from the French border, Barcelona continues to sizzle with creativity: its bars and the public parks speak more of bold contemporary design than of tradition.

Casa Milà (see p73) is the most avant-garde of all the works of Antoni Gaudí (see p72). Barcelona has more Art Nouveau buildings than any other city in the world.

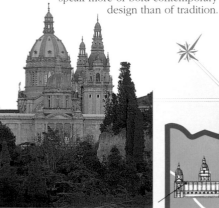

Palau Nacional (see p80), on the hill of Montjuïc, dominates the monumental halls and the fountain-filled avenue built for the 1929 International Exhibition. It now houses the Museu Nacional d'Art de Catalunya, an exceptional collection of medieval art, rich in Romanesque frescoes.

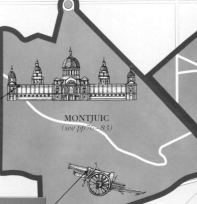

MONTJUIC
(see pp76–83)

Christopher Columbus surveys the waterfront from the top of a 60-m (200-ft) column (see p65) in the heart of the Port Vell (Old Port). From the top, visitors can look out over the new promenades and quays that have revitalized the area.

Montjuïc Castle (see p81) is a massive fortification dating from the 17th century. Sited on the crest of the hill of Montjuïc, it offers panoramic views of the city and port, and forms a sharp contrast to the ultra-modern sports halls built nearby for the 1992 Olympic Games.

0 kilometres   1

0 miles   0.5

◁ La Rambla de Mar crossing the water in the Old Port to the Maremàgnum leisure complex

The Sagrada Família (see pp74–5), Gaudí's unfinished masterpiece, begun in 1882, rises above the streets of the Eixample. Its polychrome ceramic mosaics and sculptural forms inspired by nature are typical of his work.

EIXAMPLE
(see pp66–75)

Barcelona cathedral (see pp56–7) is a magnificent 14th-century building in the heart of the Barri Gòtic (Gothic Quarter). It has 28 side chapels which encircle the nave and contain some splendid Baroque altarpieces. The keeping of white geese in the cloisters is a centuries-old tradition.

OLD TOWN
(see pp50–65)

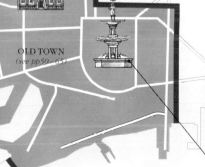

Parc de la Ciutadella (see p62), between the Old Town and the Vila Olímpica, has something for everyone. The gardens full of statuary offer relaxation, the boating lake and the zoo are fun, while the three museums within its gates cover art, geology and zoology.

La Rambla (see pp58–9) is the most famous street in Spain, alive at all hours of the day and night. A stroll down its length to the seafront, taking in its palatial buildings, shops, cafés and street vendors, makes a perfect introduction to Barcelona life.

La Ruta del Modernisme

THE 50 EXAMPLES of Modernista architecture in Barcelona, mapped here, lie along a route designed by the city's tourist office. A *Multi-ticket*, which allows you to plan your own itinerary as time allows, is the best way to see them. The Casa Lleó Morera, where the tickets are sold, Palau Güell and Palau de la Música Catalana all have guided tours, and there is free entry to the selected museums. Many of the other premises are shops, cafés and hotels in private hands, and often, tantalizingly, the interiors are not open to the public. The best-known sites are described in detail elsewhere in this book.

Casa Vicens
This bright, angular, turreted building by Antoni Gaudí, with ceramic mosaics and patterned brickwork, shows Moorish influence. The iron gate and fencing are hallmarks of his work ㊽

Palau Baró de Quadras
Built in 1906, this handsome house is by Josep Puig i Cadafalch. The intricate, sculptured frieze above the first floor windows has close affinities to Spanish early Renaissance Plateresque style ㊶

Casa Lleó Morera
The first-floor dining room of this house is one of Barcelona's most stunning interiors. The stained-glass windows are by Lluís Rigalt and the eight ceramic mosaic wall panels, depicting idyllic country scenes, are by Gaspar Homar ⑲

Antiga Casa Figueres
The mosaic, stained-glass and wrought iron decoration of this, the most famous of the city's Modernista stores, was carried out in 1902 by Antoni Ros i Güell. It is today the elegant Pastisseria Escribà ⑦

KEY

- - - Walking route

_24_ Bus route

— Metro route

0 metres   500

0 yards   500

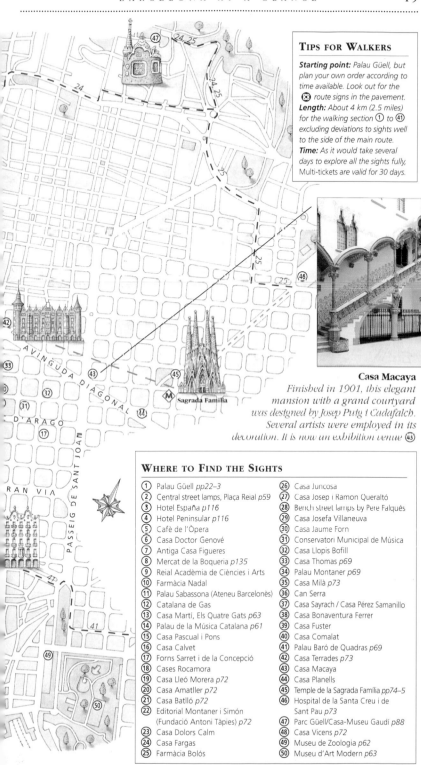

TIPS FOR WALKERS

Starting point: *Palau Güell, but plan your own order according to time available. Look out for the* ⊙ *route signs in the pavement.*
Length: *About 4 km (2.5 miles) for the walking section* ① *to* ㊶ *excluding deviations to sights well to the side of the main route.*
Time: *As it would take several days to explore all the sights fully, Multi-tickets are valid for 30 days.*

Casa Macaya
Finished in 1901, this elegant mansion with a grand courtyard was designed by Josep Puig i Cadafalch. Several artists were employed in its decoration. It is now an exhibition venue ㊸

WHERE TO FIND THE SIGHTS

① Palau Güell pp22–3
② Central street lamps, Plaça Reial p59
③ Hotel España p116
④ Hotel Peninsular p116
⑤ Cafè de l'Òpera
⑥ Casa Doctor Genové
⑦ Antiga Casa Figueres
⑧ Mercat de la Boqueria p135
⑨ Reial Acadèmia de Ciències i Arts
⑩ Farmàcia Nadal
⑪ Palau Sabassona (Ateneu Barcelonès)
⑫ Catalana de Gas
⑬ Casa Martí, Els Quatre Gats p63
⑭ Palau de la Música Catalana p61
⑮ Casa Pascual i Pons
⑯ Casa Calvet
⑰ Forns Sarret i de la Concepció
⑱ Cases Rocamora
⑲ Casa Lleó Morera p72
⑳ Casa Amatller p72
㉑ Casa Batlló p72
㉒ Editorial Montaner i Simón (Fundació Antoni Tàpies) p72
㉓ Casa Dolors Calm
㉔ Casa Fargas
㉕ Farmàcia Bolós

㉖ Casa Juncosa
㉗ Casa Josep i Ramon Queraltó
㉘ Bench street lamps by Pere Falqués
㉙ Casa Josefa Villanueva
㉚ Casa Jaume Forn
㉛ Conservatori Municipal de Música
㉜ Casa Llopis Bofill
㉝ Casa Thomas p69
㉞ Palau Montaner p69
㉟ Casa Milà p73
㊱ Can Serra
㊲ Casa Sayrach / Casa Pérez Samanillo
㊳ Casa Bonaventura Ferrer
㊴ Casa Fuster
㊵ Casa Comalat
㊶ Palau Baró de Quadras p69
㊷ Casa Terrades p73
㊸ Casa Macaya
㊹ Casa Planells
㊺ Temple de la Sagrada Família pp74–5
㊻ Hospital de la Santa Creu i de Sant Pau p73
㊼ Parc Güell/Casa-Museu Gaudí p88
㊽ Casa Vicens p72
㊾ Museu de Zoologia p62
㊿ Museu d'Art Modern p63

OLD TOWN

THE OLD TOWN, traversed by the city's most famous avenue, La Rambla, is one of the most extensive and harmonious medieval city centres in Europe. The Barri Gòtic (Gothic Quarter) contains the cathedral and ancient royal palace. Adjoining it is La Ribera, full of 14th-century mansions, one of which is occupied by the Museu Picasso. This area is bounded by the pleasant Parc de la Ciutadella, which contains the Museu d'Art Modern and the zoo. The revitalized seafront is a stimulating mix of old and new. Trendy shops and restaurants and a fashionable marina contrast with the historic shipyards, while reclaimed beaches flank the new Olympic Port.

SIGHTS AT A GLANCE

Museums and Galleries
Museu d'Art Contemporani **9**
Museu d'Art Modern **21**
Museu Frederic Marès **2**
Museu de Geologia **19**
Museu d'Història de la
  Ciutat **4**
Museu Marítim and
  Drassanes **28**
Museu Picasso **14**
Museu de Zoologia **18**

Harbour Sights
Golondrinas **27**
Port Olímpic **23**
Port Vell **25**

Streets and Districts
Barceloneta **24**
Carrer Montcada **13**
La Rambla **10**

El Raval and Barri Xinès **8**

Churches
Basílica de Santa Maria
  del Mar **12**
Cathedral (pp56–7) **7**

Historic Buildings
Casa de l'Ardiaca **1**
Casa de la Ciutat **5**
La Llotja **11**
Palau de la Generalitat **6**
Palau de la Música Catalana **15**
Palau Reial Major **3**

Monuments
Arc del Triomf **16**
Homenatge a Picasso **20**
Monument a Colom **26**

Parks and Gardens
Parc de la Ciutadella **17**
Parc Zoològic **22**

GETTING THERE
The area is well served by Metro lines 1, 3 and 4; Jaume I station is in the heart of the Barri Gòtic. Many buses pass through the Plaça de Catalunya on the edge of the Barri Gòtic.

KEY

▨	Street-by-Street map pp52–3
Ⓜ	Metro station
🚉	Train station
▥	Main bus stop
🛈	Tourist information
🅿	Parking

◁ **Els Quatre Gats café in one of the narrow streets of Barcelona's Barri Gòtic**

Street-by-Street: Barri Gòtic

THE BARRI GOTIC (Gothic Quarter) is the true heart of Barcelona. The oldest part of the city, it was the site chosen by the Romans in the reign of Augustus (27 BC–AD 14) on which to found a new *colonia* (town), and has been the location of the city's administrative buildings ever since. The Roman forum was on the Plaça de Sant Jaume, where now stand the medieval Palau de la Generalitat, Catalonia's parliament, and the Casa de la Ciutat,

Wax candle, Cereria Subirà

Barcelona's town hall. Close by are the Gothic cathedral and royal palace, where Columbus was received by Fernando and Isabel on his return from his voyage to the New World in 1492 *(see p40)*.

Casa de l'Ardiaca
Built on the Roman city wall, the Gothic-Renaissance archdeacon's residence now houses Barcelona's historical archives ❶

To Plaça de Catalunya

★ **Cathedral**
The façade and spire are 19th-century additions to the original Gothic building. Among the artistic treasures inside are medieval Catalan paintings ❼

SANT SEVER

CARRER DEL BISBE

PIETA

SANT DOMÈNEC DEL CALL

SANT HONORAT

Palau de la Generalitat
Catalonia's parliament retains superb Gothic features, which include the chapel and a stone staircase rising to an open-air, arcaded gallery ❻

CARRER DE FERRAN

PLAÇA DE SANT JAUME

To La Rambla

CARRER DE LA CIUTAT

Casa de la Ciutat
Barcelona's town hall was built in the 14th and 15th centuries. The façade is a Neo-Classical addition. In the entrance hall stands Three Gypsy Boys *by Joan Rebull (1899–1981), a 1976 copy of a sculpture he originally created in 1946* ❺

KEY

 Suggested route

Museu Frederic Marès

This medieval doorway is from an extensive display of Spanish sculpture – the mainstay of this museum's extraordinarily eclectic and high-quality collections ❷

LOCATOR MAP
See Street Finder map 5

Roman city wall

Saló del Tinell

TAPINERIA

CARRER DELS COMTES DE BARCELONA

★ Palau Reial Major

The 14th-century Capella Reial de Santa Àgata, with a 1466 altarpiece, is one of the best surviving sections of the palace ❸

Capella Reial de Santa Àgata

Plaça del Rei

Palau del Lloctinent

Cereria Subirà candle shop

VIA LAIETANA

CARRER DE JAUME I

Jaume I
Metro

CARRER DAGUERIA

SOTS-TINENT NAVARRO

Museu d'Història de la Ciutat

Housed in a 14th-century mansion, which was moved here in 1931, the museum focuses on Barcelona's development in the 13th and 14th centuries. The foundations of the Roman city can be seen in the basement ❹

The Centre Excursionista de Catalunya, housed in a medieval mansion, displays Roman columns from the Temple of Augustus, whose site is marked by a millstone in the street outside.

STAR SIGHTS

★ Cathedral

★ Palau Reial Major

---

0 metres   100
0 yards   100

Decorated marble mailbox, Casa de l'Ardiaca

Casa de l'Ardiaca ❶

Carrer de Santa Llúcia 1. **Map** 5 B2.
📞 93 318 11 95. 🚇 Jaume I.
🕐 Sep–Jul: 9am–8:45pm Mon–Fri,
9am–1pm Sat; Aug: 9am–2pm
Mon–Fri. 🔴 public hols.

STANDING BESIDE what was
originally the Bishop's
Gate in the Roman wall is
the Archdeacon's House.
It was built in the 12th
century, but its present
form dates from around
1500 when it was remodel-
led, including the addition
of a colonnade. In 1870
this was extended to
form the Flamboyant
Gothic patio around a
fountain. The Modernista
architect Domènech i Montaner
(1850–1923) added the fanciful
marble mailbox, carved with
three swallows and a tortoise,
beside the Renaissance portal.
Upstairs is the Arxiu Històric
de la Ciutat (City Archives).

Museu Frederic Marès ❷

Plaça de Sant Iu 5. **Map** 5 B2.
📞 93 310 58 00. 🚇 Jaume I.
🕐 10am–5pm Tue–Sat, 10am–2pm
Sun & public hols. 🔴 1 Jan, Good
Fri, 1 May, 25 Dec. 🈚

THE SCULPTOR Frederic Marès
i Deulovol (1893–1991) was
also a traveller and collector,
and this extraordinary museum
is a monument to his eclectic
taste. The building is part of
the Royal Palace complex and
was occupied by 13th-century
bishops, 14th-century counts
of Barcelona, 15th-century
judges and 18th-century nuns,

Virgin, Museu Frederic Marès

who lived here until they
were expelled in 1936. Marès,
who had a small apartment in
the building, opened
this museum in 1948.
It is one of the most
fascinating in the city
and has an outstand-
ing collection of
Romanesque and
Gothic religious art.
In the crypt there
is an extensive as-
semblage of stone
sculptures and two
complete Roman-
esque portals.
Exhibits on the
three floors above
range from clocks,
crucifixes and cos-
tumes to antique
cameras, pipes, tobacco jars
and pin-up postcards. There is
also a wonderful amusement
room full of children's toys.

Palau Reial Major ❸

Plaça del Rei. **Map** 5 B2. 📞 93 315
11 11. 🚇 Jaume I. 🕐 10am–2pm
& 4–8pm Tue–Sat, 10am–2pm Sun.
🔴 1 Jan, Good Fri, 25 & 26 Dec. 🈚

THE ROYAL PALACE was the
residence of the count-
kings of Barcelona from its
foundation in the 13th century.
The complex includes the 14th-
century Gothic Saló del Tinell,
a massive room with semicircular arches spanning 17 m
(56 ft). This is where Isabel and
Fernando (see p40) received
Columbus after his triumphal
return from America. It is also
where the Holy Inquisition sat,
believing the walls would
move if lies were told.
On the right, built into the
Roman city wall, is the royal
chapel, the Capella de Santa
Àgata, with a painted wood

**Gothic nave of the Capella de
Santa Àgata, Palau Reial**

BARCELONA'S EARLY JEWISH COMMUNITY

From the 11th to the 13th centuries Jews
dominated Barcelona's commerce and
culture, providing doctors and founding
the first seat of learning. But in 1243, 354
years after they were first documented in
the city, violent anti-Semitism led to the
Jews being consigned to a ghetto, El Call.
Ostensibly to provide protection, the
ghetto had only one entrance, which led
into the Plaça de Sant Jaume. Jews were
heavily taxed by the monarch, who viewed
them as "royal serfs"; but in return they also received
privileges, as they handled most of Catalonia's lucrative trade
with North Africa. However, official and popular persecution
finally led to the disappearance of the ghetto in 1401, 91
years before Judaism was fully outlawed in Spain (see p40).
   Originally there were three synagogues, the main one being
in Carrer Sant Domènec del Call, but only the foundations
are left. A 14th-century Hebrew tablet is embedded in the wall
at No. 1 Carrer de Marlet, which reads: "Holy Foundation
of Rabbi Samuel Hassardi, for whom life never ends".

Hebrew tablet

ceiling and an altarpiece (1466) by Jaume Huguet *(see p24)*. Its bell tower is formed by part of a watchtower on the Roman wall. Stairs through a small door on the right of the altar lead to the 16th-century tower of Martí the Humanist (who reigned from 1396–1410), the last ruler of the 500-year dynasty of the count-kings of Barcelona. From the top of the tower there are fine views over the royal complex.

Museu d'Història de la Ciutat ❹

Plaça del Rei. **Map** 5 B2. **[** 93 315 11 11. **∅** Jaume I. **⟳** 10am–2pm & 4–8pm Tue–Sat, 10am–2pm Sun. **⬤** 1 Jan, Good Fri, 25 & 26 Dec. **⬛**

THE CITY MUSEUM occupies the Casa Clariana-Padellàs, a Gothic building that, in 1931, was brought stone by stone to its present location from its original site in Carrer dels Mercaders. During the excavation of its new site, the remains of Roman water and drainage systems, baths, mosaic floors and a road were found. These can be seen in the basement that extends beneath the Plaça de l'Àngel. A short stretch of the Roman city wall is accessible from the upper floors, which are devoted to Barcelona's post-Roman development.

Casa de la Ciutat ❺

Plaça de Sant Jaume. **Map** 5 A2. **[** 93 402 70 00. **∅** Jaume I. **⟳** 12 Feb (St Eulàlia's Day), 23 Apr (St Jordi's Day). **⬛ ⬛**

THE MAGNIFICENT 14th-century city hall *(ajuntament)* faces the Palau de la Generalitat across the Plaça de Sant Jaume. Flanking the entrance of the Casa de la Ciutat are statues of Jaume I *(see p39)*, who granted the city rights to elect councillors in 1249, and Joan Fiveller, who levied taxes on court members in the 1500s.

Inside is the huge council chamber, the 14th-century Saló de Cent, built for the city's 100 councillors. The Saló de les Cròniques, on the first floor, was commissioned for the 1929 International Exhibition and decorated by Josep-Maria Sert *(see p25)* with murals of great events in Catalan history.

Palau de la Generalitat ❻

Plaça de Sant Jaume. **Map** 5 A2. **[** 93 402 46 00. **∅** Jaume I. **⟳** 23 Apr (St Jordi's Day) (write in advance for permission). **⬛ ⬛**

SINCE 1403 the Generalitat has been the seat of the Catalonian Government. Above the entrance, in its Renaissance

The Italianate façade of the Palau de la Generalitat

façade, is a statue of Sant Jordi (St George) – the patron saint of Catalonia – and the Dragon. The late Catalan-Gothic courtyard is by Marc Safont (1416).

Among the fine interiors are the Gothic chapel of Sant Jordi, also by Safont, and Pere Blai's Italianate Saló de Sant Jordi. The building is open to the public only on the saint's feast day. At the back, one floor above street level, lies the *Pati dels Tarongers*, the Orange Tree Patio, by Pau Mateu, which has a bell tower built by Pere Ferrer in 1568.

The Catalan president has offices here as well as in the Casa dels Canonges. The two buildings are connected across Carrer del Bisbe by a bridge built in 1928 and modelled on the Bridge of Sighs in Venice.

The magnificent council chamber, the Saló de Cent, in the Casa de la Ciutat

Barcelona Cathedral ❼

THIS COMPACT GOTHIC CATHEDRAL, with a Romanesque chapel (the Capella de Santa Llúcia) and beautiful cloister, was begun in 1298 under Jaume II, on the foundations of a Roman temple and Moorish mosque. It was not finished until the early 20th century, when the central spire was completed. A white marble choir screen, sculpted in the 16th century, depicts the martyrdom of St Eulàlia, the city's patron. Next to the font, a plaque records the baptism of six native Caribbeans, brought back from the Americas by Columbus in 1493.

Statue of St Eulàlia

The twin octagonal bell towers date from 1386–93. The bells were installed in this tower in 1545.

The main façade was not completed until 1889, and the central spire until 1913. It was based on the original 1408 plans of the French architect Charles Galters.

Nave Interior
The Catalan-style Gothic interior has a single wide nave with 28 side chapels. These are set between the columns supporting the vaulted ceiling, which rises to 26 m (85 ft).

★ **Choir Stalls**
The top tier of the beautifully carved 15th-century stalls contains painted coats of arms (1518) of several European kings.

Capella del Santíssim Sagrament
This small chapel houses the 16th-century Christ of Lepanto crucifix.

Capella de Sant Benet
This chapel, dedicated to the founder of the Benedictine Order and patron saint of Europe, houses a magnificent altarpiece showing The Transfiguration *by Bernat Martorell (1452).*

VISITORS' CHECKLIST

Plaça de la Seu. **Map** 5 A2. **☎**
93 315 15 54. **Ⓜ** Jaume I. **🚌**
17, 19, 45. **◯** 8am–1:30pm, 5–
7:30pm daily. **🚫 ✔ ♿ Sacristy
Museum** ◯ 10am–1pm, 4–7pm
daily (Sun am only). **🚫 Choir** ◯
10am–1pm, 4–7pm daily (Sun
am only). **🚫 ✝** 9am, 10am,
11am, noon daily; 6pm, 7pm Sat.

★ Crypt
In the crypt, beneath the main altar, is the alabaster sarcophagus (1339) of St Eulàlia, martyred for her beliefs by the Romans during the 4th century AD.

★ Cloisters
The fountain, set in a corner of the Gothic cloisters and decorated with a statue of St George, provided fresh water.

Porta de Santa Eulàlia,
entrance to cloisters

The Sacristy Museum has a small treasury. Pieces include an 11th-century font, tapestries and liturgical artifacts.

Capella de Santa Llúcia

STAR FEATURES

★ Choir Stalls

★ Crypt

★ Cloisters

TIMELINE

400	700	1000	1300	1600	1900
559 Basilica dedicated to St Eulàlia and Holy Cross		**1339** St Eulàlia's relics transferred to alabaster sarcophagus		**1913** Central spire completed	
	877 St Eulàlia's remains brought here from Santa Maria del Mar	**1046–58** Romanesque cathedral built under Ramon Berenguer I		**1889** Main façade completed, based on plans dating from 1408 by architect Charles Galters	
4th century Original Roman (paleo-Christian) basilica built	**985** Building destroyed by the Moors	**1257–68** Romanesque Capella de Santa Llúcia built	**1493** Indians brought back from the Americas are baptized		
		1298 Gothic cathedral begun under Jaume II		*Plaque of the Caribbeans' baptism*	

El Raval and the Barri Xinès ❽

Map 2 F3. ⚙ *Catalunya, Liceu.*

THE DISTRICT of El Raval lies to the right of La Rambla, if you are heading towards the sea, and includes the old red-light area near the port – the Barri Xinès (Chinese quarter).

From the 14th century, the city hospital was in Carrer de l'Hospital, which still has several herbal and medicinal shops. It was here that Gaudí *(see p72)* was brought after being fatally hit by a tram in 1926, just before the hospital closed. The buildings, with quiet courtyards, now house the Biblioteca de Catalunya (Catalonian Library), but the elegant former dissecting room has been fully restored.

Towards the port in Carrer Nou de la Rambla is Gaudí's extraordinary, six-storey Palau Güell *(see p23)*. At the end of the street is the city's most complete Romanesque church, the 12th-century Sant Pau del Camp, where resident Franciscans sing a plainsong mass.

Museu d'Art Contemporani ❾

Plaça dels Angels 1. **Map** 2 F2.
📞 *93 412 08 10.* ⚙ *Universitat, Catalunya, Liceu.* ☐ *11:30am–7:30pm Tue–Sat, 10am–3pm Sun & public hols.* ♿ ♿

THIS DRAMATIC, white, glass-fronted building in the heart of El Raval was designed by the American architect Richard Meier and completed in 1995. Its light, airy galleries on three floors display paintings, installation art and other modern works. Much of the space is devoted to changing exhibitions, but there is a growing permanent collection of works from the 1950s onwards. The focus is on Catalan art and the foreign trends and artists that have influenced it.

Adjacent to it is an 18th-century hospice, the Casa de la Caritat, which has been made into a centre for contemporary culture. It holds imaginative temporary exhibitions.

La Rambla ❿

THE HISTORIC AVENUE of La Rambla, leading to the sea, is busy around the clock, especially in the evenings and at weekends. Newsstands, caged bird and flower stalls, tarot readers, musicians and mime artists throng the wide, tree-shaded central walkway. Among its famous buildings are the Liceu Opera House, the huge Boqueria food market and some grand mansions.

Exploring La Rambla
The name of this long avenue, also known as Les Rambles, comes from the Arabic *ramla*, meaning the dried-up bed of a seasonal river. Barcelona's 13th-century city wall follow-ed the left bank of one such river that flowed from the Collserola hills down to the sea. Convents, monasteries and the university were built on the opposite bank in the 16th century. As time passed, the riverbed was filled in and those buildings demolished, but they are remembered in the names of the five consecu-tive Rambles that make up the great avenue between the Port Vell (Old Port) and Plaça de Catalunya. Visitors should be vigilant of their personal secu-rity *(see p144)* on La Rambla.

Palau Güell C/ Nou de la Rambla 3. **Map** 2 F3. 📞 *93 317 39 74.* ⚙ *Liceu.* ☐ *10am–1pm & 4–6:30pm Mon–Fri.* ⬤ *public hols.* ♿ **Museu de Cera** Pg de la Banca 7. **Map** 2 F4. 📞 *93 317 26 49.* ⚙ *Drassanes.* ☐ *10am–1:30pm & 4–7:30pm Mon–Fri, 10am–1:30pm & 4:30–8pm Sat, Sun & public hols.* ♿

The monument to Columbus at the bottom of the tree-lined Rambla

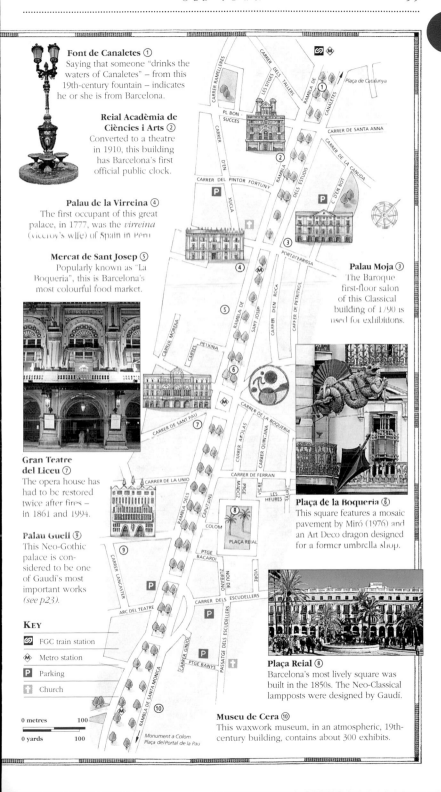

Font de Canaletes ①
Saying that someone "drinks the waters of Canaletes" – from this 19th-century fountain – indicates he or she is from Barcelona.

Reial Acadèmia de Ciències i Arts ②
Converted to a theatre in 1910, this building has Barcelona's first official public clock.

Palau de la Virreina ④
The first occupant of this great palace, in 1777, was the *virreina* (viceroy's wife) of Spain in Peru.

Mercat de Sant Josep ⑤
Popularly known as "La Boqueria", this is Barcelona's most colourful food market.

Gran Teatre del Liceu ⑦
The opera house has had to be restored twice after fires – in 1861 and 1994.

Palau Güell ⑨
This Neo-Gothic palace is considered to be one of Gaudí's most important works *(see p23).*

Palau Moja ③
The Baroque first-floor salon of this Classical building of 1790 is used for exhibitions.

Plaça de la Boqueria ⑥
This square features a mosaic pavement by Miró (1976) and an Art Deco dragon designed for a former umbrella shop.

Plaça Reial ⑧
Barcelona's most lively square was built in the 1850s. The Neo-Classical lampposts were designed by Gaudí.

Museu de Cera ⑩
This waxwork museum, in an atmospheric, 19th-century building, contains about 300 exhibits.

KEY

🔄 FGC train station

Ⓜ Metro station

🅿 Parking

✝ Church

0 metres	100
0 yards	100

Monument a Colom
Plaça del Portal de la Pau

Statue of Poseidon in the courtyard of La Llotja

La Llotja ⓫

Carrer del Consolat de Mar 2. **Map** 5 B3. Ⓜ *Jaume I.*

L
A LLOTJA (meaning commodity exchange) was built in the 1380s as the headquarters of the Consolat de Mar, the guild of Catalan sea-traders *(see p39)*. It was remodelled in Neo-Classical style in 1771 and housed the city's stock exchange until 1994, the original, three-aisled Gothic hall having been retained to act as the main trading room. It can still be glimpsed through the large ground-floor windows.

The upper floors housed the Barcelona School of Fine Arts from 1849 to 1970, attended by the young Picasso and Joan Miró *(see p25)*. La Llotja is now occupied by a public library and local government offices.

Basílica de Santa Maria del Mar ⓬

Carrer Montcada 1. **Map** 5 B3.
[93 310 23 90. Ⓜ *Jaume I.*
◯ *9am–noon & 4:30–8:15pm daily.*

T
HIS BEAUTIFUL building, the city's favourite church with superb acoustics for concerts, is the only example of a church entirely in the Catalan Gothic style. It took just 55 years to build, with money donated by merchants and shipbuilders. The speed – unrivalled in the Middle Ages – gave it a unity of style both inside and out. The west front has a 15th-century rose window of the Coronation of the Virgin. More stained glass, dating from the 15th to the 18th centuries, lights the wide nave and high aisles.

When the choir and furnishings were burned in the Civil War *(see p43)*, it added to the sense of space and simplicity.

A wedding service in the Gothic interior of Santa Maria del Mar

Carrer Montcada ⓭

Map 5 B3. Ⓜ *Jaume I.* **Museu Tèxtil i d'Indumentària** [93 310 45 16. ◯ 10am–8pm Tue–Sat, 10am–3pm Sun & public hols. ■ 1 & 5 Jan, 25 Dec.

T
HE MOST AUTHENTIC medieval street in Barcelona is a narrow lane, overshadowed by gargoyles and protruding roofs which almost touch overhead. The Gothic palaces that line it, entered through great wooden doors and built around magnificent courtyards, date back to Catalonia's expansion in the 13th century. A mural of the conquest of Mallorca, a rare secular Romanesque painting once in the 13th–15th-century Palau Berenguer d'Aguilar, is now in the Museu Nacional d'Art de Catalunya *(see p80)*.

Carrer Montcada's buildings were all modified over the years, particularly in the 17th

Pablo Picasso, *Self-Portrait* in charcoal (1899–1900)

PABLO PICASSO IN BARCELONA

Picasso (1881–1973) was 13 when he arrived in Barcelona, where his father, José Ruiz y Blasco, had found work teaching in the city art school situated above the Llotja. The city was rich, but it also possessed a large, poor working class which was becoming organized and starting to rebel. Shortly after the family's arrival, a bomb was thrown into a Corpus Christi procession. They settled at No 3 Carrer de la Mercè, a gloomy, five-storeyed house not far from the Llotja. Picasso's precocious talent gave him admittance to the upper school, where all the other pupils were aged at least 20. Here he immediately made friends with another artist, Manuel Pallarès Grau, and the two lost their virginity to the whores of Carrer d'Avinyó, who were to inspire *Les Demoiselles d'Avignon* (1906–7), considered by many art critics to be the wellspring of modern art. Picasso travelled with Pallarès to the Catalan's home town of Horta, where he painted some early landscapes, now in the Museu Picasso. The two remained friends for the rest of their lives.

century when the Renaissance style prevailed. The only one with its original façade is Casa Cervelló-Guidice at No. 25. The **Museu Tèxtil i d'Indumentària** in Palau dels Marquesos de Lló at No. 12 (also called the Palau Mora) displays textiles and clothing from the 4th century AD onwards. The street also has the city's best-known champagne and *cava* bar, El Xampanyet (*see p137*).

Museu Picasso ⑭

Carrer Montcada 15–19. **Map** 5 B2.
█ *93 319 63 10.* ⊕ *Jaume I.*
⚪ *10am–8pm Tue–Sat & public hols, 10am–3pm Sun.* ⚫

O NE OF BARCELONA'S most popular attractions, the Picasso Museum is housed in three adjoining medieval palaces on Carrer Montcada: Berenguer d'Aguilar, Baró de Castellet and Meca.

The museum opened in 1963 showing works donated by Jaime Sabartes, a great friend of Picasso. Following Sabartes' death in 1968, Picasso himself donated paintings, including early examples which had been kept by his sister. These were complemented by graphic works, left in his will, and 141 ceramic pieces given by his widow, Jacqueline.

The works are divided into three sections: paintings and drawings, engravings and ceramics. But the strength of the 3,000-piece collection is Picasso's early drawings and paintings. These show how, even at the ages of 15 and 16, he was painting major works

Painting in Picasso's series *Las Meninas* (1957), Museu Picasso

Glorious stained-glass dome, Palau de la Música Catalana

such as *The First Communion* (1896) and *Science and Charity* (1897). There are only a few pictures from his Blue and Rose periods. The most famous work is his series of 44 paintings, *Las Meninas*, inspired by Velázquez's masterpiece.

Palau de la Música Catalana ⑮

Carrer de Sant Francesc de Paula 2. **Map** 5 B1. █ *93 268 10 00.* ⊕ *Catalunya, Urquinaona.* ⚪ *for concerts, or tours by appointment at 2pm and 3pm Tue–Thu, occasionally noon on Sat.* ⚫ *Aug.* ⚫

T HIS IS A real palace of music, a Modernista celebration of tilework, sculpture and glorious stained glass. It is the only concert hall in Europe lit by natural light. Designed by Lluís Domènech i Montaner, it was completed in 1908 on the site of a monastery dissolved in the 19th century. Although a few extensions have been

added, the building still retains its original appearance. The elaborate red-brick façade is hard to appreciate fully in the confines of the narrow street. It is lined with mosaic-covered pillars topped by busts of Palestrina, Bach and Beethoven. The large stone sculpture of St George and other figures at the corner of the building is an allegory of Catalan folk-song by Miquel Blay.

But it is the interior of the building that is truly inspiring. The auditorium on the first floor is lit by a huge inverted dome of stained glass depicting angelic choristers.

The sculptures of the composers Wagner and Clavé on the proscenium arch were designed by Domènech but finished by Pau Gargallo. The work of Josep Anselm Clavé (1824–74) in promoting Catalan song led to the creation of the Orfeó Català choral society in 1891, which became a focus of Catalan nationalism and the inspiration behind the Palau.

The pink brick façade of the late 19th-century Arc del Triomf

Arc del Triomf ⑯

Passeig Lluís Companys. **Map** 5 C1.
Ⓜ *Arc de Triomf.*

THE MAIN GATEWAY to the 1888 Universal Exhibition, which filled the Parc de la Ciutadella, was designed by Josep Vilaseca i Casanovas. It is built of brick in Mudéjar (Spanish Moorish) style, with sculpted allegories of crafts, industry and business. The frieze by Josep Reynés on the main façade represents the city of Barcelona welcoming foreign visitors. The one at the rear by Josep Llimona is of a prize-giving ceremony.

Parc de la Ciutadella ⑰

Avda del Marquès de l'Argentera. **Map** 6 D2. Ⓜ *Barceloneta, Ciutadella-Vila Olímpica.* ⏰ *9am–9pm daily.* ♿

THIS POPULAR park has a large boating lake, orange groves and scores of naturalized parrots living in the palm trees. The 30-ha (75-acre) park was pre-

viously the site of a massive star-shaped citadel. Designed by Prosper Verboom, this was built for Felipe V between 1715 and 1720 following a 13-month siege of the city, brought about by Barcelona's opposition to the Bourbon succession *(see p41)*. The fortress was intended to house soldiers to help keep law and order, but was never used for this purpose. It was converted into a prison, which became particularly notorious during the Napoleonic occupation *(see p41)*, and during the 19th-century liberal repressions, when it was hated as a symbol of centralized power.

In 1878, under the enlightened dictator General Prim, whose statue stands in the middle of the park, the citadel was pulled down and the park given to the city, to become, in 1888, the venue of the Universal Exhibition *(see p42)*.

Three buildings, however, survived: the arsenal, which was redesigned in 1932 for use by the Catalan parliament and is today shared by the Museu d'Art Modern; the Governor's Palace, which is now a school; and the chapel, still sometimes used by the military.

The gardens in the Plaça de Armes were laid out by the French landscape gardener Jean Forestier. They centre on a cascade based around a triumphal arch and partly inspired by the Trevi Fountain in Rome. It was designed by architect Josep Fontseré, with the help of Antoni Gaudí, who was then still a young student.

One of the galleries inside the spacious Museu de Zoologia

Museu de Zoologia ⑱

Passeig de Picasso. **Map** 5 C2. 📞 *93 319 69 12.* Ⓜ *Arc de Triomf.* ⏰ *10am–2pm Tue–Sun & public hols.* ♿

AT THE ENTRANCE to the Parc de la Ciutadella is the fortress-like Castell dels Tres Dragons (Castle of the Three Dragons), named after a play by Frederic Soler that was popular at the time it was built.

This brick edifice, crenellated and decorated with a frieze of ceramic shields, was built as a café-restaurant for the 1888 Universal Exhibition by Lluís Domènech i Montaner. His inspiration was Valencia's Gothic Llotja (commodities exchange). He later used it as a workshop for Modernista design, and it became a focus of the movement. It has housed the city's Zoological Museum since 1937.

Ornamental cascade in the Parc de la Ciutadella designed by Josep Fontseré and Antoni Gaudí

Museu de Geologia ⑲

Parc de la Ciutadella. **Map** 5 C3.
📞 93 319 68 95. Ⓜ️ *Arc de Triomf, Jaume I.* 🕐 *9am–2pm Tue–Sun & public hols.* ● *1 May, 25 Dec.* 🅰️

BARCELONA'S OLDEST MUSEUM opened in 1882, the same year the Parc de la Ciutadella became a public space for the city. It has a large collection of fossils and minerals, including specimens from Catalonia and around the country.

Beside it is the Hivernacle, an iron-framed glasshouse by Josep Amargós now often used for concerts, and the Umbracle, a brick and wood conservatory by the park's architect, Josep Fontseré. Both date from 1884

Glass cube of the Homenatge a Picasso, Parc de la Ciutadella

Homenatge a Picasso ⑳

Passeig de Picasso. **Map** 5 C3.
Ⓜ️ *Barceloneta.*

AT THE EDGE OF THE Parc de la Ciutadella, opposite Avinguda Marqués de l'Argentera, is the intriguing 1983 work *Homage to Picasso (see p25)* by Catalan artist Antoni Tàpies *(see p25)*.

Built to pay homage to Picasso's Cubist works, it is an intellectual sculpture that does not immediately suggest its title. A large, plain glass cube sits in a square pond, with water streaming down the sides. The cube contains an old sofa, chairs and a sideboard skewered by metal poles and draped with a blanket. The elements have not treated it kindly, and an air-conditioning system has had to be installed to prevent the glass from cracking.

***Dusk on the River Loing* by Alfred Sisley (1839–99), Museu d'Art Modern**

Museu d'Art Modern ㉑

Parc de la Ciutadella. **Map** 6 D3.
📞 93 319 50 23. Ⓜ️ *Arc de Triomf.* 🕐 *10am–7pm Tue–Sat & public hols, 10am–2pm Sun.* 🅰️

THIS IS A COLLECTION of Catalan art *(see pp24–5)* of the 19th and early 20th centuries in which the main players, Miró, Picasso, Dalí and Tàpies, are under represented as they each have separate museums. However, the collection of Modernista fine and decorative art is second to none and gives a comprehensive overview of the movement.

Among the earlier painters is Marià Fortuny i Marsal (1838–74), noted for his studies of Morocco. Catalonia's two early 20th-century artists, Santiago Rusiñol (1861–1931) and Ramon Casas (1866–1932), are considered the founders of modern Catalan painting. Casas' line drawings of the great men of his day include one of Pablo Picasso newly arrived in Montmartre, Paris. There is also a painting Casas did of himself riding a tandem with Pere Romeu; the two men opened Els Quatre Gats café *(see p50)*, where the painting was originally hung. Picasso's contemporaries, the painters Joaquim Mir (1873–1940) and Isidre Nonell (1873–1911), are represented here. There is also a landscape by Alfred Sisley (1839–99) called *Dusk on the River Loing*.

A fine sculpture gallery exhibits works by Josep Llimona (1864–1934) and Miquel Blay (1866–1936). There are also some bold pieces of Modernista furniture acquired from houses in the Eixample.

Parc Zoològic ㉒

Parc de la Ciutadella. **Map** 6 D3.
📞 93 225 67 80. Ⓜ️ *Ciutadella-Vila Olímpica.* 🕐 *Oct–Feb: 10am–5pm, Mar: 10am–6:30pm, Apr: 10am–7pm, May–Sep: 10:30am–7:30pm.* 🅰️

BARCELONA'S ZOO was laid out in the 1940s to a relatively enlightened design in which the animals are separated by moats instead of iron bars. The zoo is strong on primates and for years its mascot has been Floquet de Neu (Snowflake), a rare albino gorilla. Dolphin and whale shows are held in one of the aquariums. Roig i Soler's romantic 1885 sculpture by the entrance *The Lady with the Umbrella (see p15)* is so well-loved that it has become a symbol of Barcelona.

Floquet de Neu, Barcelona zoo's rare albino gorilla

Fashionable yachts at the Port Olímpic overlooked by Spain's two tallest skyscrapers

Port Olímpic 23

Map 6 F4. Ⓜ *Ciutadella-Vila Olímpica.*

THE MOST DRAMATIC rebuilding for the 1992 Olympics was the demolition of the old industrial waterfront and the laying out of 4 km (2 miles) of promenade and pristine sandy beaches. Suddenly Barcelona seemed like a seaside resort. At the heart of the project was a 65-ha (160-acre) new estate of 2,000 apartments and parks called Nova Icària. The area is still popularly known as the Vila Olímpica because the buildings originally housed the Olympic athletes.

On the sea front there are twin 44-floor buildings, Spain's tallest skyscrapers, one occupied by offices, the other by the Arts hotel *(see p117)*. They stand beside the Port Olímpic, which was also built for 1992. This has shops and nightclubs, but the main reasons for visiting are two levels of restaurants around the marina which have made it the latest popular place to eat out. The wonderful outdoor setting attracts business people at lunchtime and pleasure seekers in the evenings and at weekends.

Lunch can be walked off along the string of beaches that is edged by a palm-fringed promenade with cafés. Behind it, the new coastal road heads around a park that lies beside

the last three beaches, divided by rocky breakwaters. Swimming is safe on the gently sloping, sandy strands.

Barceloneta 24

Map 5 B5. Ⓜ *Barceloneta.*

BARCELONA'S fishing "village", which lies on a triangular tongue of land jutting into the sea just below the city centre, is renowned for its little restaurants and cafés. The area was designed in 1753 by the architect and military engineer Juan Martín de Cermeño to rehouse people made homeless by the construction, just inland, of the Ciutadella fortress *(see p62)*. Since then it has housed largely workers and fishermen. Laid out in a grid system with narrow two- and three-storey houses, in which each room has a window on the street, the area has a friendly, intimate air.

In the small Plaça de la Barceloneta, at the centre of the district, is the Baroque church of Sant Miguel del Port, also by Cermeño. A market is often held in the square here.

Today, Barceloneta's fishing fleet is still based in the nearby Dàrsena Industrial (Industrial Docks) by a small clock tower. On the opposite side of this harbour is the Torre de Sant Sebastià, terminus of the cable car that runs right across the port, via the World Trade Centre, to Montjuïc.

Port Vell 25

Map 5 A4. Ⓜ *Barceloneta, Drassanes.* **Aquàrium** 🎫 *93 221 74 74.* ⏰ *9:30am – 9:30pm daily.* 🅶 **Museu d'Història de Catalunya** *Plaça Pau Vila 3.* 🎫 *93 225 47 00.* ⏰ *10am – 7pm Tue –Thu, 10am – 8pm Fri & Sat, 10am – 2pm Sun & public hols.* 🅶

BARCELONA'S MARINA is at the foot of La Rambla, just beyond the old customs house. This was built in 1902 at the Portal de la Pau, the city's former maritime entrance, where steps lead into the water. To the south, the Moll de Barcelona, with a new World Trade Centre, serves as the passenger pier for visiting liners. In front of the customs house, La Rambla is connected to the yacht clubs on the Moll d'Espanya by a swing bridge and a pedestrian jetty, known as La Rambla de Mar. The Moll d'Espanya (*moll* meaning quay, wharf or pier) has a new shopping and restaurant complex, the Maremàgnum, plus an IMAX cinema and the largest aquarium in Europe.

On the shore, the Moll de Fusta (Timber Wharf), with terrace cafés, has red structures inspired by the marina at Arles painted by Van Gogh. At the end of the wharf is *El Cap de Barcelona (Barcelona Head)*, a colourful, 20-m (66-ft) tall sculpture by American Pop artist Roy Lichtenstein.

The attractive Sports Marina on the other side of the Moll d'Espanya was once lined with warehouses. The only one left, built by Elies Rogent in the 1880s, has been conserved

Fishing boat moored in Barceloneta harbour

and given a new lease of life as the Palau de Mar. Restaurants provide alfresco dining overlooking the port, but the building is otherwise given over to the Museu d'Història de Catalunya. Exhibits on three floors start from Lower Palaeolithic times and continue to the region's heydays as a maritime power and industrial pioneer. There is a reconstruction of a Roman boat, a schoolroom showing how lessons were taught during the Franco era and a 1960s mock-up bar.

A *golondrina* tour boat departing from the Portal de la Pau

The Columbus Monument lit by fireworks during La Merce fiesta

Monument a Colom ㉖

Plaça del Portal de la Pau. **Map** 2 F4.
■ 93 302 52 24. ⓜ *Drassanes.*
◷ Oct–May: 10am 2pm & 3:30–6:30pm Tue–Sun, Jun–Sep: 9am 8:30pm daily. 🅿

T HE COLUMBUS monument at the bottom of La Rambla was designed by Gaietà Buigas for the 1888 Universal Exhibition *(see p42).* At that time Catalans considered Columbus to be Catalan rather than Italian.

The 60-m (200-ft) monument, a cast iron column on a stone plinth, marks the spot where Columbus stepped ashore in 1493 after discovering America, bringing with him six Caribbean Indians. He was accorded a state welcome by the Catholic Monarchs in the Saló del Tinell *(see p54).* The Indians' subsequent conversion to Christianity is commemorated in the cathedral *(see pp56–7).* A lift gives access to a viewing

platform at the top of the monument. The bronze statue, pointing out to sea, was designed by Rafael Arché.

Golondrinas ㉗

Plaça del Portal de la Pau. **Map** 2 F5.
■ 93 442 31 06. ⓜ *Drassanes.*
◷ Jun–Sep: 11am 8pm daily; Oct–May: 10am 1pm Mon–Fri, 11am–5:30pm Sat & Sun. 🅿

S IGHTSEEING TRIPS around Barcelona's harbour and to the Port Olímpic can be made on *golondrinas* ("swallows") – small double-decker boats that moor beside the steps of the Portal de la Pau at the foot of La Rambla.

Half-hour tours go out beneath the steep, castle-topped hill of Montjuïc towards the industrial port. They usually stop off at the breakwater, which reaches out to sea from Barceloneta, to allow passengers to disembark for a stroll.

A two-hour trip with commentary takes in the beaches and commercial port and stops off at the Port Olímpic.

Museu Marítim and Drassanes ㉘

Avinguda de les Drassanes. **Map** 2 F4.
■ 93 301 18 71. ⓜ *Drassanes.*
◷ Oct–Jun: 10am–6pm Tue–Sat, 10am–2pm Sun; Jul–Sep: 10am–11pm Tue & Fri, 10am–7pm Wed, Thu, Sat, Sun & public hols. 🅿 🅱 🅿

T HE GREAT GALLEYS that made Barcelona a major seafaring power were built in the sheds of the Drassanes (shipyards) that now house the maritime

museum. These royal dry docks are the largest and most complete surviving medieval complex of their kind in the world. They were founded in the mid-13th century, when dynastic marriages uniting the kingdoms of Sicily and Aragón meant that better maritime communications between the two became a priority. Three of the yards' four original corner towers survive.

Among the vessels to slip from the Drassanes' vaulted halls was the *Real,* flagship of Don Juan of Austria, who led the Christian fleet to victory against the Turks at Lepanto in 1571. The museum's showpiece is a full-scale replica decorated in red and gold.

The *Llibre del Consolat de Mar,* a book of nautical codes and practice, is a reminder that Catalonia was once the arbiter of Mediterranean maritime law *(see p39).* There are pre-Columbian charts and maps, including one from 1439 that was used by the navigator Amerigo Vespucci.

Stained-glass window in the Museu Marítim

EIXAMPLE

BARCELONA CLAIMS to have the greatest collection of Art Nouveau buildings of any city in Europe. The style, known in Catalonia as Modernisme, flourished after 1854, when it was decided to tear down the medieval walls to allow the city to develop into what had previously been a construction-free military zone.

The designs of the civil engineer Ildefons Cerdà i Sunyer (1815–76) were chosen for the new expansion (*eixample*) inland. These plans called for a rigid grid system of streets, but at each intersection the corners were chamfered to allow the buildings there to overlook the junctions or squares. The few exceptions

Jesus of the Column,
Sagrada Família

to this grid system include the Diagonal, a main avenue running from the wealthy area of Pedralbes down to the sea, and the Hospital de la Santa Creu i de Sant Pau by Modernista architect Domènech i Montaner (1850–1923). He hated the grid system and deliberately angled the hospital to look down the diagonal Avinguda de Gaudí towards Antoni Gaudí's church of the Sagrada Família, the city's most spectacular Modernista building (*see pp74–5*). The wealth of Barcelona's commercial elite, and their passion for all things new, allowed them to give free rein to the age's most innovative architects in designing their residences as well as public buildings.

SIGHTS AT A GLANCE

Museums and Galleries
Fundació Antoni Tàpies **2**

Churches
Sagrada Família pp74–5 **6**

Modernista Buildings
Casa Milà, "La Pedrera" **3**
Casa Terrades, "Casa de les Punxes" **4**
Hospital de la Santa Creu i de Sant Pau **5**
Illa de la Discòrdia **1**

KEY

▮ Street-by-Street map *pp162–3*
Ⓜ Metro station
🚉 Train station
🚌 Main bus stop
ℹ Tourist information
🅿 Parking

GETTING THERE

Metro line 3 has stations at either end of the Passeig de Gràcia (Catalunya and Diagonal), and one in the middle, at the Illa de la Discòrdia (Passeig de Gràcia). Metro line 5 takes you straight to the Sagrada Família and Hospital de Sant Pau (a long walk from other sights).

0 metres	500
0 yards	500

◁ **Nativity façade of the Sagrada Família – the only façade to be more or less completed in Gaudí's lifetime**

Street-by-Street: Quadrat d'Or

THE HUNDRED OR SO city blocks centring on the Passeig de Gràcia are known as the Quadrat d'Or, "Golden Square", because they contain so many of the best Modernista buildings *(see pp22–3)*. This was the area within the Eixample favoured by the wealthy bourgeoisie, who embraced the new artistic and architectural style with enthusiasm, not only for their residences, but also for commercial buildings. Most remarkable is the Illa de la Discòrdia, a single block with houses by Modernisme's most illustrious exponents. Many interiors can be visited by the public, revealing a feast of stained glass, ceramics and ornamental ironwork.

Perfume bottle, Museu del Perfum

Diagonal Metro

Passeig de Gràcia, the Eixample's main avenue, is a showcase of highly original buildings and smart shops. The graceful street lamps are by Pere Falqués (1850–1916).

Vinçon home decor store *(see p135)*

Fundació Tàpies
Topped by Antoni Tàpies' wire sculpture Cloud and Chair, *this 1879 building by Domènech i Montaner houses a wide variety of Tàpies' paintings, graphics and sculptures* ❷

Casa Amatller

Museu del Perfum

Casa Ramon Mulleras

★ Illa de la Discòrdia
In this city block, four of Barcelona's most famous Modernista houses vie for attention. All were created between 1900 and 1910. This ornate tower graces the Casa Lleó Morera by Domènech i Montaner ❶

To Plaça de Catalunya

Casa Batlló

Casa Lleó Morera

Passeig de Gràcia Metro

Museu de la Música is housed in the Palau Baró de Quadras designed by Puig i Cadafalch in 1904. This carving adorns the doorway. The museum has displays of historical instruments collected from around the world.

LOCATOR MAP
See Street Finder map 3

EIXAMPLE

OLD TOWN

AVINGUDA DIAGONAL

CARRER DE PAU CLARIS

CARRER DE PROVENÇA

CARRER DE MALLORCA

CARRER DE ROGER DE LLÚRIA

CARRER DE VALÈNCIA

CARRER DEL BRUC

CARRER D'ARAGÓ

Casa Thomas

To Sagrada Família

Palau Ramon de Montaner

Casa Terrades
Built in red brick with carved stone ornamentation, this 1905 house by Puig i Cadafalch echoes the Gothic buildings of northern Europe ❹

★ Casa Milà "La Pedrera"
Gaudí put all his architectural daring into this, his most famous house. The result is a remarkable wave-like façade and a roofscape of chimneys and vents resembling abstract sculptures ❸

0 metres 100
0 yards 100

KEY

– – – Suggested route

STAR SIGHTS

★ **Illa de la Discòrdia**

★ **Casa Milà "La Pedrera"**

Sumptuous interior of the Casa Lleó Morera, Illa de la Discòrdia

Illa de la Discòrdia ❶

Passeig de Gràcia, between Carrer d'Aragó and Carrer del Consell de Cent. **Map** 3 A4. 🚇 Passeig de Gràcia. **Centre del Modernisme** 📞 93 488 01 39. 🕐 10am–7pm Mon–Sat. 📷

BARCELONA'S MOST FAMOUS group of Modernista (see pp22–3) buildings illustrates the wide range of styles used by the movement's architects. The city block in which the houses stand is known as the Illa de la Discòrdia (Island of Discord), owing to the startling visual argument between them.

The three finest were remodelled in Modernista style from existing houses early in the 20th century. No. 35 Passeig de Gràcia is Casa Lleó Morera (1902 – 6), the first residential work of Lluís Domènech i Montaner. The ground floor was gutted to create a shop in 1943, but the Modernista interiors upstairs still exist. The first floor is open to the public and houses the Centre del Modernisme. Tickets for the Modernisme route (see pp48–9) can be bought here.

Beyond the next two houses, one of which is a beauty shop containing a perfume museum, is Casa Amatller, designed by Puig i Cadafalch in 1898. Its façade, under a stepped gable roof, features a harmonious blend of Moorish and Gothic windows. Inside the wrought-iron main doors is a fine stone staircase beneath a stained-glass roof. The building, now

used by the Institut Amatller d'Art Hispànic, has a beautiful wood-panelled library. Next door is Antoni Gaudí's Casa Batlló (1904–1906). Its façade is typically fluid, with heavily tiled walls and curving iron balconies pierced with holes to look like masks or skulls. The hump-backed, scaly-looking roof is thought to represent a dragon, with St George as a chimney. Step inside to see the blue-tiled entrance hall.

Fundació Antoni Tàpies ❷

Carrer d'Aragó 255. **Map** 3 A1. 📞 93 487 03 15. 🚇 Passeig de Gràcia. 🕐 11am–8pm Tue–Sun & public hols (Sun in Aug: 11am–3pm). 🌑 1 & 6 Jan, 25 & 26 Dec. 📷 ♿

ANTONI TÀPIES (see p25), born in 1923, is Barcelona's best-known living artist. Inspired by Surrealism, his abstract work is executed in a variety of materials, including concrete and metal (see p68). Difficult to appreciate at first, the exhibits should help viewers obtain a clearer perspective of Tàpies' work, even if there is not enough here to gain a full understanding. The collection is housed in Barcelona's first domestic building to be constructed with iron (1880), designed by Domènech i Montaner for his brother's publishing firm.

ANTONI GAUDÍ (1852–1926)

Born in Reus (Tarragona) into an artisan family, Antoni Gaudí i Cornet was the leading exponent of Catalan Modernisme. After a blacksmith's apprenticeship, he studied at Barcelona's School of Architecture. Inspired by a nationalistic search for a romantic medieval past, his work was supremely original. His first major achievement was the Casa Vicens (1888) at No. 24 Carrer de les Carolines (see p48). But his most celebrated building is the church of the Sagrada Família (see pp74–5), to which he devoted his life from 1914. When he had put all his money into the project, he went from house to house begging for more. He was killed by a tram in 1926 (see p58).

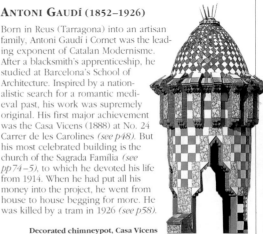

Decorated chimneypot, Casa Vicens

◁ **Extraordinary sculptured and ceramic-encrusted chimneys of Gaudí's Casa Milà**

The rippled façade of Gaudí's apartment building, Casa Milà

Casa Milà ❸

Passeig de Gràcia 92. **Map** 3 B3.
📞 93 484 59 80. Ⓜ *Diagonal.*
🕐 10am–7:30pm. 🔴 *public hols.*

USUALLY CALLED *La Pedrera* (the Stone Quarry), the Casa Milà is Gaudí's greatest contribution to Barcelona's civic architecture, and his last work before he devoted himself entirely to the Sagrada Família (*see pp74–5*).

Built between 1906 and 1910, *La Pedrera* completely departed from the established construction principles of the time and, as a result, was ridiculed and strongly attacked by Barcelona's intellectuals.

Gaudí designed this corner apartment block, eight floors high, around two circular courtyards. In the basement he incorporated the city's first underground car park. The intricate ironwork balconies, by Josep Maria Jujol, are like seaweed against the wave-like walls of white, undressed stone. There are no straight walls anywhere in the building.

The Milà family had an apartment on the first floor. There are regular guided tours from an office on the ground floor which take in the extraordinary roof. The multitude of sculptured air ducts and chimneys on the roof have such a threatening appearance they are known as *espantabruixes*, or witch-scarers.

Casa Terrades ❹

Avinguda Diagonal 416. **Map** 3 B3.
Ⓜ *Diagonal.* 🔴 *to public.*

THIS FREE-STANDING, six-sided apartment block by Modernista architect Josep Puig i Cadafalch gets its nickname, *Casa de les Punxes* (House of the Points), from the spires on its six corner turrets. It was built between 1903 and 1905 by converting three existing houses on the site and was Puig's largest work. It is an eclectic mixture of medieval and Renaissance styles. The towers

Spire on the main tower, Casa Terrades

and gables are influenced in particular by the Gothic architecture of northern Europe. However, the deeply carved, floral stone ornamentation of the exterior, in combination with red brick used as the principal building material, are typically Modernista.

Hospital de la Santa Creu i de Sant Pau ❺

Carrer de Sant Antoni Maria Claret 167.
Map 4 F1. 📞 93 291 90 00. Ⓜ
Hospital de Sant Pau. **Grounds** 🔴
daily; write in advance for permission to visit pavilions not in medical use. 🚻 🎫

LLUÍS DOMÈNECH I MONTANER began designing a new city hospital in 1902. Totally innovative in concept, his scheme consisted of 26 attractive Mudéjar-style pavilions set in large gardens, as he strongly disliked huge wards and believed that patients would recover better among fresh air and trees. All the connecting corridors and service areas were hidden underground.

Also believing art and colour to be therapeutic, he decorated the pavilions profusely. The turreted roofs were tiled with ceramics, and the reception pavilion embellished with mosaic murals and sculptures by Pau Gargallo. After Domènech's death, the vast project was completed in 1930 by his son, Pere.

Statue of the Virgin, Hospital de la Santa Creu i de Sant Pau

Sagrada Família 6

A carved whelk

EUROPE'S MOST unconventional church, the Temple Expiatori de la Sagrada Família, is an emblem of a city that likes to think of itself as individualistic. Crammed with symbolism inspired by nature and striving for originality, it is the greatest work of Gaudí *(see pp22–3)*. In 1883, a year after work had begun on a Neo-Gothic church on the site, the task of completing it was given to Gaudí who changed everything, extemporizing as he went along. It became his life's work and he lived like a recluse on the site for 16 years. He is buried in the crypt. At his death only one tower on the Nativity façade had been completed, but work resumed after the Civil War and several more have since been finished to his original plans. Work continues today, financed by public subscription.

Bell Towers
Eight of the 12 spires, one for each apostle, have been built. Each is topped by Venetian mosaics.

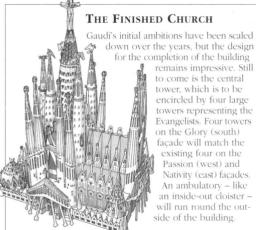

THE FINISHED CHURCH

Gaudí's initial ambitions have been scaled down over the years, but the design for the completion of the building remains impressive. Still to come is the central tower, which is to be encircled by four large towers representing the Evangelists. Four towers on the Glory (south) façade will match the existing four on the Passion (west) and Nativity (east) façades. An ambulatory – like an inside-out cloister – will run round the outside of the building.

Tower with lift

The apse was the first part of the church Gaudí completed. Stairs lead down from here to the crypt below.

The altar canopy, designed by Gaudí, is still waiting for the altar.

★ **Passion Façade**
This bleak façade was completed in the late 1980s by artist Josep Maria Subirachs. A controversial work, its sculpted figures are angular and often sinister.

Entrance to Crypt Museum

Main entrance

Spiral Staircases
*Steep stone steps –
400 in each – allow
access to the towers
and upper galleries.
Majestic views
reward those who
climb or take the lift.*

VISITORS' CHECKLIST

C/ Mallorca 401. **Map** 4 E3. ☎ 93
455 02 47. Ⓜ Sagrada Familia.
🚌 19, 34, 43, 50, 51, 54. ⭘
Apr–Aug: 9am–8pm daily; Sep:
9am–7pm daily; Oct–Mar: 9am–
6pm daily. ⬤ 1 Jan, 25 Dec (pm).
✝ 9am, 8:15pm Mon–Sat; 9am,
10:30am, 11:45am, 1pm, 8:15pm
Sun. 📷 ♿ except crypt & towers.

Tower
with lift

★ Nativity Façade
*The most complete part of
Gaudí's church, finished in
1904, has doorways which
represent Faith, Hope and
Charity. Scenes of the Nativity
and Christ's childhood are
embellished with symbolism,
such as white doves that
represent the congregation.*

★ Crypt
*The crypt, where Gaudí is buried,
was built by the original architect,
Francesc de Paula Villar i Lozano,
in 1882. This is where services are
currently held. On the lower floor
a small museum traces the careers
of both architects and the church's
complicated history.*

The final parts of the
structure to be built will
be the nave and the south
(Glory) façade – which was
originally planned as the main
entrance. The finished building
will be in the form of a Latin
cross. A forest of intricately
fluted pillars will support four
galleries above the side aisles.

STAR FEATURES

★ **Passion Façade**

★ **Nativity Façade**

★ **Crypt**

MONTJUÏC

THE HILL OF MONTJUÏC, rising to 213 m (699 ft) above the commercial port on the south side of the city, is Barcelona's biggest recreation area. Its museums, art galleries, gardens and nightclubs make it a popular place in the evenings as well as during the day.

There was probably a Celt-iberian settlement here before the Romans built a temple to Jupiter on their Mons Jovis, which may have given Montjuïc its name – though another theory suggests that a Jewish cemetery on the hill inspired the name Mount of the Jews.

The absence of a water supply meant that there were few buildings on Montjuïc until the castle was erected on the top in 1640.

Statue, gardens of the Palau Nacional

The hill finally came into its own as the site of the 1929 International Fair. With great energy and flair, buildings were erected all over the north side, with the grand Avinguda de la Reina Maria Cristina, lined with huge exhibition halls, leading into it from the Plaça d'Espanya. In the middle of the avenue is the Font Màgica (Magic Fountain), which is regularly illuminated in colour. Above it is the Palau Nacional, home of the city's historic art collections. The Poble Espanyol is a crafts centre housed in copies of buildings from all over Spain. The last great surge of building on Montjuïc was for the 1992 Olympic Games, which left Barcelona with international-class sports facilities.

SIGHTS AT A GLANCE

Historic Buildings
Castell de Montjuïc ❼

Modern Architecture
Estadi Olímpic de Montjuïc ❽
Pavelló Mies van der Rohe ❹

Museums and Galleries
Fundació Joan Miró ❶
Museu Arqueològic ❷
Museu Nacional d'Art de Catalunya ❸

Squares
Plaça d'Espanya ❻

Theme Parks
Poble Espanyol ❺

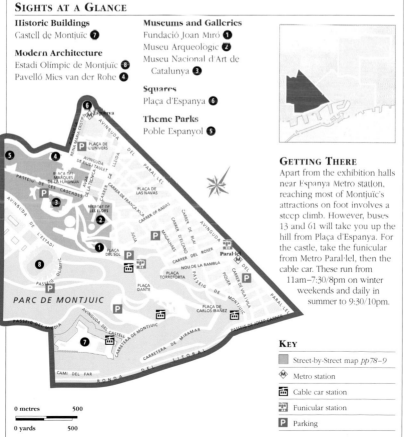

GETTING THERE

Apart from the exhibition halls near Espanya Metro station, reaching most of Montjuïc's attractions on foot involves a steep climb. However, buses 13 and 61 will take you up the hill from Plaça d'Espanya. For the castle, take the funicular from Metro Paral·lel, then the cable car. These run from 11am–7:30/8pm on winter weekends and daily in summer to 9:30/10pm.

KEY

▨	Street-by-Street map *pp78–9*
Ⓜ	Metro station
🚡	Cable car station
🚞	Funicular station
🅿	Parking

◁ **Changing colours of the Font Màgica (Magic Fountain) on the grand avenue leading up to Montjuïc**

Street-by-Street: Montjuïc

Mᴏɴᴛᴊᴜɪᴄ ɪꜱ ᴀ ꜱᴘᴇᴄᴛᴀᴄᴜʟᴀʀ vantage point from which to view the city. It has a wealth of art galleries and museums, as well as theatres. Many of the buildings were designed for the 1929 International Exhibition, and the 1992 Olympics were held on its southern slopes. Montjuïc is approached from the Plaça d'Espanya between brick pillars based on the campanile of St Mark's in Venice. They give a foretaste of the eclecticism of building styles from the Palau Nacional, which houses magnificent Romanesque art, to the Poble Espanyol, which illustrates the architecture of Spain's regions.

Pavelló Mies van der Rohe
This elegant statue by Georg Kolbe stands serenely in the steel, glass, stone and onyx pavilion built in the Bauhaus style as the German contribution to the 1929 International Exhibition ➍

AVINGUDA DEL MARQUÈS DE COMILLAS

AVINGUDA DELS MONTANYANS

PASSEIG DE LES CAS

AVINGUDA DE L'ESTADI

★ Poble Espanyol
Containing replicas of buildings from many regions of Spain, this "village" provides a fascinating glimpse of vernacular styles ➎

★ Museu Nacional d'Art de Catalunya
On show in the Palau Nacional (National Palace), the main building of the 1929 International Exhibition, is Europe's finest collection of Romanesque frescoes. These were a great source of inspiration for Joan Miró ➌

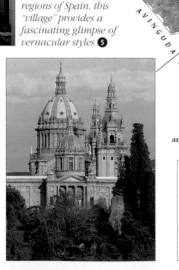

To Montjuïc castle and Olympic stadium

Sᴛᴀʀ Sɪɢʜᴛꜱ

★ Poble Espanyol

★ Museu Nacional d'Art de Catalunya

★ Fundació Joan Miró

Fountains and cascades descend in terraces from the Palau Nacional. Below them is the Font Màgica (Magic Fountain). On Thursday to Sunday evenings in summer and Friday and Saturday evenings in winter, its jets are programmed to a multi-coloured music and light show. This marvel of engineering was built by Carles Buigas (1898–1979) for the 1929 International Exhibition.

LOCATOR MAP
See Street Finder map 1

To Plaça d'Espanya

RIUS I TAULET

Museu Etnològic displays artifacts from Oceania, Africa, Asia and Latin America.

Museu Arqueològic
The museum displays important finds from prehistoric cultures in Catalonia and the Balearic Islands. The Dama d'Evissa, a 4th-century sculpture, was found in Ibiza's Carthaginian necropolis ❷

AVINGUDA DE LA TÈCNICA

CARRER DE LLEIDA

Mercat de les Flors theatre (see p136)

Teatre Grec is an open-air theatre set among gardens.

PASSEIG DE LA SANTA MADRONA

PASSEIG DE LA SANTA MADRONA

PASSEIG DE LA SANTA MADRONA

★ **Fundació Joan Miró**
This tapestry by Joan Miró hangs in the centre he created for the study of modern art. In addition to Miró's works in various media, the modern building by Josep Lluís Sert is of architectural interest ❶

AVINGUDA DE MIRAMAR

To Montjuïc castle and cable car

KEY

— — — Suggested route

0 metres 100

0 yards 100

Flame in Space and Naked Woman (1932) by Joan Miró

Fundació Joan Miró ❶

Parc de Montjuïc. **Map** 1 B3. 【 93 329 19 08. ⚫ *Espanya, then bus 55.* ⏰ *Jul–Sep: 10am–8pm Tue–Sat; Oct–Jun: 10am–7pm Tue, Wed, Fri & Sat, 10am–9:30pm Thu, 10:30am–2:30pm Sun & public hols.* ⚫ *1 & 6 Jan, 25 Dec.* 🖼 ♿

THE SON OF A GOLDSMITH, Joan Miró (1893–1983) went to La Llotja's art school *(see p60)*, but from 1919 spent much time in Paris. Though opposed to Franco, he returned to Spain in 1940 and from then on lived mainly in Mallorca, where he died. An admirer of primitive Catalan art and Modernisme *(see pp22–3)*, Miró remained a Catalan painter *(see pp24–5)* but invented and developed a Surrealistic style, with vivid colours and fantastical forms that suggested dream-like situations. During the 1950s he concentrated on ceramics.

In 1975, after the return of democracy to Spain, his friend, the architect Josep Lluís Sert, designed this stark, white

building to house a permanent collection of graphics, paintings, sculptures and tapestries lit by natural light. Miró himself donated the works and some of the best pieces on display include his *Barcelona Series* (1939–44), a set of 50 black-and-white lithographs. Exhibitions of other artists' work are also held from time to time.

Museu Arqueològic ❷

Passeig Santa Madrona 39. **Map** 1 B3. 【 93 423 21 49. ⚫ *Espanya, Poble Sec.* ⏰ *9:30am–1:30pm & 3:30–7pm Tue–Sat, 9am–2pm Sun.* ⚫ *public hols.* 🖼 *except Sun.* ♿

HOUSED IN the Renaissance-inspired 1929 Palace of Graphic Arts, the museum has artifacts from prehistory to the Visigothic period (AD 415–711). Highlights are finds from the Greco-Roman town of Empúries *(see p102)*, Hellenistic Mallorcan jewels and Iberian silver treasure. There is also a splendid collection of Visigothic jewellery.

Museu Nacional d'Art de Catalunya ❸

Parc de Montjuïc. **Map** 1 A2. 【 93 423 71 99. ⚫ *Espanya.* ⏰ *10am–7pm Tue–Sat, 10am–9pm Thu, 10am–2:30pm Sun.* 🖼 ♿

THE AUSTERE Palau Nacional was built for the 1929 International Exhibition, but in 1934 it was used to house an art collection that has since become the most important in the city.

The museum includes what is probably the greatest display of Romanesque *(see pp20–21)* items in the world, centred around a series of magnificent 12th-century frescoes. These have been taken from Catalan Pyrenean churches and pasted onto replicas of the original vaulted ceilings and apses they decorated, to save them from plunder and the ravages of time. The most remarkable are the wall paintings from Sant Climent de Taüll and Santa Maria de Taüll *(see p95)*.

There is also an impressive Gothic collection, covering the whole of Spain but particularly good on Catalonia. Notable artists of the time are exhibited, including the 15th-century Spanish artists Lluís Dalmau and Jaume Huguet *(see p24)*.

Distinguished works by El Greco, Velázquez and Zurbarán are on display in the Baroque and Renaissance collection. A photographic collection, started in 1996, has room for expansion in this spacious museum.

12th-century *Christ in Majesty*, Museu Nacional d'Art de Catalunya

Morning by Georg Kolbe (1877–1945), Pavelló Mies van der Rohe

Pavelló Mies van der Rohe **4**

Avinguda del Marquès de Comillas.
Map 1 B2. 93 423 40 16.
Espanya. Apr–Oct: 10am–8pm daily; Nov–Mar: 10am–6pm daily.

I F THE ELEGANTLY simple lines of the glass and polished stone German Pavilion look modern today, they must have shocked visitors to the 1929 International Exhibition. Designed by Ludwig Mies van der Rohe (1886–1969), director of the avant-garde Bauhaus school, it included his famous *Barcelona Chair*. The building was demolished after the exhibition, but a replica was built on the centenary of his birth.

Poble Espanyol **5**

Avinguda del Marquès de Comillas.
Map 1 A2. 93 325 78 66.
Espanya. 9am–8pm Mon, 9am–2am Tue–Thu, 9am–4am Fri & Sat, 9am–midnight Sun.

T HE IDEA BEHIND the Poble Espanyol (Spanish Village) was to illustrate and display local Spanish architectural styles and crafts. It was laid out for the 1929 International Exhibition, but has proved to be enduringly popular.
Building styles from all over Spain are illustrated by 116 houses. These are arranged on streets radiating from a main square and were created by many well-known architects

and artists of the time. The village was refurbished at the end of the 1980s and is now a favourite place to visit for both tourists and native *barcelonins*.
Resident artisans produce a wide range of crafts including hand-blown glass, ceramics, sculpture, Toledo damascene and Catalan canvas sandals (*espardenyes*). The Torres de Avila, which form the huge main entrance, have been converted into a highly popular nightspot, with an interior by designers Alfredo Arribas and Javier Mariscal *(see p17)*. There are also shops, cafés, bars and a children's theatre.

Looking down from the Palau Nacional towards Plaça d'Espanya

Plaça d'Espanya **6**

Avinguda de la Gran Via de les Corts Catalanes. **Map** 1 B1. Espanya.

T HE FOUNTAIN in the middle of this road junction, the site of public gallows until they were transferred to Ciutadella in 1715, is by Josep Maria Jujol, one of Gaudí's followers. The sculptures are by Miquel Blay. The 1899 bullring to one side is by Font i Carreras, but Catalans have never taken to bullfighting and the arena is now used as a music venue.
On the Montjuïc side of the roundabout is the Avinguda de la Reina Maria Cristina. This is flanked by two 47-m (154-ft) high brick campaniles by Ramon Raventós, modelled on the bell towers of St Mark's in Venice and built as the entrance way to the 1929 International Exhibition. The avenue, lined with exhibition buildings, leads up to Carles Buigas's illuminated *Font Màgica* (Magic Fountain) in front of the Palau Nacional.

Castell de Montjuïc **7**

Parc de Montjuïc. **Map** 1 B5. 93 329 86 13. Paral·lel, then funicular & cable car (only Sat & public hols in winter). **Museum** 9:30am–7:30pm Tue–Sun.

T HE SUMMIT of Montjuïc is occupied by a huge, 18th-century castle with fabulous views over the port. The first castle was built in 1640, but destroyed by Felipe V in 1705
The present star-shaped fortress was built on the ruins for the Bourbon family. During the War of Independence it was taken by French troops. After the Civil War it became a prison and the defeated Catalan leader Lluís Companys *(see p43)* was executed there in 1940. The castle is now a military museum with displays of ancient weaponry and models of Catalan castles.

Estadi Olímpic de Montjuïc **8**

Passeig Olímpic 17–19. **Map** 1 A3. 93 426 20 89. Espanya, Poble Sec. 10am–6pm daily.

T HE NEO-CLASSICAL FAÇADE has been preserved from the original stadium, built by Pere Domènech i Roura for the 1936 "Alternative" Olympics, which were cancelled at the outbreak of the Spanish Civil War. The arena was refitted to increase its capacity to 70,000 for the 1992 Olympics.
Nearby are the steel-and-glass Palau Sant Jordi indoor stadium, by Japanese architect Arata Isozaki, and swimming pools by Ricard Bofill.

Entrance to the Olympic Stadium, refurbished in 1992

FURTHER AFIELD

RADICAL REDEVELOPMENTS throughout Barcelona in the late 1980s and 1990s have given it a wealth of new buildings, parks and squares. Sants, the city's main station, was rebuilt and the neighbouring Parc de l'Espanya Industrial and Parc Joan Miró were created containing futuristic sculpture and architecture. In the east, close to the revitalized area of Poblenou, the city now has a new national theatre and concert hall. In the

Parc Güell gateway sign

west, where the streets climb steeply, are the historic royal palace and monastery of Pedralbes, and Gaudí's Torre Bellesguard and Parc Güell. Beyond, the Serra de Collserola, the city's closest rural area, is reached by two funiculars. Tibidabo, the highest point, has an amusement park, the Neo-Gothic church of the Sagrat Cor and a nearby steel-and-glass communications tower. It is a popular place among *barcelonins* for a day out.

SIGHTS AT A GLANCE

Museums and Galleries
Museu de la Ciència **8**
Museu del Futbol Club
   Barcelona **3**

Historic Buildings
Monestir de Pedralbes **5**
Palau Reial de Pedralbes **4**
Torre Bellesguard **9**

Modern Buildings
Torre de Collserola **6**

Parks and Gardens
Parc de l'Espanya Industrial **2**
Parc Güell **10**
Parc de Joan Miró **1**

Squares and Districts
Estació del Nord **11**
Plaça de les Glòries Catalanes **12**
Poblenou **13**

Theme Parks
Tibidabo **7**

KEY

▨	Street-by-Street maps
☐	Built-up area
🚉	Train station
🚡	Funicular station
═	Motorway (highway)
▬	Major road
—	Minor road

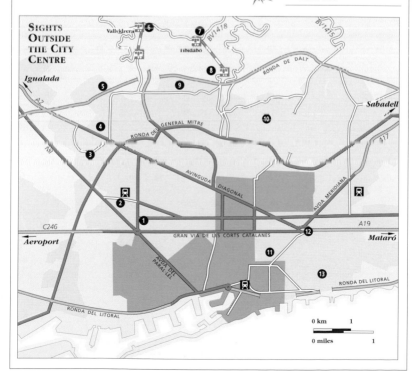

The Neo-Gothic Temple Expiatori del Sagrat Cor dominating the summit of Tibidabo

Dona i Ocell (1983) by Joan Miró
in the Parc de Joan Miró

Parc de Joan Miró ❶

Carrer d'Aragó 1. Ⓜ *Tarragona.*

BARCELONA'S 19th-century slaughterhouse *(escorxa-dor)* was transformed in the 1980s into this unusual park, hence its alternative name, Parc de l'Escorxador.

It is constructed on two levels, the lower of which is devoted to football pitches interspersed with landscaped sections of palms, pines, eucalyptus trees and flowers. The upper level is completely paved and is dominated by a magnificent 1983 sculpture by the Catalan artist Joan Miró *(see p25)* entitled *Dona i Ocell (Woman and Bird)*. Standing 22 m (72 ft) high in the middle of a pool, its surface is covered with colourful glazed tiles.

Parc de l'Espanya Industrial ❷

Plaça de Joan Peiró. Ⓜ *Sants-Estació.*

THIS MODERN PARK, designed by the Basque architect Luis Peña Ganchegui, owes its name to the textile mill that used to stand on the 5-hectare (12-acre) site.

Laid out in 1986 as part of Barcelona's policy to provide more open spaces within the city, the park has canals and a rowing lake – with a Classical statue of Neptune at its centre. Tiers of steps rise around the lake like an amphitheatre and on one side a row of ten futur-istic watchtowers dominates the entire area. Their only function is to serve as public viewing platforms and lamp standards.

Six contemporary sculptors are represented in the park, among them Andrés Nagel, whose enormous metal dragon incorporates a children's slide.

Museu del Futbol Club Barcelona ❸

Avda de Arístides Maillol. 📞 93 496 36 00. Ⓜ *Maria Cristina, Collblanc.* 🕙 10am–6:30pm Mon–Sat, 10am–2pm Sun & public hols. ⬤ 1 & 6 Jan, 25 Dec. 🎫 ♿

CAMP NOU, Europe's largest football stadium, is home to the city's famous football club, Barcelona FC (Barça, as it is known locally). Founded in 1899, it is one of the world's richest soccer clubs, and has more than 100,000 members.

The stadium is a magnificent, sweeping structure, built in 1957 to a design by Francesc Mitjans.

Line of watchtowers in the Parc de l'Espanya Industrial

An extension was added in 1982 and it can now comfort-ably seat 98,000 fans, with standing room for 17,000 more.

The club's museum, which displays club memorabilia and trophies on two floors, and has a souvenir shop, is one of the most popular in Barcelona. There are also paintings and sculptures of famous club footballers commissioned for the Blau-grana Biennial, an exhibition held in celebration of the club in 1985 and 1987, and others donated by Catalan artists. *Blau-grana* (blue-burgundy) are the colours of Barça's strip. The club's flags were used as an expression of local nationalist feelings when the Catalan flag was banned during the Franco dictatorship.

As well as hosting its own high-profile matches (mainly at weekends), Camp Nou also accommodates affiliated local soccer clubs and promotes other sports in its sports centre, ice rink and mini-stadium.

View across Camp Nou stadium, prestigious home of the Futbol Club Barcelona

Palau Reial de Pedralbes ➍

Avda Diagonal 686. 📞 *93 280 13 64.*
Ⓜ *Palau Reial.* ⬤ *closed for unspeci-
fied period.* **Museu de Ceràmica &
Museu de Arts Decoratives** ◻
*10am–6pm Tue–Sat, 10am–3pm Sun
& public hols.* ⬤ *1 Jan, 1 May, 24 Jun,
25 & 26 Dec.* 📷 ✔

THE PALACE OF PEDRALBES was
once the main house on
the estate of Count Eusebi
Güell. In 1919 he offered it to
the Spanish royal family. The
first visit was from Alfonso XIII
in 1926, before which the interior was refurbished and a new
throne, supported by golden
lions, was created for him.

The building was opened to
the public in 1937 and the
Museu de Arts Decoratives installed. Exhibits include period
furniture from other great
houses in the city and fine
household items from the
Middle Ages to the present.
A genealogical tree traces the
500-year dynasty of the count-
kings of Barcelona *(see p38)*.

The palace also houses the
Museu de Ceràmica, which
displays old Catalan and
Moorish pottery and modern
ceramics, including works by
Miró and Picasso *(see p80)*.

The palace gardens are well
laid out with small ponds and
paths. Just behind the gardens,
in Avinguda de Pedralbes, is
the entrance to the original
Güell estate. It is guarded by a
black wrought-iron gate, its top
formed into a great open-jawed
dragon, and two gate houses,
all by Gaudí *(see pp22–3)*.

Madonna of Humility, **Monestir de
Santa Maria de Pedralbes**

Monestir de Santa Maria de Pedralbes ➎

Carrer de Montevideo 14. 📞 *93 203
77 79 (Monastery), 93 203 92 82
(Thyssen-Bornemisza Collection).*
Ⓜ *Reina Elisenda.* ◻ *10am–2pm
Tue–Sun.* 📷

APPROACHED through an arch
in its ancient walls, the
lovely monastery of Pedralbes
retains the air of an enclosed
community. This is heightened
by the good state of preserva-
tion of its furnished kitchens,
cells, infirmary and refectory.
But the nuns of the Order of
St Clare moved to an adjoining

building back in 1983. The
monastery was founded in
1326 by Elisenda de Montcada
de Piños, fourth wife of Jaume
II of Catalonia and Aragón. Her
alabaster tomb lies in the wall
between the church and the
cloister. On the church side her
effigy is dressed in royal robes;
on the other, in a nun's habit.

The most important room in
the monastery is the Capella
(chapel) de Sant Miquel, with
murals of the *Passion* and the
Life of the Virgin, both painted
by Ferrer Bassa in 1346, when
Elisenda's niece, Francesca
Saportella, was abbess.

In 1989, some 60 paintings
forming part of the Thyssen-
Bornemisza Collection (most
of which is in Madrid) were
donated to the monastery.
They now hang in the former
dormitory and one of Queen
Elisenda's rooms and are mainly religious in theme. The collection is strong in Italian and
Spanish works, with examples
by Fra Angelico, Tiepolo, Lotto,
Titian, Canaletto, Veronese,
Velázquez and Zurbarán.

Torre de Collscrola ➏

Carretera de Vallvidrera al Tibidabo.
📞 *93 406 93 54.* Ⓜ *Peu del
Funicular, then Funicular de Vallvidrera
& bus 211.* ◻ *11am–2:30 & 3:30–
6pm Wed–Fri, 11am–6pm Sat, Sun &
public hols.* 📷 ♿

IN A CITY that enjoys thrills,
the ultimate ride is offered
by the communications tower
near Tibidabo mountain *(see
p88)*. A glass-sided lift takes
less than two minutes to reach
the top of this 288-m (944-ft)
tall structure standing on the
summit of a 445-m (1,460-ft)
hill – not a pleasant experience
for those who fear heights.

The tower was designed by
English architect Norman
Foster for the 1992 Olympic
Games. Needle-like in form,
it is a tubular steel mast on a
concrete pillar. There are 13
levels. The top one has an
observatory with a powerful
telescope, and a public viewing platform with a 360° view
encompassing Barcelona, the
sea and the mountain chain
on which Tibidabo sits.

BARCELONA v REAL MADRID

FC Barcelona

Més que un club is the motto of Barcelona FC:
"More than a club". It has above all, however,
been a symbol of the struggle of Catalan
nationalism against the central government in
Madrid. To fail to win the league is one thing.
To come in behind Real Madrid is a
complete disaster. Each season the
big question is which of the two
teams will win the title. Under the Franco
regime in a memorable episode in 1941, Barça
won 3–0 at home. At the return match in
Madrid, the crowd was so hostile that the police
and referee "advised" Barça to prevent trouble.
Demoralized by the intimidation, they lost 11–1.
Loyalty is paramount: one Barça player who
left to join Real Madrid received death threats.

Real Madrid

Merry-go-round, Tibidabo

Tibidabo **❼**

Plaça del Tibidabo. **❤** *93 211 79 42.* **⏱** *Avda Tibidabo, then Tramvia Blau & Funicular; or Peu del Funicular, then Funicular & bus 211.* **Amusement Park ⏱** *1–5 Apr: noon–8pm; May–Jun: noon–8pm Sat & Sun; Jul–Aug: noon–10pm Mon–Thu, noon–1am Fri–Sun; Sep: noon–8pm daily; Oct: noon–7pm Sat & Sun.* **⏺** *17 Oct–20 Mar.* **♿ Temple del Sagrat Cor ⏱** *10am–7pm daily.*

Tʜᴇ ʜᴇɪɢʜᴛs ᴏꜰ ᴛɪʙɪᴅᴀʙᴏ can be reached by Barcelona's last surviving tram. The name, inspired by Tibidabo's views of the city, comes from the Latin *tibi dabo* (I shall give you) – a reference to the Temptation of Christ when Satan took Him up a mountain and offered Him the world spread at His feet.

The hugely popular Parc d'Atraccions (Amusement Park, *see p137*) first opened in 1908. The rides were renovated in the 1980s. While the old ones retain their charm, the newer ones provide the latest in vertiginous experiences. Their hilltop location at 517 m (1,696 ft) adds to the thrill. Also in the park is the Museu d'Autòmats displaying automated toys, juke boxes and slot machines.

Tibidabo is crowned by the Temple Expiatori del Sagrat Cor (Church of the Sacred Heart), built with religious zeal but little taste by Enric Sagnier between 1902 and 1911. A lift takes you up to the feet of an enormous figure of Christ.

Just a short bus ride away is another viewpoint – the Torre de Collserola (*see p87*).

Museu de la Ciència **❽**

Carrer Teodor Roviralta 55. **❤** *93 212 60 50.* **⏱** *Avinguda del Tibidabo, then Tramvia Blau.* **⏱** *10am–8pm Tue–Sun.* **♿ ♿**

Tʜᴇ ᴄɪᴛʏ's science museum provides some excellent hands-on experiences. Here you can test your senses and physical abilities and learn about world ecology. Separate floors are devoted to sound and optics. There is a weather station, and a planetarium staging 30-minute shows. Outside is a full-sized submarine which you can explore.

Wrought-iron entrance door at Antoni Gaudí's Torre Bellesguard

Torre Bellesguard **❾**

Carrer de Bellesguard 16. **⏱** *Avinguda del Tibidabo.* **⏺** *closed to public.*

Bᴇʟʟᴇsɢᴜᴀʀᴅ means "beautiful spot" and here, half way up the Collserola hills, is the place chosen by the medieval Catalan kings as their summer home. Their castle, built in 1408, was in particular a favourite residence of Barcelona's Martí the Humanist (*see p55*).

The surrounding district of Sant Gervasi was developed in the 19th century after the coming of the railway. In 1900 Gaudí built the present house on the site of the castle, which had fallen badly into ruin. Its castellated look and the elongated, Gothic-inspired windows refer clearly to

the original castle. Gaudí kept the vestiges of its walls in his structure. The roof, with a walkway behind the parapet, is topped by a distinctive Gaudí tower. Ceramic fish mosaics by the main door symbolize Catalonia's past sea power.

Parc Güell **❿**

Carrer d'Olot. **❤** *93 424 38 09.* **Ⓜ** *Lesseps.* **⏱** *10am–8pm daily.* **♿ ♿ Casa-Museu Gaudí ❤** *93 219 38 11.* **⏱** *10am–6pm daily (to 7pm Mar, Apr & Oct, 8pm May–Sep).* **⏺** *1 Jan.* **♿**

Dᴇsɪɢɴᴀᴛᴇᴅ ᴀ World Heritage Site by UNESCO, the Parc Güell is Antoni Gaudí's (*see pp22–3*) most colourful creation. He was commissioned in the 1890s by Count Eusebi Güell to design a garden city on 20 hectares (50 acres) of family estate. In the event, little of the grand design for decorative public buildings and 60 houses in landscaped gardens became reality. What we see today was completed between 1910 and 1914 and the park opened in 1922.

Most atmospheric is the Room of a Hundred Columns, a cavernous covered market hall of 84 crooked pillars, brightened by glass and ceramic mosaics. Up a flight of steps flanked by ceramic animals is the Gran Plaça Circular, an open space with a snaking

Mosaic-encrusted chimney by Gaudí at the entrance of the Parc Güell

Catalonia's new National Theatre near the Plaça de les Glòries Catalanes

balcony of coloured mosaics, whose contours are bordered by a bench measuring 152 m (499 ft), said to be the longest in the world. It was executed by Josep Jujol, one of Gaudí's chief collaborators. The view from here is panoramic.

The two mosaic-decorated pavilions at the entrance are by Gaudí, but the gingerbread-style house where he lived from 1906 to 1926, now the Casa-Museu Gaudí, is by Francesc Berenguer. It contains Gaudí furniture and drawings.

Estació del Nord ⓫

Avinguda de Vilanova. **Map** 6 D1. Ⓜ *Arc de Triomf.*

ONLY THE 1861 façade over-looking a park and the grand 1915 entrance remain of this former railway station. The rest has been remodelled as a sports centre, a police head-quarters, and the city's bus station. Two elegant, blue-tiled sculptures, *Espiral arbrada (Branched Spiral)* and *Cel obert (Open Sky)* by Beverley Pepper (1992) sweep through the pleasant park. In front of

the station, at Avinguda de Vilanova 12, is a carefully restored building occupied by Catalonia's power generating company. It was built as a power station in 1897 by the architect Pere Falqués. Though the great machinery inside is not visible, the exterior of this iron and brick structure is unmistakably Modernista.

Plaça de les Glòries Catalanes ⓬

Gran Via de les Corts Catalanes. **Map** 4 F5. Ⓜ *Glòries.*

THIS WHOLE AREA, where the Diagonal crosses the Gran Via de les Corts Catalanes, has recently been redeveloped as the city expands northeast-wards and the Diagonal is extended down to the sea, completing the vision of the Eixample's planner Ildefons Cerdà *(see p67)*. On the north side, a new shopping centre contrasts with the Encants Vells flea market *(see p135)*, which sprawls beside the highway heading north out of town. It is open 8am–8pm four days a week, and much

of the merchandise of furniture, clothes, and bric-à-brac is simply laid out on the ground. It is busiest early in the day and bartering is all part of the fun.

To the south of the *plaça* is the new Teatre Nacional de Catalunya, a vast temple to culture by the Barcelona archi-tect Ricard Bofill. Beside it is the Auditori de Barcelona, with two concert halls by Rafael Moneo which were inaug-urated in 1999. The Museu de la Música *(see p69)* will move here after the millennium.

La Rambla del Poblenou, a good place for a stroll and a cup of coffee

Poblenou ⓭

Rambla del Poblenou. Ⓜ *Poblenou.*

POBLENOU IS the trendy part of town where artists and photographers have built their studios in the defunct ware houses of the city's former industrial heartland. The area is centred on the Rambla del Poblenou, a quiet avenue of plane trees which now extends from Avinguda Diagonal down to the sea. Here palm trees back a stretch of sandy beach.

Halfway down the Rambla, at the crossroads with Carrer de Ramon Turró is the Casino de l'Aliança, an historic social and cultural centre next to a good restaurant and, opposite, El Tio Che, a well-known ice cream parlour. A walk around the quiet streets leading from the Rambla will reveal a few protected pieces of industrial architecture, legacies from the time Barcelona was known as "the Manchester of Spain".

At the bottom of the Rambla along the parallel Carrer del Ferrocarril is the pretty, tree-shaded Plaça de Prim with low, whitewashed houses reminis-cent of a small country town.

Blue-tiled sculpture by Beverley Pepper, Parc de l'Estació del Nord

CATALONIA

·······································

LLEIDA · ANDORRA · GIRONA
BARCELONA PROVINCE · TARRAGONA

THERE IS A *wealth of natural beauty in Catalonia's four provinces, plus the small Catalan-speaking country of Andorra. They offer rocky coasts and mountains, fertile plains and sandy shores. Many who visit don't stray far from the coast, but the rewards for venturing further afield are immense.*

Beyond the constant bustle of Barcelona, Catalonia is essentially a rural region, with no large cities and few industrial blights. Of the four provinces, all named after their principal city, Lleida is the largest and least populated. Among its jewels are the Romanesque churches of the Boí valley and the Aigüestortes National Park.

Santa Maria, Ripoll

The province of Girona is blessed with mountains and sea. This eastern end of the Pyrenees has the magical Cerdanya valley and the ancient monasteries of Ripoll and Sant Joan de les Abadesses, as well as medieval villages and a handsome and too-often overlooked capital city. Its coast, the Costa Brava, is rocky and full of delights.

Barcelona province has its own coasts; the Maresme to the north is rather spoiled by the railway running beside the sea, but the Garraf to the south is more exciting – Sitges is a highly fashionable spot. Inland are the Holy Mountain of Montserrat (Catalonia's spiritual heart), the Penedès winelands, and the country town of Vic.

Tarragona, the most southerly of the provinces, has one of Spain's former Roman capitals. Here the land rolls more gently, supporting fruit and nut orchards and the monastic communities of Poblet and Santes Creus, before falling away towards the rice lands of the Ebre. The coastline is more gentle, too, with miles of long, sandy beaches.

Fruit trees in blossom near Balaguer in the province of Lleida

◁ **A fisherman inspects his nets in Cadaqués on the Costa Brava**

Exploring Catalonia

CATALONIA INCLUDES a long stretch of the Spanish Pyrenees, whose green, flower-filled valleys hide picturesque villages with Romanesque churches. The Parc Nacional d'Aigüestortes and Vall d'Aran are paradises for naturalists, while Baqueira-Beret offers skiers reliable snow. Sun-lovers can choose between the rugged Costa Brava or the long sandy stretches of the Costa Daurada. Tarragona is rich in Roman monuments. Inland are the monasteries of Poblet and Santes Creus and the well-known vineyards of Penedès.

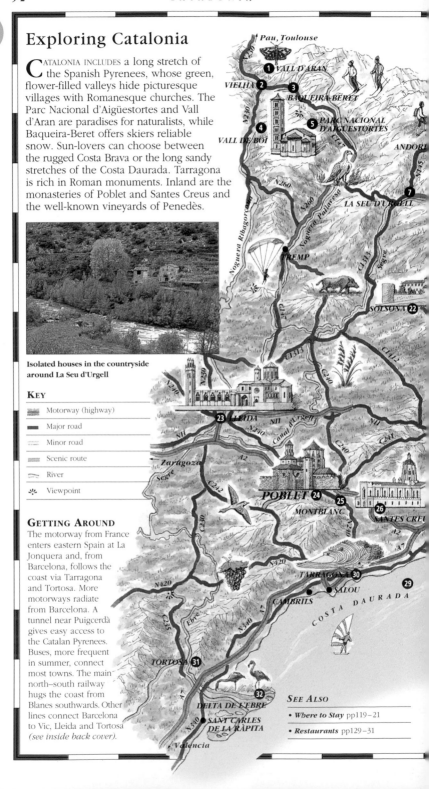

Isolated houses in the countryside around La Seu d'Urgell

KEY

▧	Motorway (highway)
▬	Major road
═══	Minor road
▧	Scenic route
⌇	River
⁂	Viewpoint

GETTING AROUND

The motorway from France enters eastern Spain at La Jonquera and, from Barcelona, follows the coast via Tarragona and Tortosa. More motorways radiate from Barcelona. A tunnel near Puigcerdà gives easy access to the Catalan Pyrenees. Buses, more frequent in summer, connect most towns. The main north–south railway hugs the coast from Blanes southwards. Other lines connect Barcelona to Vic, Lleida and Tortosa (*see inside back cover*).

Pau, Toulouse

① VALL D'ARAN
VIELHA ②
③ BAQUEIRA-BERET
④ ⑤ PARC NACIONAL D'AIGÜESTORTES
VALL DE BOÍ
ANDORRA
⑦
LA SEU D'URGELL
TREMP
SOLSONA ㉒
㉓ LLEIDA
Zaragoza
POBLET ㉔ ㉕
MONTBLANC ㉖ SANTES CREUS
TARRAGONA ㉚
CAMBRILS · SALOU ㉙
COSTA DAURADA
TORTOSA ㉛
㉜
DELTA DE L'EBRE
SANT CARLES DE LA RÀPITA
Valencia

SEE ALSO
• *Where to Stay* pp119–21
• *Restaurants* pp129–31

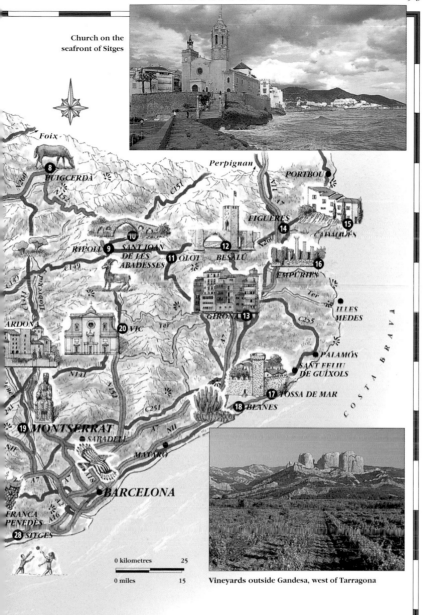

Church on the seafront of Sitges

Vineyards outside Gandesa, west of Tarragona

0 kilometres 25

0 miles 15

SIGHTS AT A GLANCE

The Vall d'Aran, surrounded by the snow-capped mountains of the Pyrenees

Vall d'Aran ❶

Lleida. 🚌 *Vielha.*
ℹ️ *Vielha (973 64 01 10).*

THIS VALLEY OF VALLEYS – *aran* means valley – is a lovely 600-sq km (230-sq mile) haven of forests and meadows filled with flowers, surrounded by towering mountain peaks.

The Vall d'Aran was formed by the Riu Garona, which rises in the area and flows out to France as the Garonne. With no proper link to the outside world until 1924, when a road was built over the Bonaigua Pass, the valley was cut off from the rest of Spain for most of the winter. Snow blocks the narrow pass from November to April, but today access is easy through the Túnel de Vielha from El Pont de Suert.

The fact that the Vall d'Aran faces north means that it has a climate similar to that on the Atlantic coast. Many rare wild flowers and butterflies flourish in the perfect conditions that are created by the shady slopes and damp breezes. It is also a famous habitat for many species of narcissus.

Tiny villages have grown up beside the Riu Garona, often around Romanesque churches, notably at **Bossòst**, **Salardú**, **Escunhau** and **Arties**. The valley is also ideal for outdoor sports such as skiing and is popular with walkers.

Vielha ❷

Lleida. 🏔️ *2,300.* 🚌 ℹ️ *Carrer Sarriulera 10 (973 64 01 10).* 🚊 *Thu.* 🎉 *Festa de Vielha (8 Sep).*

NOW A modern ski resort, the capital of the Vall d'Aran preserves relics of its medieval past. The Romanesque church of **Sant Miquel** has an octagonal bell tower, a tall, pointed roof and a superb wooden 12th-century crucifix, the *Mig Aran Christ*. It once formed part of a larger carving, since lost, which represented the Descent from the Cross. The **Museu de la Vall d'Aran** is a museum devoted to Aranese history and folklore.

🏛️ **Museu de la Vall d'Aran**
Carrer Major 26. 📞 *973 64 18 15.*
⬜ *Jul–mid-Sep: daily; mid-Sep–Jun: Tue–Sun.*
⬤ *public hols.* ♿

Mig Aran Christ (12th-century), Sant Miquel church, Vielha

Baqueira-Beret ❸

Lleida. 🎿 100. 🚌 🛈 Baqueira
(973 64 44 55). 📅 Romeria de
Nostra Senyora de Montgarri (2 Jul).

Tʜɪs ᴇxᴛᴇɴsɪᴠᴇ ski resort, one
of the best in Spain, is
popular with both the public
and the Spanish royal family.
There is reliable winter snow
cover and a choice of over 40
pistes at altitudes from 1,520 m
to 2,470 m (4,987 ft to 8,104 ft).

Baqueira and Beret were
separate mountain villages
before skiing became popular,
but they have now merged to
form a single resort. The Romans took full advantage of
the thermal springs located
here, which are nowadays
appreciated by tired skiers.

Vall de Boí ❹

Lleida. 🚌 La Pobla de Segur.
🚌 El Pont de Suert. 🛈 Barruera
(973 69 40 00).

Tʜɪs sᴍᴀʟʟ ᴠᴀʟʟᴇʏ on the
edge of the Parc Nacional
d'Aigüestortes is dotted with
tiny villages, many of which
are built around magnificent
Catalan Romanesque churches.

Dating from the 11th and
12th centuries, these churches
are distinguished by their tall
belfries, such as the six-storey
bell tower of the **Església de
Santa Eulàlia** at Erill-la-Vall.

The two churches at Taüll,
Sant Climent (see p20) and
Santa Maria, have superb
frescoes. Between 1919 and
1923 the originals were taken
for safekeeping to the Museu
Nacional d'Art de Catalunya in
Barcelona (see p80). Replicas
now stand in their place. You
can climb the towers of Sant
Climent for superb views of
the surrounding countryside.

Other churches in the area
worth visiting include those at
Coll, for its fine ironwork,
Barruera, and **Durro**, which
has another massive bell tower.

At the head of the valley is
the hamlet of **Caldes de Boí**,
popular for its thermal springs
and ski facilities. It is also a
good base for exploring the
Parc Nacional d'Aigüestortes,
the entrance to which is only
5 km (3 miles) from here.

**The tall belfry of Sant Climent
church at Taüll in the Vall de Boí**

Parc Nacional
d'Aigüestortes ❺

Lleida. 🚌 La Pobla de Segur.
🚌 El Pont de Suert, La Pobla de Segur.
🛈 Barruera (973 69 40 00)

Tʜᴇ ᴘʀɪsᴛɪɴᴇ mountain scenery of Catalonia's only
national park is among the
most spectacular to be seen
anywhere in the Pyrenees.

Established in 1955, the park
covers an area of 102 sq km
(40 sq miles). Its full title is
Parc Nacional d'Aigüestortes i
Estany de Sant Maurici, named
after the lake (estany) of Sant
Maurici in the east and the
Aigüestortes (literally, twisted
waters) area in the west. The
main village is the mountain

settlement of Espot, on the
park's eastern edge. Dotted
around the park are waterfalls
and the sparkling, clear waters
of around 150 lakes and tarns
which, in an earlier era, were
scoured by glaciers to depths
of up to 50 m (164 ft).

The finest scenery is around
Sant Maurici lake, which lies
beneath the twin shards of
the Serra dels Encantats,
(Mountains of the Enchanted).
From here, there is a variety
of walks, particularly along
the string of lakes that leads
north to the towering peaks
of Agulles d'Amitges. To the
south is the dramatic vista of
Estany Negre, the highest and
deepest tarn in the park.

Early summer in the lower
valleys is marked by a mass of
pink and red rhododendrons,
while later in the year wild
lilies bloom in the forests of
fir, beech and silver birch.

The park is also home to a
variety of wildlife. Chamois
(also known as izards) live on
the mountain screes and in
the meadows, while beavers
and otters can be spotted by
the lakes. Golden eagles nest
on mountain ledges, and
grouse and capercaillie are
found in the woods.

During the summer the
park is popular with walkers,
while in winter, the snow-
covered mountains are ideal
for cross-country skiing.

A crystal-clear stream, Parc Nacional d'Aigüestortes

LES QUATRE BARRES

Catalonia's national emblem

The four red bars on the *senyera*, the Catalan flag, represent the four provinces: Barcelona, Girona, Lleida and Tarragona. The design came about through a legend of Guifré el Pelós, first Count of Barcelona *(see p38)*. It relates how he received a call for help from Charles the Bald, who was King of the West Franks and grandson of Charlemagne. Guifré went to his aid and turned the tide of battle, but was mortally wounded. As he lay dying, Charles dipped his fingers in Guifré's blood and dragged them across his plain gold shield, giving him a grant of arms.

Andorra ❻

Principality of Andorra. 🏘 *65,000.* 🚻 *Andorra la Vella.* 🚌 *Pl de la Rotonda, Andorra la Vella (07-376 82 71 17).*

ANDORRA OCCUPIES 464 sq km (179 sq miles) of the Pyrenees between France and Spain. In 1993, it became fully independent and held its first ever democratic elections. Since 1278, it had been an autonomous feudal state under the jurisdiction of the Spanish bishop of La Seu d'Urgell and the French Count of Foix (a title adopted by the President of France). These are still the ceremonial joint heads of state.

Andorra's official language is Catalan, though French and Castilian are also spoken, and it uses both the French franc and the peseta as currency.

For many years Andorra has been a tax-free paradise for shoppers, a fact reflected in the crowded shops and supermarkets of the capital **Andorra la Vella**. Les Escaldes (near the capital), as well as Sant Julià de Lòria and El Pas de la Casa (the towns nearest the Spanish and French borders), have also become shopping centres.

Most visitors never see Andorra's rural charms, which match those of other parts of the Pyrenees. The region is excellent for walkers. One of the main routes leads to the **Cercle de Pessons**, a bowl of lakes in the east, and past Romanesque chapels such as **Sant Martí** at La Cortinada. In the north is the picturesque Sorteny valley where traditional farmhouses have been converted into snug restaurants.

La Seu d'Urgell ❼

Lleida. 🏘 *11,000.* 🚌 🚻 *Parc del Segre (973 36 00 92).* 🚢 *Tue & Sat.* 🎉 *Festa major (last week of Aug).*

THIS ANCIENT Pyrenean town was made a bishopric by the Visigoths in the 6th century. Feuds between the bishops of Urgell and the Counts of Foix over land ownership led to the emergence of Andorra in the 13th century.

The 12th-century **cathedral** has a much venerated Romanesque statue of Santa Maria d'Urgell. The **Museu Diocesà** contains medieval works of art and manuscripts, including a 10th-century copy of St Beatus of Liébana's 8th-century *Commentary on the Apocalypse*.

🏛 Museu Diocesà
Plaça del Deganat. 📞 *973 35 32 42.* ⭘ *daily.* ⬤ *public hols.* 📷

Carving, La Seu d'Urgell cathedral

Puigcerdà ❽

Girona. 🏘 *6,500.* 🚌 🚌 🚻 *Pl de l'Ajuntament (972 88 05 42).* 🚢 *Sun.* 🎉 *Festa del Llac (third Sun of Aug).*

PUIG IS CATALAN for hill. Although Puigcerdà sits on a relatively small hill compared with the encircling mountains, which rise to 2,900 m (9,500 ft), it nevertheless has a fine view right down the beautiful Cerdanya valley, watered by the trout-filled Riu Segre.

Puigcerdà, very close to the French border, was founded in 1177 by Alfons II as the capital of Cerdanya, an important agricultural region, which shares a past and its culture with the French Cerdagne. The Spanish enclave of **Llívia**, an attractive little town with a medieval pharmacy, lies 6 km (3.5 miles) inside France.

Cerdanya is the largest valley in the Pyrenees. At its edge is the **Cadí-Moixeró** nature reserve *(see p138)*, a place for ambitious walks.

Portal of Monestir de Santa Maria

Ripoll ❾

Girona. 🏘 *11,000.* 🚌 🚌 🚻 *Plaça del Abat Oliva (972 70 23 51).* 🚢 *Sat.* 🎉 *Sant Eudald (11–12 May).*

ONCE A TINY mountain base from which raids against the Moors were made, Ripoll is now best known for the **Monestir de Santa Maria** *(see p20)*, founded in 879. The town is called the "cradle of Catalonia" as the monastery was the power base and cultural centre of Guifré el Pelós (Wilfred the Hairy), founder of the House of Barcelona *(see p38)*. He is also buried here.

In the later 12th century, the west portal was decorated with what are regarded as the finest Romanesque carvings in Spain. This and the cloister are the only parts of the medieval monastery to have survived. The rest is a 19th-century reconstruction.

ENVIRONS: In the mountains to the west is **Sant Jaume de Frontanyà** *(see p20)*, another superb Romanesque church.

The medieval town of Besalú on the banks of the Riu Fluvià

Sant Joan de les Abadesses ⑩

Girona. 🚶 3,800. 🚉 🚌 ﹗ Passeig del Comte Guifré 5 (972 72 05 99). 🚍 Sun. 🎉 Festa major (second week of Sep).

A FINE, 12th-century Gothic bridge arches over the Riu Ter to this unassuming market town, whose main attraction is its **monastery**.

Founded in 885, it was a gift from Guifré, first count of Barcelona, to his daughter, the first abbess. The church is unadorned except for a superb wooden calvary, *The Descent from the Cross*. Though made in 1150, it looks modern. The figure of a thief on the left was burnt in the Civil War and re-placed so skillfully that it is hard to tell it is new. The monastery's museum has Baroque and Renaissance altarpieces.

12th-century calvary, Sant Joan de les Abadesses monastery

ENVIRONS: To the north are **Camprodon** and **Beget**, both with Romanesque churches *(see p21)*. Camprodon also has some grand houses, and its region is noted for sausages.

Olot ⑪

Girona. 🚶 27,000. 🚉 🚌 ﹗ Carrer del Bisbe Lorenzana 15 (972 26 01 41). 🚍 Mon. 🎉 Corpus Christi (May/Jun), Festa del Tura (8 Sep).

T HIS SMALL MARKET TOWN is at the centre of a landscape pockmarked with the conical hills of extinct volcanoes. But it was an earthquake in 1474 which last disturbed the town, destroying its medieval past.

During the 18th century the town's textile industry spawn-ed the "Olot School" of art *(see p24)*: finished cotton fabrics were printed with drawings, and in 1783 the Public School of Drawing was founded.

Much of the school's work, which includes sculpted saints and paintings such as Joaquim Vayreda's *Les Falgueres*, is in the **Museu Comarcal de la Garrotxa**, housed in an 18th-century hospice. There are also pieces by *Modernista* sculptor Miquel Blay, whose damsels support the balcony at No. 38 Passeig Miquel Blay.

🏛 **Museu Comarcal de la Garrotxa**
Edifici Hospici 8. 📞 972 27 91 30. 🔵 Wed–Mon. 🎫 ♿

Besalú ⑫

Girona. 🚶 2,000. 🚌 ﹗ Plaça de la Llibertat 1 (972 59 12 40). 🚍 Tue. 🎉 Sant Vicenç (22 Jan), Festa major (last weekend of Sep).

A MAGNIFICENT medieval town, with a striking approach across a fortified bridge over the Riu Fluvià, Besalú has two fine Romanesque churches: **Sant Vicenç** and **Sant Pere** *(see p21)*. The latter is the sole remnant of a Benedictine monastery founded in 977, but pulled down in 1835 leaving a big, empty square.

In 1964 a **mikvah**, a Jewish ritual bath, was discovered by chance. It was built in 1264 and is one of only three of that period to survive in Europe. The tourist office has the keys to all the town's attractions.

To the south, the sky-blue lake of **Banyoles**, where the 1992 Olympic rowing contests were held, is ideal for picnics.

Shop selling *llonganisses* in the mountain town of Camprodon

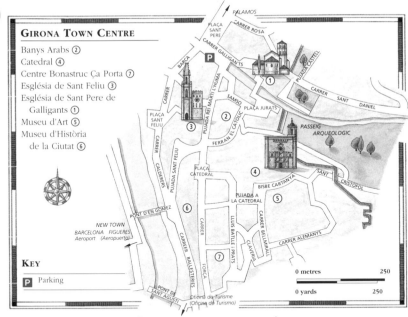

GIRONA TOWN CENTRE

Banys Arabs ②
Catedral ④
Centre Bonastruc Ça Porta ⑦
Església de Sant Feliu ③
Església de Sant Pere de
    Galligants ①
Museu d'Art ⑤
Museu d'Història
    de la Ciutat ⑥

KEY

P Parking

0 metres   250
0 yards   250

Girona ⑬

Girona. 🏛 *75,000.* ✈ 🚌 🚉 📮 🛈
*Rambla de la Llibertat 1 (972 22 65
75).* 🕐 *Tue, Sat.* 🎉 *El Pedal (last
fortnight of Sep), Sant Narcis (29 Oct).*

THIS HANDSOME TOWN puts
on its best face beside the
Riu Onyar, where tall, pastel-
coloured buildings rise above
the water. Behind them, in the
old town, the Rambla de la
Llibertat is lined with busy
shops and street cafés.

The houses were built in the
19th century to replace sections of the city wall damaged
during a seven-month siege
by French troops in 1809. Most
of the rest of the ramparts, first
raised by the Romans, are still

intact and have been turned
into the Passeig Arqueològic
(Archaeological Walk), which
runs right round the city.

The walk's starting point is
on the north side of the town,
near the **Església de Sant
Pere de Galligants** (St Peter
of the Cock Crows) *(see p21).*
The church now houses the
city's archaeological collection.

From here, a narrow street
into the old part of town goes
through the north gate, where
huge Roman foundation stones
are still visible. They mark the
route of the Via Augusta, the
important road which originally ran from Tarragona to
Rome. The most popular place
of devotion for the people of
Girona is the **Església de**

Sant Feliu, which brims with
history. The church, begun in
the 14th century, was built
over the tombs of St Felix and
St Narcissus, both patrons of
the city. Next to the high altar
are eight Roman sarcophagi
embedded in the apse wall.

Despite their name, the
nearby **Banys Àrabs** (Arab
Baths), lit by a fine octagonal
lantern, were built in the late
12th century, about 300 years
after the Moors had left.

🏛 Centre Bonastruc Ça Porta

Carrer de Sant Llorenç. 📞 *972 21
67 61.* 🕐 *daily.* 🌐
This centre charts the history of
Jews in Girona. The buildings it
occupies in the maze of alley-
ways and steps in the old town
were once part of El Call, the
Jewish ghetto, which was in-
habited by the city's Jews from
the late 9th century until their
expulsion from Spain in 1492.

⛪ Catedral

Girona Cathedral's west face is
pure Catalan Baroque, but the
rest of the building is Gothic.
The single nave, built in 1416
by Guillem Bofill, possesses
the widest Gothic span in the
Christian world. Behind the
altar is a marble throne known
as "Charlemagne's Chair". It is
named after the Frankish king

Painted houses packed tightly along the bank of the Riu Onyar in Girona

whose troops took Girona in 785. In the chancel is a 14th-century jewel-encrusted silver and enamel altarpiece, the best example in Catalonia. Among the fine Romanesque paintings and statues in the cathedral's museum are a 10th-century illuminated copy of St Beatus of Liébana's *Commentary on the Apocalypse*, and a 14th-century statue of the Catalan king, Pere the Ceremonious.

The collection's most famous item is a tapestry, called *The Creation*, decorated with lively figures. The rich colours of this large 11th- to 12th-century work are well preserved.

Tapestry of *The Creation*

🏛 Museu d'Art

Pujada de la Catedral 12. ☎ 972 20 95 36. ⬤ Tue–Sun. 🎫 ♿

This former episcopal palace is one of Catalonia's best art galleries, with works from the Romanesque period up to the 20th century. The many items from churches ruined by war or neglect tell of the richness of church interiors long ago.

🏛 Museu del Cinema

Carrer Sèquia 1. ☎ 972 41 27 77. ⬤ Tue–Sun.

Next to Església de Mercadel in the new town, this intriguing collection includes film and artifacts from the mid-19th century to the present day.

🏛 Museu d'Història de la Ciutat

Carrer de la Força 27. ☎ 972 22 22 29. ⬤ Tue–Sun.

The city's history museum is in an 18th-century former convent. The recesses where the decomposing bodies of members of the Capuchin Order were placed can still be seen. Exhibits include scientific items and old *sardana* (see p111) instruments.

Figueres ⓮

Girona. 🏘 35,000. 🚉 🚌 ℹ Plaça del Sol (972 50 31 55). 🚏 Thu. 🎉 Santa Creu (3 May), Sant Pere (29 Jun).

FIGUERES IS THE market town of the Empordà plain. Beside the plane-tree-shaded Rambla is the former Hotel de Paris, now home to the **Museu de Joguets** (Toy Museum). At the bottom of the Rambla is a statue of Narcís Monturiol i Estarriol (1819–95) who, it is said, invented the submarine.

Figueres was the birthplace of Salvador Dalí, who in 1974 turned the town theatre into the **Teatre-Museu Dalí**. Under its eye-catching glass dome is an eclectic mix of works by Dalí and other painters. The whole entertaining place, from *Rainy Taxi* to the Mae West room, is a monument to Catalonia's most eccentric artist.

ENVIRONS: The **Casa-Museu Castell Gala Dalí**, 55 km (35 miles) south of Figueres, is the medieval castle Dalí bought for his wife in the 1970s. It contains their furnishings and some of his paintings and

***Rainy Taxi*, a monument in the garden of the Teatre-Museu Dalí**

drawings. East of Figueres is the Romanesque monastery of **Sant Pere de Rodes** (see p21).

🏛 Museu de Joguets

C/ Sant Pere 1. ☎ 972 50 45 85. ⬤ Wed–Mon. ● Feb. 🎫 ♿

🏛 Teatre-Museu Dalí

Pl Gala-Salvador Dalí. ☎ 972 51 18 00. ⬤ Tue–Sun. ● 1 Jan, 25 Dec 🎫

🏛 Casa-Museu Castell Gala Dalí

C/ Gala Dalí, Púbol (La Pera). ☎ 972 48 82 11. ⬤ 15 Mar–14 Jun Tue Sat; 15 Jun–15 Sep daily. 🎫

THE ART OF DALI

Salvador Dalí i Domènech was born in Figueres in 1904 and mounted his first exhibition at the age of 15. After studying at the Escuela de Bellas Artes in Madrid, and dabbling with Cubism, Futurism and Metaphysical painting, the young artist embraced Surrealism in 1929, becoming the movement's best-known painter. Never far from controversy, the self-publicist Dalí became famous for his hallucinatory images – such as *Woman-Animal Symbiosis* – which he described as "hand-painted dream photographs". Dalí's career also included writing and film-making, and established him as one of the 20th century's greatest artists. He died in his home town in 1989.

Ceiling fresco in the Wind Palace Room, Teatre-Museu Dalí

Cadaqués ⑮

Girona. 🏛 *1,800.* 🚌 ℹ️ *Carrer Cotxe 2 (972 25 83 15).* 🏛 *Mon.* 🎪 *Santa Esperança (18 Dec).*

THIS PRETTY, whitewashed resort, overlooked by the Baroque **Església de Santa Maria**, is the most easterly in the Iberian peninsula. In the 1960s it was dubbed the "St Tropez of Spain", largely because of the young crowd that sought out Salvador Dalí in nearby Port Lligat. The house where he lived from 1930 until his death in 1989 is open to the public as the **Casa-Museu Salvador Dalí**. A "bus-train" takes visitors there from Cadaqués. As tours are in small groups, advance booking is essential.

The **Centre d'Art Perrot-Moore** contains examples of Dalí's work, some excellent Picassos, and a room dedicated to contemporary artists.

🏛 **Casa-Museu Salvador Dalí**
Port Lligat. 📞 *972 25 80 63.* ⭕ *mid-Mar–Oct: Tue–Sun.* 🎫
🏛 **Centre d'Art Perrot-Moore**
Carrer Vigilant 1. 📞 *972 25 82 31.* ⭕ *Easter–Oct: Tue–Sun.* 🎫 ♿

Empúries ⑯

Girona. 🚌 *L'Escala.* 📞 *972 77 02 08.* ⭕ *daily.* 🎫 *for ruins.*

THE EXTENSIVE ruins of the Greco-Roman town of Empúries *(see p37)* occupy an imposing site beside the sea. Three separate settlements were built between the 7th and

An excavated Roman pillar in the ruins of Empúries

Looking south along the Costa Brava from Tossa de Mar

3rd centuries BC: the old town (known to archaeologists as Palaiapolis); the new town (Neapolis); and the Roman town, which was founded by Julius Caesar in 49 BC.

The **old town** was founded by the Greeks in 600 BC as a trading port. It was built on what was then a small offshore island, and is now the site of the tiny walled hamlet of Sant Martí de Empúries. In 550 BC this was replaced by a larger new town on the shore which the Greeks named Emporion, meaning "trading place". In 218 BC, the Romans landed at Empúries and built a city next to the new town. From here they began their subjugation of the Iberian peninsula.

A museum near the ruins exhibits some finds from the site, but the best are now in the Museu Arqueològic of Barcelona *(see p80).*

Tossa de Mar ⑰

Girona. 🏛 *3,500.* 🚌 ℹ️ *Avinguda Pelegri 25 (972 34 01 08).* 🏛 *Thu.* 🎪 *Festa de estiu (29 Jun).*

AT THE END of a tortuous corniche, the Roman town of Turissa is one of the prettiest places along the Costa Brava. Above the modern town is the **Vila Vella** (old town), a protected national monument. The medieval walls, which have three towers, enclose fishermen's cottages, a 14th-century church and countless bars.

The **Museu Municipal** in the old town exhibits local archaeological finds and

modern art including *The Flying Violinist* by 20th-century Russian artist Marc Chagall.

🏛 **Museu Municipal**
Plaça Roig y Soler. 📞 *972 34 07 09.* ⭕ *Tue–Sun.* ● *25 Dec.* 🎫

Blanes ⑱

Girona. 🏛 *30,000.* 🚌 ℹ️ *Plaça de Catalunya 21 (972 33 03 48).* 🏛 *Mon.* 🎪 *Santa Ana (24–28 Jul).*

THE WORKING PORT of Blanes has one of the longest beaches on the Costa Brava. However, the highlight of the town is the **Jardí Botànic Mar i Murtra**. These beautiful gardens, designed by the German Karl Faust in 1928, are spectacularly sited above cliffs. There are around 7,000 species of Mediterranean and tropical plants here, including a collection of African cacti.

🌿 **Jardí Botànic Mar i Murtra**
Pg Karl Faust 10. 📞 *972 33 08 26.* ⭕ *daily.* ● *1 & 6 Jan, 24 & 25 Dec.*

A few of the many species of cacti, Jardí Botànic Mar i Murtra

◁ **Surrealist decoration on one of the buildings of the Teatre-Museu Dalí in Figueres**

The Costa Brava

THE COSTA BRAVA ("wild coast") runs for some 200 km (125 miles) from Blanes northwards to the region of Empordà, which borders France. It is a mix of rugged cliffs, pine-backed sandy coves, golden beaches and crowded, modern resorts. The busiest resorts – Lloret de Mar, Tossa de Mar and Platja d'Aro – are to the south. Sant Feliu de Guíxols and Palamós are still working towns behind the summer rush. Just inland there are medieval villages to explore, such as Peralada, Peratallada and Pals. Wine, olives and fishing were the mainstays of the area before the tourists came in the 1960s.

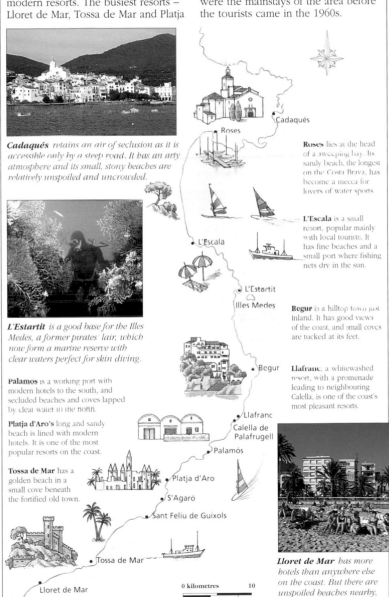

Cadaqués *retains an air of seclusion as it is accessible only by a steep road. It has an arty atmosphere and its small, stony beaches are relatively unspoiled and uncrowded.*

Roses lies at the head of a sweeping bay. Its sandy beach, the longest on the Costa Brava, has become a mecca for lovers of water sports.

L'Escala is a small resort, popular mainly with local tourists. It has fine beaches and a small port where fishing nets dry in the sun.

L'Estartit *is a good base for the Illes Medes, a former pirates' lair, which now form a marine reserve with clear waters perfect for skin diving.*

Begur is a hilltop town just inland. It has good views of the coast, and small coves are tucked at its feet.

Palamós is a working port with modern hotels to the south, and secluded beaches and coves lapped by clear water to the north.

Llafranc, a whitewashed resort, with a promenade leading to neighbouring Calella, is one of the coast's most pleasant resorts.

Platja d'Aro's long and sandy beach is lined with modern hotels. It is one of the most popular resorts on the coast.

Tossa de Mar has a golden beach in a small cove beneath the fortified old town.

Cadaqués
Roses
L'Escala
L'Estartit
Illes Medes
Begur
Llafranc
Calella de Palafrugell
Palamós
Platja d'Aro
S'Agaró
Sant Feliu de Guíxols
Tossa de Mar
Lloret de Mar
Blanes

0 kilometres　10

0 miles　5

Lloret de Mar *has more hotels than anywhere else on the coast. But there are unspoiled beaches nearby, such as Santa Cristina.*

Monestir de Montserrat 🏛

A Benedictine monk

THE "SERRATED MOUNTAIN" (*mont serrat*), its highest peak rising to 1,236 m (4,055 ft), is a superb setting for Catalonia's holiest place, the Monastery of Montserrat, which is surrounded by chapels and hermits' caves. The monastery was first mentioned in the 9th century, enlarged in the 11th century, and in 1409 became independent of Rome. In 1811, when the French attacked Catalonia in the War of Independence (*see p41*), the monastery was destroyed and the monks killed. Rebuilt and repopulated in 1844, it was a beacon of Catalan culture during the Franco years. Today Benedictine monks live here. Visitors can hear the Escolania singing the *Virolai* (the Montserrat hymn) at 1pm and the *Salve Regina* at 7:10pm every day, except in July and during the Christmas period, in the basilica.

Plaça de Santa Maria
The focal points of the square are two wings of the Gothic cloister built in 1477. The modern monastery façade is by Francesc Folguera.

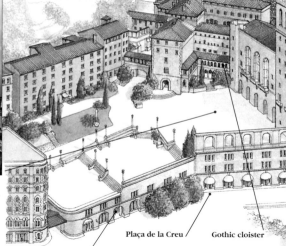

Plaça de la Creu   **Gothic cloister**

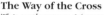

The Museum has a collection of 19th- and 20th-century Catalan paintings and many Italian works. It also displays liturgical items brought from the Holy Land.

The Way of the Cross
This path passes 14 statues representing the Stations of the Cross. It begins near the Plaça de l'Abat Oliba.

STAR FEATURES

★ Basilica Façade

★ Black Virgin

View of Montserrat
The complex includes shops, cafés and a hotel. Funicular railways take visitors from the Plaça de la Creu to the Cova Santa and the hermitage of Sant Joan.

★ **Basilica Façade**
Agapit and Venanci Vallmitjana sculpted Christ and the Apostles on the basilica's Neo-Renaissance façade. It was built in 1900 to replace the Plateresque façade of the original church, consecrated in 1592.

★ **Black Virgin**
La Moreneta looks down from behind the altar, protected behind glass; her wooden orb protrudes for pilgrims to touch.

Terminus for cable car from Aeri de Montserrat railway station

VISITORS' CHECKLIST

Montserrat (Barcelona province).
🚌 93 835 02 51. 🚉 Aeri de Montserrat, then cable car.
🚌 from Barcelona. **Basilica**
🕐 Oct– Jun: 8am–6:30pm daily; Jul–Sep: 7:30am–8:30pm daily.
✝ throughout the day, from 9am Mon–Fri, from 7:30am Sat, from 8am Sun & religious hols.
📷 ♿ **Museum** 🕐 Jan–Feb: 10am–4:45pm daily; Mar–Dec: 10am–6pm daily. 📷 ♿ 🍽

Basilica Interior
The sanctuary in the domed basilica is adorned by a richly enamelled altar and paintings by Catalan artists.

The Escolania is the famous choir of 50 boy choristers, who sing twice a day in the basilica.

THE VIRGIN OF MONTSERRAT

The small wooden statue of La Moreneta (the dark maiden) is the soul of Montserrat. It is said to have been made by St Luke and brought here by St Peter in AD 50. Centuries later, the statue is believed to have been hidden from the Moors in the nearby Santa Cova (Holy Cave). Carbon dating suggests, however, that the statue was carved around the 12th century. In 1881 Montserrat's Black Virgin became patroness of Catalonia.

The blackened Virgin of Montserrat

Inner Courtyard
On one side of the courtyard is the baptistry (1902), with sculptures by Carles Collet. Pilgrims may approach the Virgin through a door to the right.

Vic ⑳

Barcelona. 🏛 *30,000.* 🚉 🚌
🅘 *C/ Ciutat 4 (93 886 20 91).* 🚌 *Tue & Sat.* 🎪 *Mercat del Ram (Sat before Easter), Sant Miquel (5–15 Jul), Música Viva (3 days mid-Sep).*

MARKET DAYS are the best time to go to this small country town. This is when the excellent local sausages *(embotits)*, for which the area is renowned, are piled high in the large Gothic Plaça Major, along with other produce from the surrounding plains.

In the 3rd century BC Vic was the capital of an ancient Iberian tribe, the Ausetans. The town was then colonized by the Romans – the remains of a Roman temple survive today. Since the 6th century the town has been a bishop's see. In the 11th century, Abbot Oliva commissioned El Cloquer tower, around which the cathedral was built in the 18th century. The interior of the cathedral is covered with vast murals by Josep-Maria Sert (1876–1945, *see p25*). Painted in reds and golds, they represent scenes from the Bible.

Adjacent to the cathedral is the **Museu Episcopal de Vic** *(see p21)*, which has one of the best Romanesque collections in Catalonia. The large display of mainly religious art and relics includes bright, simple murals and wooden carvings from rural churches. Also on display are 11th- and 12th-century frescoes and some superb altar frontals.

Cardona dominating the surrounding area from its hilltop site

🏛 **Museu Episcopal**
Plaça Bisbe Oliva. 📞 *93 886 22 14.*
⏺ *for restoration.*

Cardona ㉑

Barcelona. 🏛 *4,500.* 🚉 🅘 *Avinguda Rastrillo (93 869 27 98).* 🚌 *Sun.* 🎪 *Festa major (second Sun of Sep).*

THIS 13TH-CENTURY, ruddy-stoned castle of the Dukes of Cardona, constables to the crown of Aragón, is set on the top of a hill. The castle was rebuilt in the 18th century and is now a luxurious parador *(see p114)*. Beside the castle is an elegant, early 11th-century church, the **Església de Sant Vicenç**, where the Dukes of Cardona are buried.

The castle gives views of the town and of the Muntanya de Sal (Salt Mountain), a huge salt deposit beside the Riu Cardener that has been mined since Roman times.

Solsona ㉒

Lleida. 🏛 *7,000.* 🚉 🅘 *Avinguda Pont (973 48 23 10).* 🚌 *Tue & Fri.* 🎪 *Carnival (late Feb); Corpus Christi (May/Jun), Festa major (8–10 Sep).*

NINE TOWERS and three gateways remain of Solsona's moated fortifications. Inside the walls is an ancient town of noble mansions. The cathedral houses a beautiful black stone Virgin. The adjoining **Museu Diocesà i Comarcal** contains Romanesque paintings and local archaeological finds. Solsona has a fine collection of knives at the **Museu Ganivets**.

🏛 **Museu Diocesà i Comarcal**
Plaça del Palau 1. 📞 *973 48 21 01.*
🕐 *Tue–Sun.* ♿
🏛 **Museu Ganivets**
C/ Llovera 14. 📞 *973 48 15 69.*
🕐 *Tue–Sun.* 🎫

Lleida ㉓

Lleida. 🏛 *112,000.* 🚉 🚌 🅘 *Avda de Madrid 36 (973 27 09 97).* 🚌 *Thu & Sat.* 🎪 *Sant Anastasi (11 May), Sant Miquel (29 Sep).*

DOMINATING LLEIDA, the capital of Catalonia's only inland province, is **La Suda**, a fort, now in ruins, taken from the Moors in 1149. The old cathedral, **La Seu Vella**, founded in 1203, lies within the fort's walls, high above the town. It was transformed into barracks by Felipe V in 1707 but today is desolate. It remains imposing, however, with magnificent Gothic windows in the cloister.

A lift descends from La Seu Vella to the Plaça de Sant Joan

Twelfth-century altar frontal, Museu Episcopal de Vic

in the busy, pedestrianized shopping street that sweeps round the foot of the hill. The new cathedral is here, as are manorial buildings such as the reconstructed 13th-century town hall, the **Paeria**.

Poblet ㉔

See pp108–9.

Montblanc ㉕

Tarragona. 🚶 6,000. 🚌 🚉 🅸
Muralla Santa Tecla 24 (977 86 12 32).
🖐 Fri. 🎊 Festa major (8 Sep).

THE MEDIEVAL grandeur of Montblanc lives on within its walls, which are considered to be Catalonia's finest piece of military architecture. At the **Sant Jordi** gate St George allegedly slew the dragon. The **Museu Comarcal de la Conca de Barberà** has interesting displays on local crafts.

🏛 Museu Comarcal de la Conca de Barberà
Carrer de Josa 6. 🕻 977 86 03 49.
◯ daily. 🈁

Santes Creus ㉖

Tarragona. 🚶 100. 🚌 🅸 *Plaça de Sant Bernard (977 63 83 01).* 🖐 Sat & Sun; Santa Llúcia (13 Dec).

THE TINY VILLAGE of Santes Creus is home to the prettiest of the "Cistercian triangle"

monasteries. The other two, Vallbona de les Monges and Poblet *(see pp108–9)*, are nearby. The **Monestir de Santes Creus** was founded in 1150 by Ramon Berenguer IV *(see p38)* during his reconquest of Catalonia. The Gothic cloisters are decorated with figurative sculptures, a style first permitted by Jaume II, who ruled from 1291 to 1327. His finely carved tomb is in the 12th-century church whose interior is decorated with a beautiful rose window.

⛪ Monestir de Santes Creus
🕻 977 63 83 29. ◯ Tue–Sun. 🈁

Vilafranca del Penedès ㉗

Barcelona. 🚶 30,000. 🚌 🚉
🅸 *Carrer Cort 14 (93 892 03 58).*
🖐 Sat. 🎊 Festa major (end Aug).

THIS BUSY MARKET town is set in the heart of Penedès, the main wine-producing region of Catalonia. The **Museu del Vi** (Wine Museum), in the 14th century palace of the kings of Aragón, documents the long history of the area's wine trade. Local *bodegues* can be visited for wine tasting.

Sant Sadurní d'Anoia, the capital of Spain's sparkling wine, *cava (see pp28–9)*, is 8 km (5 miles) to the north.

🏛 Museu del Vi
Plaça de Jaume I. 🕻 93 890 05 82.
◯ Tue–Sun. 🈁

Anxaneta climbing to the top of a tower of *castellers*

HUMAN TOWERS

The province of Tarragona is famous for its *casteller* festivals, in which teams of men stand on each other's shoulders in an effort to build the highest human tower *(castell)*. Configurations depend on the number of men who form the base. The participants, dressed in coloured shirts, are called *els xiquets* (the lads), and the small boy who has to undertake the hazardous climb to the top, where he makes the sign of the cross, is called the *anxaneta* (weathercock).

Castellers assemble in competition for Tarragona province's major festivals throughout the year. In the wine town of Vilafranca del Penedès they turn out for Sant Fèlix (30 August), and in Tarragona city for Santa Tecla, its *festa major* on 23 September. Rival teams in Valls appear on St John's Day (24 June), but strive for their best achievement at the end of the tower-building season on St Ursula's Day (21 October), when teams from all over Catalonia converge on the town square.

Monestir de Santes Creus, surrounded by poplar and hazel trees

Monestir de Poblet 🄬

THE MONASTERY OF SANTA MARIA DE POBLET is a haven of tranquillity and a resting place of kings. It was the first and most important of three sister monasteries, known as the "Cistercian triangle" *(see p107)*, that helped to consolidate power in Catalonia after it had been recaptured from the Moors by Ramon Berenguer IV. In 1835, during the Carlist upheavals, it was plundered and seriously damaged by fire. Restoration of the impressive ruins, largely complete, began in 1930 and monks returned in 1940.

The dormitory is reached by stairs from the church. The vast 87-m (285-ft) gallery dates from the 18th century. Half of it is still in use by the monks.

The 13th-century refectory is a vaulted hall with an octagonal fountain and a pulpit.

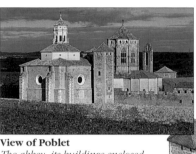

View of Poblet
The abbey, its buildings enclosed by fortified walls that have hardly changed since the Middle Ages, is in an isolated valley near the Riu Francolí's source.

Museum

Wine cellar

Library
The Gothic scriptorium was converted into a library in the 17th century, when the Duke of Cardona donated his book collection.

Former kitchen

Royal doorway   Royal palace

TIMELINE

Royal tombs

1100	1300	1500	1700	1900

1157 Founding of sister monastery at Vallbona de les Monges

1168 Santes Creus founded – third abbey in Cistercian triangle

14th century Main cloister finished

1479 Juan II, last king of Aragón, buried here

1812 Poblet desecrated by French troops

1940 Monks return

1196 Alfonso II is the first king to be buried here

1336–87 Reign of Pere the Ceremonious, who designates Poblet a royal pantheon

1953 Tombs reconstructed. Royal remains returned

1151 Poblet monastery founded by Ramon Berenguer IV

1788–1808 Reign of Carlos IV, who has main reredos installed

1835 Disentailment *(p41)* of monasteries. Poblet ravaged

Chapterhouse
This perfectly square room, with slender columns, has tiers of benches for the monks. It is paved with the tombstones of 11 abbots who died between 1393 and 1693.

VISITORS' CHECKLIST

Off N240, 10 km (6 miles) from Montblanc. ℹ 997 87 02 54. **Monastery** 📞 977 87 00 89. 🚌 L'Espluga de Francolí, then walk or taxi. 🚻 ⏰ 10am–12:30pm, 3–5:30pm (6pm Jun–Sep) daily. 🚫 ✝ Jul–Sep: 8am, 10am & 7pm; Oct–Jun: 8am, 10am & 6pm. 🍴

Parlour cloister

Sant Esteve cloister

New sacristy

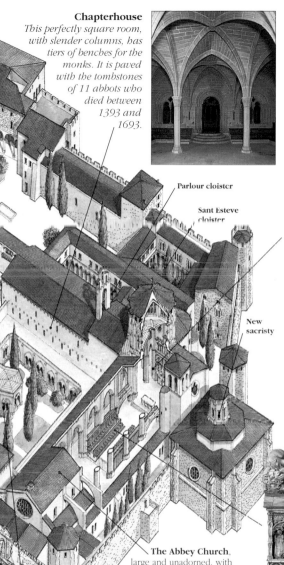

★ **High Altar Reredos**
Behind the stone altar, supported by Romanesque columns, an impressive alabaster reredos fills the apse. It was carved by Damià Forment in 1527.

The Abbey Church, large and unadorned, with three naves, is a typical Cistercian building.

★ **Royal Tombs**
The tombs in the pantheon of kings were begun in 1359. In 1950 they were reconstructed by the sculptor Frederic Marès.

Baroque church façade

★ **Cloisters**
The evocative, vaulted cloisters were built in the 12th and 13th centuries and were the centre of monastic life. The capitals are beautifully decorated with carved scrollwork.

STAR FEATURES

★ High Altar Reredos

★ Royal Tombs

★ Cloisters

Palm trees lining the waterfront at Sitges

Sitges 28

Barcelona. 🎿 *15,000*. 🚗 🚉 🛈 C/
Sinia Morera 1 (93 89 50 04). 🚌 alter-
nate Thu. 🎪 Festa major (23–24 Aug).

LIVELY BARS line the seafront
at Sitges which is popular
with both locals and foreigners.
Modernista artist Santiago
Rusiñol (see p25) spent much
time here. He bequeathed his
eclectic collection of wrought-
iron, ceramics, sculptures and
paintings to the colourful
Museu Cau Ferrat, which
also has works by El Greco.

🏛 **Museu Cau Ferrat**
Carrer Fonollar. 【 93 894 03 64.
🕐 Tue–Sun. 🌑 public hols. 🈳

Costa Daurada 29

Tarragona. 🚉 🚗 Calafell, Sant Vicenç
de Calders, Salou. 🛈 Tarragona
(977 23 34 15).

THE COAST OF Tarragona province, with its long, sandy
beaches, is known as the
Costa Daurada (the Golden
Coast). **Vilanova i la Geltrú**
and **El Vendrell** are two of the
active ports along its coastline.
The **Museu Pau Casals** in
Sant Salvador (El Vendrell) is
dedicated to the famous cellist.
   Port Aventura, south of
Tarragona, is one of Europe's
largest theme parks. Its attractions are exotically-inspired
and named Mediterrània, Wild

West, México, Polynesia and
China. **Cambrils** and **Salou**
to the south are the liveliest
resorts – the others are mostly
low-key, family holiday spots.

🏛 **Museu Pau Casals**
Avinguda Palfuriana 59–61.
【 977 68 34 68. 🌑 for restoration.
🎢 **Port Aventura**
Autovia Salou–Vila-seca. 【 977 77
90 00. 🕐 mid-Mar–Oct. 🈳 ♿

Tarragona 30

Tarragona. 🎿 *110,000*. ✈ 🚉 🚗
🛈 Carrer Fortuny 4 (977 23 34 15).
🚌 Tue & Thu. 🎪 Sant Magí (9 Aug),
Santa Tecla (23 Sep).

TARRAGONA IS NOW a major
industrial port, but it has
preserved many remnants of
its Roman past, when it was

the capital of Tarraconensis.
The Romans chose it as their
base for the conquest of the
peninsula, which began in the
3rd century BC (see p37).
   The avenue of Rambla Nova
ends abruptly above the sea on
the clifftop Balcó de Europa,
from which the extensive ruins
of the **Amfiteatre Romà** can
be seen. Within them is the
ruined 12th-century church of
Santa Maria del Miracle.
   Nearby is the Praetorium,
a Roman tower that was converted into a palace in medieval times. It is sometimes
known as the Castell de Pilato
(named after Pontius Pilate),
and it now houses the **Museu
de la Romanitat**. This displays Roman and medieval
finds, and gives access to the
cavernous passageways of the
excavated Roman circus, built

The remains of the Roman amphitheatre, Tarragona

in the 1st century AD. Adjoining the Praetorium is the **Museu Nacional Arqueològic,** containing the most important collection of Roman artifacts in Catalonia. It has a large collection of bronze implements, stone busts and beautiful mosaics, including a *Head of Medusa*.

Among the most impressive remains in the city are the gigantic pre-Roman stones on which the Roman wall is built. An archaeological wall runs along a 1-km (1,100-yd) long stretch of the wall and its towers.

Behind it is the 12th-century **cathedral**, built on the site of a Roman temple to Jupiter and a subsequent Arab mosque. The structure evolved over many centuries, as seen from the harmonious blend of styles of the exterior. Inside is an alabaster altarpiece of St Tecla, carved by Pere Joan in 1434. The large 13th century cloister, which is filled with orange trees, has early Gothic vaulting, but the doorway is Romanesque (*see pp20–21*) in its geometric decoration.

In the west of town is a 3rd- to 6th-century Christian cemetery (ask about opening times in the archaeological museum). Some of the carved sarcophagi in the site museum were originally used as pagan tombs.

ENVIRONS: The well-preserved **Aqüeducte de les Ferreres** lies just outside the city, next to the A7 motorway. (There is a lay-by for viewing.) This 2nd-century aqueduct was built to bring water to the city from the Riu Gaià, 30 km (19 miles) to the north. The **Arc de Berà**, a 1st-century triumphal arch on the Via Augusta, is 20 km (12 miles) northeast on the N340.

🏛 **Museu Nacional Arqueològic de Tarragona**
Plaça del Rei 5. 🅲 977 23 62 09.
◯ Tue–Sun. 🈺 🅱
🏛 **Museu de la Romanitat**
Plaça del Rei. 🅲 977 24 19 52.
◯ Tue–Sun. 🈺

Tortosa ③¹

Tarragona. 🚹 30,000. 🚻 Plaça Bimil·lenari (977 51 08 22). 🚌 Mon. 🎪 Nostra Senyora de la Cinta (first week of Sep).

A RUINED CASTLE and medieval walls are clues to Tortosa's historical importance. Sited at the lowest crossing point on the Riu Ebre, it has been strategically significant since Iberian times. The Moors held the city from the 8th century until 1148. The old Moorish castle, known as La Suda, is all that remains of their defences. It has now been renovated as a parador (*see p121*). The Moors also built a mosque in Tortosa in 914. Its foundations were used for the present cathedral, on which work began in 1347. Although it was not completed for two centuries, the style is pure Gothic. Tortosa was badly damaged in 1938–39 during one of the fiercest battles of the Civil War (*see p43*), when the Ebre formed the front line between the opposing forces.

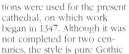

Ruins of the Palaeo-Christian Necropolis

Delta de L'Ebre ③²

Tarragona. 🚉 Aldea. 🚌 Deltebre, Aldea. 🚻 Deltebre (977 48 96 79).

T HE DELTA of the Riu Ebre is a prosperous rice-growing region and wildlife haven. Some 70 sq km (27 sq miles) have been turned into a nature reserve, the **Parc Natural del Delta de L'Ebre**. In Deltebre there is an information centre and an interesting **Eco-Museu**, with an aquarium containing species found in the delta.

The main towns in the area are **Amposta** and **Sant Carles de la Ràpita**, both of which serve as good bases for exploring the reserve.

The best places to see the huge variety of wildlife are along the shore, from the Punta del Fangar in the north to the Punta de la Banya in the south. Everywhere is accessible by car except the Illa de Buda. Flamingoes breed on this island and, together with other water birds such as black-winged stilts, herons and avocets, can be seen from tourist boats that leave from Riumar and Deltebre.

🏛 **Eco-Museu**
Carrer Martí Buera 22. 🅲 977 48 96 79. ◯ daily. ⬤ 25 Dec. 🈺 🅱

THE SARDANA

Catalonia's national dance is more complicated than it appears. Its success depends on the dancers forming a circle and accurately counting the complicated short- and long-step skips and jumps which accounts for their serious faces. Music is provided by a *cobla*, an 11-person band consisting of a leader playing a three-holed flute (*flabiol*) and a little drum (*tabal*), five woodwind players and five brass players. The *sardana* is performed during most *festes* and at special day-long gatherings called *aplecs*. In Barcelona it is danced every Sunday evening at 6:30 in the Plaça de Sant Jaume.

A group of *sardana* dancers captured in stone

TRAVELLERS' NEEDS

WHERE TO STAY

CATALONIA HAS AN unrivalled variety of accommodation to offer visitors. The Barcelona and Catalonia tourist authorities have complete listings of hotels, country houses and camp sites as well as information on a range of other options. In Barcelona you can stay in the modern luxury of Spain's highest skyscraper,

Sign for a luxury five-star hotel

while on the coast you can try a self-catering holiday village (efficiencies) with all sorts of sports and entertainments provided. Family-run *cases de pagès*, which are stone-built farm or village houses or country manors, are Catalonia's most distinctive alternative. Some of the best hotels in every price range are listed on pages 116–21.

Façade of the Hotel Lloret in Barcelona's Rambla de Canaletes

HOTEL GRADING AND FACILITIES

THE DIFFERENT TYPES of hotel in Catalonia are denoted by the blue plaques near their doors. These show a star-rating which reflects the number and range of facilities available rather than quality of service. *Hotels* (H) and *hotel-residències* (HR) are graded from one to five stars; *motels* (M), *hostals* (H) and *hostal-residències* HR) from one to three stars; and *pensions* (P), with the simplest accommodation, have one or two stars. Hotels, *hostals*, *pensions* and motels have restaurants that are open to non-residents. *Hotel-residències* and *hostal-residències* do not have full dining rooms, but some serve breakfast.

PRICES AND PAYING

SPANISH LAW requires all hotels to display their prices at reception and in every room. As a rule, the higher the star-rating, the greater the price. Rates are almost invariably quoted per room (but meal

prices per person). A double room in a one-star *hostal* can be as little as 3,000 pesetas a night; one in a five-star hotel will cost more than 20,000 pesetas a night. Prices vary according to region, season or special feature such as a view or balcony. The prices given on pages 116–21 are based on mid-season or high (tourist)-season rates. Prices for rooms and meals are usually quoted without including VAT *(IVA)*, currently seven per cent.

BOOKING AND CHECK-IN

HOTELS IN BARCELONA can be very busy during the many trade fairs held all year round, so booking in advance is advisable. Off-season in rural Catalonia there is rarely any need to book ahead, but if you want a room in a busy season or in a particular hotel it is a good idea to do so. Resort hotels on the Costa Brava often close from autumn to spring. On the warmer Costa Daurada, hotels may have a shorter winter closing period. You will not normally be asked

for a deposit when you book a room. However, a deposit of 20–25 per cent may be levied for bookings during peak periods or for a stay of more than a few nights. You may lose all or some of it if you cancel at less than a week's notice. Most hotels will honour a booking only until 8pm. If you are delayed, telephone to tell them when to expect you.

When checking in you will be asked for your passport or identity card to comply with police regulations. It will normally be returned as soon as your details have been copied.

PARADORS

THERE ARE seven paradors in Catalonia – at Aiguablava, Artíes, Cardona, Seu de Urgell, Vic, Vielha and Tortosa. They form part of Spain's chain of high-quality, government-run hotels in historic buildings, or in purpose-built, new buildings in spectacular settings. Reservations for paradors can be made through the **Central de Reservas** (Madrid), **Keytel International** (London) and **Marketing Ahead** (New York).

The spacious and comfortable interior of the parador at Vic

Solid, stone-built architecture typical of traditional Catalan farmhouses

RURAL ACCOMMODATION

CASES DE PAGÈS are Catalan farmhouses *(masies)* or country houses that accept visitors, some do B&B, some an evening meal or full board. Tourist offices have the *Guia residències-casa de pagès*, published by the Generalitat de Catalunya. You can book directly or through **Turisverd**.

The **Associació Fondes de Catalunya** is a group of *cases fonda* (simple country hotels, offering wholesome regional cuisine). Potential visitors should note that the facility closes in August, so you will be unable to make a reservation for that period.

The **Xarxa d'Albergs de Catalunya** runs youth hostels, which also cater for adults and families, and the **Federació d'Entitats Excursionistes de Catalunya** runs mountain refuges for hikers.

SELF-CATERING

VILLAS AND apartments let by the week are plentiful on the Costa Daurada and Costa Brava. *Aparthotels (in hotels-apartament)* and *residències apartament* are a new breed of self-catering accommodation (efficiencies). Ranked from one to four stars, each apartment has a kitchen, but each complex also has a restaurant and often a swimming pool and other facilities. Generalitat de Catalunya tourist offices *(see p142)* and most travel agents have details of all types of villas and apartments.

Holiday (vacation) villages *(ciutats de vacances)*, such as Cala Montjoi and Club-Hotel Giverola on the Costa Brava, are similar, but accommodation is in bungalows and includes sports and entertainments.

Gites de Catalunya are superior country houses rented out on a week-by-week basis by Turisverd or **The Individual Travellers' Spain**. Many *cases de pagès* are also self-catering (run as efficiencies).

CAMP SITES

CATALONIA HAS over 300 camp sites, classified as deluxe (L), 1-star, 2-star, 3-star, or farm (M, *càmpings-masia*). All have basic amenities, guards and a safe. *Catalunya Càmpings*, published by the Generalitat *(see p142)*, is available from tourist offices. Ten sites near Barcelona are grouped under the **Associació de Càmpings de Barcelona** (which closes for the first three weeks in August). A camping carnet from your home camping association can be used instead of a passport at sites and covers you for third-party insurance. Camping is permitted only at official sites.

Sign for a camp site

DISABLED TRAVELLERS

FEW HOTELS are well equipped for disabled guests, although some youth hostels are. The **Federació ECOM** and Viajes 2000 *(see p143)* will advise on hotels throughout Catalonia for visitors with special needs.

DIRECTORY

PARADORS

Central de Reservas
Calle Requena 3,
28013 Madrid.
☎ 91 516 66 66.
FAX 91 516 66 57, 91 516 66 58.

Keytel International
402 Edgware Road,
London W2 1ED.
☎ 020 7402 8182 in UK.
FAX 020 7724 9503 in UK.

Marketing Ahead
433 Fifth Avenue,
New York, NY 10016.
☎ 800 223 1356 (toll free).
FAX (212) 686 0271 in NY.

RURAL ACCOMMODATION

Associació Fondes de Catalunya
Balmes 150 3er-3ª,
08008 Barcelona.
☎ 93 415 30 99.
FAX 93 415 94 82.

Federació d'Entitats Excursionistes de Catalunya
La Rambla 41, 1er, 08002 Barcelona.
☎ 93 412 07 77.
FAX 93 412 63 53.

Turisverd
Plaça Sant Josep Oriol 4,
08002 Barcelona.
☎ 93 412 69 84.
FAX 93 412 50 16.

Xarxa d'Albergs de Catalunya
Carrer Rocafort 116–122,
08015 Barcelona.
☎ 93 483 83 63.
FAX 93 483 83 50.

SELF-CATERING

The Individual Travellers' Spain
Bignor, Pulborough,
West Sussex RH20 1QD.
☎ 08700 773 773.
FAX 08700 780 190.

CAMPING

Associació de Càmpings de Barcelona
Gran Via Corts Catalanes 608, 3ª, 08007 Barcelona.
☎ 93 412 59 55.
FAX 93 302 13 36.

DISABLED TRAVELLERS

Federació ECOM
Gran Via de les Corts Catalanes 562, principal,
2ª, 08011 Barcelona.
☎ 93 451 55 50.
FAX 93 451 69 04.

SPANISH TOURIST OFFICES

UK
57 St James's Street,
London SW1A 1LD.
☎ 020 7499 0901.
FAX 020 7629 4257.

US
666 Fifth Ave, Floor 35,
New York, NY 10103.
☎ (212) 265 8822.
FAX (212) 265 8864.

Choosing a Hotel

THE HOTELS in this guide have been selected across a wide price range for the excellence of their facilities, location or character. Many have a highly recommended restaurant. The chart below first lists hotels in Barcelona by area, followed by a selection in the rest of Catalonia. For more details on restaurants see pages 126–131.

	Credit Cards	Number of Rooms	Private Parking	Swimming Pool	Garden or Terrace
OLD TOWN					
PENINSULAR. Map 2 F3. ℗ Carrer de Sant Pau 34, 08001. 93 302 31 38. FAX 93 412 36 99. Rooms are truly basic in this former Carmelite convent, but good value. Just off La Rambla behind the Liceu opera house, this hotel's charms lie in its luminous inner courtyard and Modernista dining room. ▤ ▤	MC V	80			
REMBRANDT. Map 5 A2. ℗ Carrer de Portaferrissa 23, 08002. 93 318 10 11. FAX 93 318 10 11. A clean, simple hotel in the Barri Gòtic, popular with students. A tiled courtyard is a sitting area. Some bedrooms share bathrooms. ▤		24			▪
ESPAÑA. Map 2 F3. ℗℗ Carrer de Sant Pau 9–11, 08001. 93 318 17 58. FAX 93 317 11 34. Lluís Domènech i Montaner, the outstanding Modernista architect, designed this hotel. The bedrooms are all modern. ▤	AE DC MC V	84			
GAUDÍ. Map 2 F3. ℗℗ Carrer Nou de la Rambla 12, 08001. 93 317 90 32. FAX 93 412 26 36. A pleasant hotel near Gaudí's Palau Güell in a street close to La Rambla with comfortable, well-equipped rooms. ▤ ▤ TV ⛬	AE DC MC V	73	▪		
JARDÍ. Map 2 F3. ℗℗ Plaça Sant Josep Oriol 1, 08002. 93 301 59 00. FAX 93 318 36 64. A popular hotel overlooking a leafy square. Some bedrooms have been renovated and have good views; the others are cheaper. ▤ TV	V	38			
LLORET. Map 5 A1. ℗℗ Rambla de Canaletes 125, 08002. 93 317 33 66. FAX 93 301 92 83. There are views of the city from the foyer of this popular hotel near the Plaça de Catalunya – but streetside bedrooms can be noisy. ▤ ▤ TV	AE MC V	52			
ATLANTIS. Map 2 F1. ℗℗℗ Carrer de Pelai 20, 08001. 93 318 90 12. FAX 93 412 09 14. This modern, inexpensive hotel is centrally located near the Plaça de Catalunya. The bedrooms have a range of facilities. ▤ ▤ TV ⛬	AE DC MC V	42	▪		
MESÓN CASTILLA. Map 2 F1. ℗℗℗ Carrer de Valdonzella 5, 08001. 93 318 21 82. FAX 93 412 40 20. A comfortable hotel, if a little old-fashioned, in a building with a Modernista façade near the Casa de la Caritat arts centre. ▤ ▤ TV	AE DC MC V	56	▪		▪
SAN AGUSTÍN. Map 2 F3. ℗℗℗ Plaça de Sant Agustí 3, 08001. 93 318 16 58. FAX 93 317 29 28. An attractive hotel with a pleasant lounge and bar looking across a square. Some bedrooms are decorated with traditional Catalan furniture. ▤ ▤ TV ⛬	AE DC MC V	77			
NOUVEL. Map 5 A1. ℗℗℗℗ Carrer de Santa Anna 18–20, 08002. 93 301 82 74. FAX 93 301 83 70. In a quiet street off La Rambla, near the Plaça de Catalunya, this well-kept, old-style hotel is tastefully decorated and furnished. ▤ ▤ TV	AE MC V	54			
ORIENTE. Map 2 F3. ℗℗℗℗ La Rambla 45-47, 08002. 93 302 25 58. FAX 93 412 38 19. A former Franciscan friary makes a romantic setting for the Oriente. The cloister has been converted into a ballroom. ▤ TV	AE DC MC V	142			▪
PARK HOTEL. Map 5 C3. ℗℗℗℗ Avda Marquès de l'Argentera 11, 08003. 93 319 60 00. FAX 93 319 45 19. A rare gem of 1950s architecture, designed by Antonio Moragas in 1951 and well preserved during his son's award-winning renovations in 1990. ▤ ▤ TV	AE DC MC V	87	▪		▪

Price categories for a standard double room per night, with tax, breakfast and service included:

- ℗ under 8,000 ptas
- ℗℗ 8,000–12,000 ptas
- ℗℗℗ 12,000–16,000 ptas
- ℗℗℗℗ 16,000–20,000 ptas
- ℗℗℗℗℗ over 20,000 ptas

CREDIT CARDS
Indicates which credit cards are accepted: *AE* American Express; *DC* Diners Club; *MC* MasterCard/Access; *V* VISA
PARKING
Parking provided by the hotel in a private car park or a private garage on the hotel site or very close by. Some hotels charge for use of private parking facilities.
SWIMMING POOL
Hotel pool outdoors unless otherwise stated.
GARDEN
Hotel with garden, courtyard or terrace, often providing tables for eating outdoors.

	CREDIT CARDS	NUMBER OF ROOMS	PRIVATE PARKING	SWIMMING POOL	GARDEN OR TERRACE
RIVOLI RAMBLAS. Map 5 A1. ℗℗℗℗ Rambla dels Estudis 128, 08002. **[** *93 302 66 43.* **FAX** *93 317 50 53, 93 318 8760.* An elegant hotel on La Rambla decorated in contemporary style, with spacious bedrooms and city views from a roof terrace. 🖼 ▤ TV ⓺	AE DC MC V	89	■	●	■
SUIZO. Map 5 B2. ℗℗℗ Plaça del Àngel 12, 08002. **[** *93 310 61 08.* **FAX** *93 268 90 62.* This hotel behind the cathedral has 19th-century Parisian style. The attic bedrooms with skylights have great character. 🖼 ▤ TV	AE DC MC V	51	■		
ARTS. Map 6 E4. ℗℗℗℗℗ Carrer de la Marina 19–21, 08005. **[** *93 221 10 00.* **FAX** *93 221 10 70* A modern, super-luxurious beachside hotel at the Port Olímpic in one of Spain's tallest buildings. 🖼 ▤ TV ⓺	AE DC MC V	483	■	●	■
COLON. Map 5 B2. ℗℗℗℗℗ Avinguda de la Catedral 7, 08002. **[** *93 301 14 04.* **FAX** *93 317 29 15.* From the Colón's front windows guests can watch the *sardana*, the traditional Catalan folk dance, performed in the Plaça de la Catedral, opposite, on Sunday mornings. 🖼 ▤ TV	AE DC MC V	147			
LE MERIDIEN. Map 5 A1. ℗℗℗℗℗ La Rambla 111, 08002. **[** *93 318 62 00.* **FAX** *93 301 77 76.* An elegant hotel on La Rambla, popular with rock and film stars. It has an enormous presidential suite and a business centre. 🖼 ▤ TV ⓺	AE DC MC V	205	■		
ROYAL. Map 5 A1. ℗℗℗℗ La Rambla 117, 08002. **[** *93 301 94 00.* **FAX** *93 317 31 79.* This hotel, near the top of La Rambla, has friendly staff and simple but elegant rooms with spacious marble bathrooms. 🖼 ▤ TV	AE DC MC V	108	■		
EIXAMPLE					
FELIPE II. Map 3 C4. ℗ Carrer de Mallorca 329, 08037. **[** *93 458 77 58.* **FAX** *93 207 21 04.* A basic, clean hotel in an old apartment block in the Eixample, with a particularly fine antique elevator. Breakfast is not available. 🖼 TV		11			
GRAN VIA. Map 3 A5. ℗℗℗ Gran Via de les Corts Catalanes 642, 08007. **[** *93 318 19 00.* **FAX** *93 318 99 97.* A hotel in a late 19th-century building with an ageing grandeur, north of the Plaça de Catalunya adjoining the Passeig de Gràcia. 🖼 ▤ TV ⓺	AE DC MC V	53			
HOSTAL CIUDAD CONDAL. Map 3 A4. ℗℗℗ Carrer de Mallorca 255, 08008. **[** *93 215 10 40.* A modest *hostal* on one of the most elegant streets of the Eixample. Rear rooms overlook leafy gardens and an Eixample patio. No breakfasts. 🖼	DC MC V	11	■		
ALEXANDRA. Map 3 A4. ℗℗℗℗ Carrer de Mallorca 251, 08008. **[** *93 467 71 66.* **FAX** *93 488 02 58.* A stylish, modern interior behind a 19th-century façade sets the tone in this hotel, which is well equipped for business meetings. 🖼 ▤ TV ⓺	AE DC MC V	81	■		
CATALUNYA PLAZA. Map 5 A1. ℗℗℗℗ Plaça de Catalunya 7, 08002. **[** *93 317 71 71.* **FAX** *93 317 78 55.* A city-centre hotel popular with business people. The 19th-century building has large sitting rooms decorated with some amazingly intricate frescoes. 🖼 ▤ TV	AE DC MC V	47			
CLARIS. Map 3 B4. ℗℗℗℗℗ Carrer Pau Claris 150, 08009. **[** *93 487 62 62.* **FAX** *93 215 79 70.* Antique kilims and elegant English and French furniture ornament this hotel off the Passeig de Gràcia. It occupies the converted Vedruna Palace and has a private museum of Egyptian art. 🖼 ▤ TV ⓺	AE DC MC V	120	■	●	■

For key to symbols see back flap

Price categories for a standard double room per night, with tax, breakfast and service included:

ℙ under 8,000 ptas
ℙℙ 8,000–12,000 ptas
ℙℙℙ 12,000–16,000 ptas
ℙℙℙℙ 16,000–20,000 ptas
ℙℙℙℙℙ over 20,000 ptas

CREDIT CARDS
Indicates which credit cards are accepted: *AE* American Express; *DC* Diners Club; *MC* MasterCard/Access; *V* VISA
PARKING
Parking provided by the hotel in a private car park or a private garage on the hotel site or very close by. Some hotels charge for use of private parking facilities.
SWIMMING POOL
Hotel pool outdoors unless otherwise stated.
GARDEN
Hotel with garden, courtyard or terrace, often providing tables for eating outdoors.

	CREDIT CARDS	NUMBER OF ROOMS	PRIVATE PARKING	SWIMMING POOL	GARDEN OR TERRACE
CONDES DE BARCELONA. Map 3 A4. Passeig de Gràcia 75, 08008. **☎** 93 488 22 00. **FAX** 93 467 47 85. This Modernista hotel has an impressive pentagonal lobby with a marble floor, illuminated by a skylight. Book well in advance so as not to miss the aesthetic thrill. 🛏 ▤ TV ⚞	ℙℙℙℙ	AE DC MC V	109	■	●	■
DUCS DE BERGARA. Map 5 A1. Carrer de Bergara 11, 08002. **☎** 93 301 51 51. **FAX** 93 317 34 42. A luxury hotel in an exquisite Modernista building, with original halls and stairways, just off the Plaça de Catalunya. It has spacious, well-furnished bedrooms and modern public rooms. 🛏 ▤ TV ⚞	ℙℙℙℙ	AE DC MC V	150		●	■
GALLERY. Map 3 A3. Carrer Rosselló 249, 08008. **☎** 93 415 99 11. **FAX** 93 415 91 84. A modern, efficient, comfortable hotel which is well situated and retains the personal atmosphere of a family-run business. An attractive terrace-garden restaurant leads into a public garden. Rooms are soundproofed. 🛏 ▤ TV ⚞	ℙℙℙℙ	AE DC MC V	113	■		■
GRAN HOTEL CALDERÓN. Map 3 A5. Rambla de Catalunya 26, 08007. **☎** 93 301 00 00. **FAX** 93 412 41 93. A modern hotel near the Plaça de Catalunya with spacious, comfortable rooms, indoor and rooftop pools, and a good restaurant. 🛏 ▤ TV ⚞	ℙℙℙℙ	AE DC MC V	253	■	●	■
GRAN HOTEL HAVANA. Map 3 B5. Gran Via de les Corts Catalanes 647, 08010. **☎** 93 412 11 15. **FAX** 93 412 26 11. Stunning light from a central glass atrium floods the avant-garde interior of this efficient, well-equipped and friendly hotel. Its most popular suite is behind the large clock face on the façade. 🛏 ▤ TV ⚞	ℙℙℙℙ	AE DC MC V	145	■		
MAJESTIC. Map 3 A4. Passeig de Gràcia 68, 08007. **☎** 93 488 17 17. **FAX** 93 488 18 80. A hotel in Neo-Classical style in a very chic street (adjoining the Carrer de València). The bedrooms are well equipped and soundproofed. 🛏 ▤ TV ⚞	ℙℙℙℙ	AE DC MC V	301	■	●	■
REGENTE. Map 3 A4. Rambla de Catalunya 76, 08008. **☎** 93 487 59 89. **FAX** 93 487 32 27. A hotel in a Modernista building, with magnificent stained-glass decoration and a small, rooftop pool overlooking Montjuïc. 🛏 ▤ TV ⚞	ℙℙℙℙ	AE DC MC V	79		●	■
RITZ. Map 3 B5. Gran Via de les Corts Catalanes 668, 08010. **☎** 93 318 52 00. **FAX** 93 318 01 48. The most elegant of Barcelona's grand hotels, recently refurbished. The large, luxurious bedrooms are decorated in classic style. 🛏 ▤ TV	ℙℙℙℙ	AE DC MC V	125	■		■
FURTHER AFIELD					
SANT GERVASI: *Rekor'd.* Carrer de Muntaner 352, 08021. **☎** 93 200 19 53. **FAX** 93 414 50 84. A small, modern hotel oriented towards business travellers in the uptown shopping area. Large rooms with office space. Some with mini-gym. 🛏 ▤ TV	ℙℙℙ	AE DC MC V	15	■		
LES CORTS: *Gran Derby.* Carrer de Loreto 28, 08029. **☎** 93 322 32 15. **FAX** 93 410 08 62. Attractive suites are the only accommodation offered here. There is no restaurant; guests may dine in the Hotel Derby over the road. 🛏 ▤ TV	ℙℙℙℙ	AE DC MC V	40	■	●	■
PEDRALBES: *Princesa Sofía Intercontinental.* Plaça de Pius XII 4, Avda Diagonal, 08028. **☎** 93 330 71 11. **FAX** 93 330 76 21. A vast, luxury hotel decorated in marble, wood and bronze, with one of its several restaurants on the 19th floor, and a nightclub. 🛏 ▤ TV ⚞	ℙℙℙℙ	AE DC MC V	506	■	●	■

CATALONIA

BEUDA: *Can Felicià.* Ⓟ 6
Segueró, 17850 (Girona). ☎ 972 59 05 23.
Beautiful views make this charming, rural hotel in a former school a good place to stay. Simple, pleasing decor. Price includes home-cooked dinners.

L'ESPLUGA DE FRANCOLÍ: *Hostal del Senglar.* Ⓟ AE DC MC V 40
Pl de Montserrat Canals 1, 43440 (Tarragona). ☎ 977 87 01 21. FAX 977 87 10 12.
A three-storey, whitewashed hotel with a garden. A menu of delicious dishes traditional to the area is served in the restaurant.

CADAQUÉS: *Misty.* ⓅⓅ DC MC V 11
Carretera Nova Port Lligat, 17488 (Girona). ☎ 972 25 89 62. FAX 972 15 90 90.
Three houses and a swimming pool surrounded by gardens make up this appealing hotel, one of the most unusual on the Costa Brava.

CASTELLÓ D'EMPÚRIES: *Allioli.* ⓅⓅ AE DC MC V 42
Urbanització Castell Nou, 17486 (Girona). ☎ 972 25 03 20. FAX 972 25 03 00.
A 17th-century Catalan farmhouse, just off the main Roses–Figueres road. The restaurant is popular for Sunday lunch among the local people.

ARTIES: *Parador Don Gaspar de Portolà.* ⓅⓅⓅ AE DC MC V 57
Ctra a Baqueira-Beret, 25599 (Lleida). ☎ 973 64 08 01. FAX 973 64 10 01.
A modern, warm, comfortable parador, near the Vall d'Aran ski resorts, ideal for après-ski rest. Beside it is a medieval chapel.

AVINYONET DE PUIGVENTÓS: *Mas Pau.* ⓅⓅⓅ AE DC MC V 20
Despoblado, 17742 (Girona). ☎ 972 54 61 54. FAX 972 54 63 26.
A beautiful hotel in a 17th-century house, surrounded by wooded farmland. The bedrooms and suites open onto a garden.

BEGUR: *Aigua Blava.* ⓅⓅⓅ AE MC V 85
Platja de Fornells, 17255 (Girona). ☎ 972 62 20 58. FAX 972 62 21 12.
A charming hotel on a small beach in an attractive spot on the Costa Brava. It has marvellous sea views.

CUBELLES: *Llicorella.* ⓅⓅⓅ AE DC MC V 15
C/ Camí de Sant Antoni 101, 08880 (Barcelona). ☎ 93 895 00 44. FAX 93 895 24 17.
This elegant hotel has striking sculptures in its garden. Most of the bedrooms are luxurious and the restaurant is excellent.

ANDORRA LA VELLA: *Andorra Park Hotel.* ⓅⓅⓅⓅ AE DC MC V 40
Les Canals 24 (Andorra). ☎ 00-376 82 09 79. FAX 00-376 82 09 83.
One of Andorra's most luxurious hotels, the Andorra Park is modern and built into a steep, wooded hillside. It has a library, a swimming pool hewn out of rock, and is beside a department store.

BAQUEIRA-BERET: *Royal Tanau.* ⓅⓅⓅⓅ AE MC V 30
Carretera de Beret, 25598 (Lleida). ☎ 973 64 44 46. FAX 973 64 43 44.
A luxurious hotel in the Tanau skiing area, with a ski lift to the pistes. It has full après-ski facilities and apartments as well as rooms.

BOLVIR DE CERDANYA: *Torre del Remei.* ⓅⓅⓅⓅ AE DC MC V 11
Camí Reial, 17539 (Girona). ☎ 972 14 01 82. FAX 972 14 04 49.
An Art Nouveau mansion with a large garden has become a refined hotel full of comforts, such as video players (VCRs) in bedrooms.

CASTELLDEFELS: *Gran Hotel Rey Don Jaime.* ⓅⓅⓅⓅ AE MC V 215
Avinguda del Hotel 22, 08860 (Barcelona). ☎ 93 665 13 00. FAX 93 664 51 51.
This hotel is in traditional Mediterranean style with arches and white-washed walls. It is on a hilltop giving views over the coast.

L'ESPLUGA DE FRANCOLÍ: *Masia del Cadet.* ⓅⓅ AE DC MC V 12
Les Masies de Poblet, 43449 (Tarragona). ☎ 977 87 08 69. FAX 977 87 08 69.
An inexpensive hotel near the monastery of Poblet in a tastefully renovated, 15th-century house. The bedrooms are austere and quiet. Traditional Catalan food is served in the restaurant.

LA GARRIGA: *Blancafort.* ⓅⓅⓅ MC V 56
Carrer Banys 59, 08530 (Barcelona). ☎ 93 871 46 00. FAX 93 871 57 50.
A 19th-century hotel in a relaxing spa town near Barcelona. There are simple bedrooms and games facilities in the lounges.

For key to symbols see back flap

Price categories for a standard double room per night, with tax, breakfast and service included:

℗ under 8,000 ptas
℗℗ 8,000–12,000 ptas
℗℗℗ 12,000–16,000 ptas
℗℗℗℗ 16,000–20,000 ptas
℗℗℗℗℗ over 20,000 ptas

CREDIT CARDS
Indicates which credit cards are accepted: *AE* American Express; *DC* Diners Club; *MC* MasterCard/Access; *V* VISA

PARKING
Parking provided by the hotel in a private car park or a private garage on the hotel site or very close by. Some hotels charge for use of private parking facilities.

SWIMMING POOL
Hotel pool outdoors unless otherwise stated.

GARDEN
Hotel with garden, courtyard or terrace, often providing tables for eating outdoors.

	CREDIT CARDS	NUMBER OF ROOMS	PRIVATE PARKING	SWIMMING POOL	GARDEN OR TERRACE
LA GARRIGA: *La Garriga.* ℗℗℗℗ Carrer Banys 23, 08530 (Barcelona). ☎ 93 871 70 86. FAX 93 871 78 87. Affluent people from Barcelona have been visiting this spa town for its waters since 1876. Children are not admitted to the hotel. 🚗 🍴 📺	AE MC V	22		●	■
GRANOLLERS: *Fonda Europa.* ℗℗℗ Carrer Anselm Clavé 1, 08400 (Barcelona). ☎ 93 870 03 12. FAX 93 870 79 01. This small hotel has been an inn for travellers since 1714. The bedrooms are on the second floor and are decorated in Art Deco style. 🚗 🍴 📺	AE DC MC V	7			
LLORET DE MAR: *Santa Marta.* ℗℗℗℗℗ Platja Santa Cristina, 17310 (Girona). ☎ 972 36 49 04. FAX 972 36 92 80. A modern hotel with tennis courts and other sporting facilities in the grounds. It is set in a pine wood that extends to a quiet cove. 🚗 🍴 📺	AE DC MC V	78	■	●	■
MONTSENY: *Sant Bernat.* ℗℗℗ Finca El Cot, 08460 (Barcelona). ☎ 93 847 30 11. FAX 93 847 32 20. A big country house in the Serra de Montseny, with a façade cloaked in greenery. There are beautiful grounds with lawns and a pond. 🚗 📺	AE DC MC V	20			■
PERAMOLA: *Can Boix de Peraluola.* ℗℗℗ Afueras, 25790 (Lleida). ☎ 973 47 02 66. FAX 973 47 02 81. Run by a family of distinguished restaurateurs, this simple, good-value hotel is convenient for walking in the Pyrenean foothills. 🚗 🍴 📺 ♿	AE DC MC V	45			■
S'AGARÓ: *Hostal de la Gavina.* ℗℗℗℗℗ Plaça de la Rosaleda, 17248 (Girona). ☎ 972 32 11 00. FAX 972 32 15 73. An elegant beach mansion in traditional Mediterranean style with an exclusive feel. It is set in its own estate, with beautiful gardens. 🚗 🍴 📺	AE DC MC V	73	■	●	■
SA TUNA (BEGUR): *Hotel Sa Tuna.* ℗℗ Passeig de Ancora 6, 17255 (Girona). ☎ & FAX 972 62 21 98. A simple, white-washed, small hotel on one of the Costa Brava's prettiest coves. Recent improvements by the grandson of the original owner have added to its charms. Rooms with own terrace overlooking the bay. Best out of season. 🚗	MC V	5			■
SANTA CRISTINA D'ARO: *Mas Torrellas.* ℗℗ Carretera Platja d'Aro, 17246 (Girona). ☎ 972 83 75 26. FAX 972 83 75 27. An 18th-century country house hotel. Its most comfortable bedroom is in a distinctive yellow tower, built at a later date. 🚗 🍴 📺	AE DC MC V	17	■	●	■
SANTA PAU: *Cal Sastre.* ℗℗ Cases Noves 1, 17811 (Girona). ☎ 972 68 01 32. FAX 972 68 04 81. This 18th-century rural house has been tastefully converted into a comfortable, intimate hotel. Dinner in the old village square comes with the room. 🚗 📺	AE DC MC V	10			■
SANT PERE DE RIBES: *Els Sumidors.* ℗℗℗ Carretera de Vilafranca, 08810 (Barcelona). ☎ 93 896 20 61. On the southern slope of a hill, with views across the landscape of the fertile Penedès wine region, this rustic 18th-century house has atmosphere and a certain charm, but few luxuries. 🚗 📺 🍴	MC V	9	■	●	■
LA SEU D'URGELL: *Parador de La Seu d'Urgell.* ℗℗℗ Carrer Sant Domènec 6, 25700 (Lleida). ☎ 973 35 20 00. FAX 973 35 23 09. Only the cloister, now the lounge, remains of a convent that occupied this site close to the 12th-century cathedral of La Seu. The dining room and indoor swimming pool have glass ceilings. 🚗 🍴 📺	AE DC MC V	80	■	●	
LA SEU D'URGELL: *El Castell.* ℗℗℗℗ Carretera N260, 25700 (Lleida). ☎ 973 35 07 04. FAX 973 35 15 74. This sumptuous hotel is a low, modern building beneath the medieval castle of Seu d'Urgell. There are impressive views across the mountains of El Cadí and the ski slopes of Andorra are nearby. 🚗 🍴 📺	AE DC MC V	37	■	●	■

SITGES: *La Santa María.* ⓅⓅ
Passeig Ribera 52, 08870 (Barcelona). ☎ 93 894 09 99. FAX 93 894 78 71.
A cheery, modern hotel hidden behind an older, five-storey, moulded-plaster frontage. The restaurant has tables on the seafront. 🛏 ▤ TV

AE DC MC V — 53

SITGES: *Capri Veracruz.* ⓅⓅⓅ
Avinguda de Sofia 13–15, 08870 (Barcelona). ☎ 93 811 02 67. FAX 93 894 51 88.
Built in the 1950s near the beach, in one of the quieter parts of Sitges, this hotel has simple bedrooms and a family atmosphere. 🛏 ▤ TV

AE MC V — 58

SITGES: *Romàntic.* ⓅⓅⓅ
Sant Isidre 33, 08870 (Barcelona). ☎ 93 894 83 75. FAX 93 894 81 67.
Something of a legend in Sitges, this memorable hotel lives up to its name. Bedrooms are simple, but attractively decorated with antiques and paintings. A gloriously shady garden is perfect for breakfast, and evening cocktails.

AE MC V — 70

SITGES: *San Sebastián Playa.* ⓅⓅⓅⓅ
Carrer Port Alegre 53, 08870 (Barcelona). ☎ 93 894 86 76. FAX 93 894 04 30.
This new hotel on the beach near the old part of the town has very attentive staff and comfortable bedrooms. 🛏 ▤ TV

AE DC MC V — 51

TAVERTET: *El Jufré.* Ⓗ
Tavertet, 08511 (Barcelona). ☎ & FAX 93 856 51 67.
This converted farmhouse with stunning views in a mountain village has been in the same family for over 800 years. Warm, comfortable rooms have replaced the former animal quarters. A perfect base for walking and exploring Osona. 🛏

0

TAVÈRNOLES: *El Banús.* Ⓟ
El Banús, 08519 (Barcelona). ☎ 93 812 20 91. FAX 93 888 70 12.
A small farmhouse, furnished with Banús family heirlooms, offering basic bedrooms, shared bathrooms, and breakfast. ● *two weeks in Sep.*

AE MC V — 5

TARRAGONA: *Lauria.* ⓅⓅⓅ
Rambla Nova 20, 43004. ☎ 977 23 67 12. FAX 977 23 67 00.
A modern, functional hotel in the town centre and close to the sea, with an elegant entrance under balustraded stone stairs. 🛏 ▤ TV

AE DC MC V — 72

TORRENT: *Mas de Torrent.* ⓅⓅⓅⓅⓅ
Afueras, 17123 (Girona). ☎ 972 30 32 92. FAX 972 30 32 93.
A superbly converted, 18th-century country house in large, terraced gardens. It has magnificent views. 🛏 ▤ TV 👨‍🦽

AE DC MC V — 30

TORTOSA: *Parador Castillo de la Zuda.* ⓅⓅⓅ
Castillo de la Zuda, 43500 (Tarragona). ☎ 977 44 44 50. FAX 977 44 44 58.
A medieval castle built by the Moors makes a magnificent hilltop parador with views of the town and the valley of the Riu Ebre. 🛏 ▤ TV

AE DC MC V — 75

TREDÒS: *Hotel de Tredòs.* ⓅⓅⓅ
Carretera a Baqueira-Beret, 25598 (Lleida). ☎ 973 64 40 14. FAX 973 64 43 00.
Skiers and mountain walkers find this hotel in the Vall d'Aran good value. It is built of stone and slate in the local style. 🛏 TV 👨‍🦽

MC V — 37

VIC: *Parador de Turismo de Vic.* ⓅⓅⓅ
Paratge Bac de Sau, 08500 (Barcelona). ☎ 93 812 23 23. FAX 93 812 23 68.
This recently refurbished parador, 14 km (9 miles) from Vic, has very comfortable rooms and magnificent views over the Sau reservoir. A peaceful retreat amid pine forests and dramatic rock formations. 🛏 ▤ TV

AE DC MC V — 36

VIELHA (VIELLA): *Parador Valle de Arán.* ⓅⓅⓅⓅ
Carretera del Túnel, 25530 (Lleida). ☎ 973 64 01 00. FAX 973 64 11 00.
This modern parador has a semicircular lounge dominated by a large window from which there are magnificent mountain views. 🛏 TV

AE DC MC V — 126

VILADRAU: *Hostal de la Glòria.* ⓅⓅ
Carrer Torreventosa 12, 17406 (Girona). ☎ 93 884 90 34. FAX 93 884 94 65.
A hotel with a family atmosphere in a traditional Catalan house above the Serra de Montseny. It is full of copper pots.
🛏 TV ● *two weeks at Christmas.*

AE DC MC V — 23

VILANOVA I LA GELTRÚ: *César.* ⓅⓅ
Carrer Isaac Peral 8, 08800 (Barcelona). ☎ 93 815 11 25. FAX 93 815 67 19.
This hotel, near the Ribes Roges beach, is owned by two sisters who pay great attention to detail, from the furniture and the fabrics in the bedrooms to the well-known restaurant. 🛏 ▤ TV

AE DC MC V — 32

For key to symbols see back flap

RESTAURANTS, CAFÉS AND BARS

ATING OUT remains both a common practice and one of the convivial joys of life in Catalonia. Catalans are proud of their regional cuisine and expect to eat well in restaurants, not only at celebratory dinners, but also at work-day meal breaks or at family Sunday lunches out. Country restaurants in particular are packed on Sundays. Barcelona has

Wall tile advertising a Barcelona restaurant

an unusually large number of restaurants. From the sophisticated feast to the simple tapa, fresh ingredients are usually in evidence as Catalans tend to despise convenience food. The restaurants and cafés listed on pages 126–33 have been selected for their food and atmosphere. Pages 26–7 and 124–5 illustrate some of Catalonia's best dishes.

Bodegues are bars that specialize in wines and do not serve food

RESTAURANTS AND BARS

BARCELONA AND Catalonia possess some of Spain's best restaurants, testifying to the quality of Catalan cooking, but the cheapest and quickest places to eat are the bars and cafés that serve *tapes* (tapas). Some bars, however, especially *pubs* (late-opening bars for socializing) do not serve food.

Family-run *bars i restaurants*, *hostals* and *fondes* – old Catalan words for the various types of inn – serve inexpensive, sit-down meals. *Xiringuitos* are beachside bars that are open only during the busy summer season.

Most restaurants close one day a week, some for lunch or dinner only, and most for an annual holiday. They also close on some public holidays. The main closing times of the restaurants on pages 126–31 are listed at the end of each entry. Always check the opening times, however, when phoning to book a table.

EATING HOURS

CATALANS, in common with other Spaniards, often eat a light breakfast *(el esmorzar)* of biscuits or toast with butter and jam and *cafè amb llet* (milky coffee), then follow with a second breakfast or snack between 10 and 11am, perhaps in a café. This may consist of a croissant, or an *entrepà* (sandwich) with sausage, ham or cheese, or a slice of the ubiquitous *truita de patates* (potato omelette). Fruit juice, coffee or beer are the usual accompaniments.

From about 1pm onwards, people will stop in the bars for a beer or an *aperitivo* with tapas. By 2pm those who can will have arrived home from work for *el almuerzo* (lunch), which is the main meal of the day. Others will choose to have lunch in a restaurant.

The cafés, *salons de te* (tea rooms) and *pastisseries* (pastry shops) fill up by about 5:30 or

Decoration, Barcelona bar

6pm for *el berenar* (tea) of sandwiches, pastries or cakes, with coffee, tea or fruit juice. Snacks such as *xurros* (fried, sugar-coated batter sticks) can also be bought from stalls.

By 7pm, bars are crowded with people having tapas with sherry, wine or beer. In Catalonia *el sopar* (dinner or supper), begins at about 9pm. However, restaurants sometimes begin serving earlier for tourists. In summer, however, families and groups of friends often do not sit down to dinner until as late as 11pm. At weekend lunch times, especially in the summer, you will often find that restaurants are filled by large and noisy family gatherings.

HOW TO DRESS

A JACKET AND TIE are rarely required, but Catalans dress smartly, especially for city restaurants. Day dress is casual in beach resorts, but shorts are frowned on in the evenings.

Eating out at Barcelona's Port Olímpic, a busy venue all year round

Outdoor tables at a *cafeteria* in Cadaqués on the Costa Brava

READING THE MENU

ASIDE FROM TAPAS, perhaps the cheapest eating options in Catalan restaurants are the fixed-price *plats combinats* and the *menú del dia*. A *plat combinat* (meat or fish with vegetables and, usually, fried potatoes) is offered only by cheaper establishments. Most restaurants – but not all – offer an inexpensive, fixed-price *menú del dia*, normally of three courses, but with little choice. Some gourmet restaurants offer a *menú de degustació* consisting of a choice of six or seven of the head chef's special dishes.

The Catalan word for menu is *la carta*. It starts with *sopes* (soups), *amanides* (salads), *entremesos* (hors d'oeuvres), *ous i truites* (eggs and omelettes) and *verdures i llegums* (vegetable dishes).

Main courses are *peix i marisc* (fish and shellfish) and *carns i aus* (meat and poultry). Daily specials are chalked on a board or clipped to menus. *Paella* and other rice dishes may be served as the first course. A useful rule is to follow rice with meat, or start with *fuet* or *secallona* (two popular types of sausage) or salad and follow with *paella*.

Desserts are called *postres*. All restaurants offer fresh fruit, but otherwise the range of *postres* is often limited – perhaps the famous *crema catalana (crème brûlée)*, or *flam* (crème caramel) and *natillas* (custard). Gourmet restaurants have more creative choices.

Vegetarians are rather poorly catered for. Some vegetable, salad and egg dishes will be vegetarian, but may contain pieces of ham or fish, so ask before you order.

All eating places welcome children and will serve small portions if requested.

Las Torres de Ávila *(see p137)*, a distinctive Barcelona bar

WINE CHOICES

DRY FINO WINES are perfect with shellfish, sausage, olives, soups and most first courses. Main dishes are often accompanied by wines from Penedès or Terra Alta *(see p28)* in Catalonia, or from Spain's other wine areas such as Rioja, Ribera del Duero and Navarra. Oloroso wines are often drunk as a *digestif. Cava (see pp28–9)* is popular for Sunday lunch.

SMOKING

IN FINE RESTAURANTS customers are offered cigars with their coffee and brandy. Many people in Spain smoke and very few restaurants have no-smoking areas or tables.

PRICES AND PAYING

IF YOU ORDER from *la carta* in a restaurant, your bill can soar way above the price of the *menú del dia*, especially if you order pricey items, such as fresh seafood, fish or *ibérico* ham. If there is an expensive fish such as sole or swordfish on the menu at a bargain price, it may be frozen. Sea bass and other popular fish and shellfish, such as large prawns, lobster and crab, are generally priced by weight

El compte (the bill) includes service charges and perhaps a small cover charge. Prices on the menu do not include seven per cent VAT *(IVA)*, which is usually added when the bill is calculated. Clients hardly ever tip restaurant waiters more than five per cent, often just rounding up the bill.

Cheques are rarely used in restaurants. Traveller's cheques in pesetas are usually accepted, but you might not be given change. The major credit cards and international direct debit cards are now accepted in most restaurants. However, do not expect to pay by credit card in smaller eating or drinking places like tapas bars, cafés, village *hostals* roadside *pubs* or *bodegues*.

WHEELCHAIR ACCESS

SINCE RESTAURANTS are rarely designed for wheelchairs, phone in advance (or ask the hotel staff to call) to check on access to tables and toilets.

Interior of Set Portes restaurant *(see p127)*, Port Vell, Barcelona

A Glossary of Typical Dishes

Olives

CATALAN CUISINE AT ITS BEST, using fresh food, is known as *cuina de mercat* (market cuisine) and there is nowhere better to see produce laid out than at Barcelona's Boqueria market *(see p135)*. Peppers glisten, fish sparkle and no meat is wasted – even cock's combs are sold for the pot. Olives come in all sorts of varieties. Spring brings *calçot* onions and broad (fava) beans, while strawberries, from Easter onwards, are eaten with *cava*. In autumn 30 varieties of mushroom spill across the stalls.

TAPES (TAPAS – SNACKS)

Bar-hopping around Barcelona is a delightful way to spend an evening, and a good way to try the many local dishes laid out on the counters.

Anxoves: anchovies.
Berberechos: cockles.
Bunyols de bacallà: salt cod fritters.
Calamars a la romana: fried squid rings.
Pa amb tomàquet: bread rubbed with tomato, garlic and olive oil – a good filler.
Panadons d'espinacs: small spinach pasties or pies.
Patatas bravas: potato chunks in spicy tomato sauce.
Pernil: ham – leg of pork seasoned and hung to dry.
Pescaditos: small fried fish.
Popets: baby octopus.
Truita: omelette.
Truita espanyola: traditional potato and onion omelette.

Pa amb tomàquet (bread with tomato), often served with ham

ENTRANTS (STARTERS)

These are often unusual dishes and two may be enough for a meal. Some may appear as main courses.

Amanida catalana: Catalan mixed salad *(see p26)*.
Arròs negre: black rice *(see p26)*. Can be a main course.

Produce at La Boqueria, Barcelona's huge covered market on La Rambla

Cargols a la llauna: snails in a spicy sauce.
Empedrat: salad of salt cod and white beans.
Escalivada: char-grilled or roasted aubergines (eggplant) and peppers, all drizzled with olive oil.
Espinacs a la catalana: spinach with pine nuts, raisins and anchovies; sometimes made with chard *(bledes)*.
Esqueixada: raw salt cod salad *(see p27)*.
Faves a la catalana: a broad (fava) bean stew of black pudding, bacon, onion and garlic.
Fideus: noodles, usually served with fish and meat.
Garotes: raw sea urchins, from the Costa Brava, eaten with bread, garlic or spring onions.
Musclos: mussels.
Ous remenats amb camasecs: scrambled eggs with wild mushrooms.
Pa de fetge: liver pâté.
Sardines escabetxades: pickled sardines.
Xató: salt cod and tuna salad with *romesco* sauce *(see p26)*.

SOPES (SOUPS)

Caldereta de llagosta: spiny lobster soup.
Escudella i carn d'olla: the liquid from Catalonia's

traditional hotpot; the meat and vegetables *(carn i olla)* are served as a main course.
Gaspatxo: a clear, cold soup with added raw vegetables.
Sopa de farigola: thyme soup.
Sopa de bolets: mushroom soup.

MAIN DISHES

Methods of cooking are: *a la brasa* (over open flames); *bullit* (boiled); *cremat* (crisp fried or caramelized); *estofat* (stewed); *farcit* (stuffed); *al forn* (in the oven); *a la graella/planxa* (cooked on a griddle, pan-fried or barbecued); *a la pedra* (on a hot stone).

PEIX I MARISCOS (FISH AND SHELLFISH)

Allipebre d'anguiles: spicy eel stew.
Anfós al forn: baked stuffed grouper.
Calamars farcits: squid stuffed with pork, tomatoes and onions.
Cassola de peix: fish casserole.
Congre amb pèsols: conger eel with peas.
Escamarlans bullits: boiled Dublin Bay prawns.
Gambes a la planxa: prawns cooked on a griddle.
Graellada de peix: mixed seafood grill.
Llagosta a la brasa: lobster cooked over open flames.
Llagostins amb maionesa: king prawns and mayonnaise.
Llobarro al forn a rodanxes: baked, sliced sea bass.
Lluç a la planxa: hake cooked on a griddle.
Molls a la brasa: red mullet cooked over open flames.
Orada a la sal: gilthead bream baked in salt, which is removed on serving.
Paella valenciana: paella with chicken and seafood.
Rap a l'all cremat: angler fish with crisped garlic.
Romesco de peix: seafood with the famous *romesco* sauce *(see p26)*. Tarragona's master *romesco* makers compete each summer.
Sarsuela: fish, shellfish and spices, everything goes into

the pot that gives its name to a light Spanish opera.

Sèpia amb pèsols: cuttlefish with peas.

Suquet de peix: Catalonia's principal fish stew, made with various fish, tomatoes, peppers, potatoes and almonds.

Verats a la brasa: mackerel cooked over open flames.

CARN (MEAT)

Ànec amb naps: duck with turnips, ideally the "black" turnips of the Empordà region; also sometimes served with pears *(ànec amb peres).*

Boles de picolat: meatballs in tomato sauce. Meatballs with cuttlefish *(sèpia)* is classic *mar i muntanya* food *(see p26).*

Butifarra amb mongetes: sausage and beans *(see p27).*

Bou a l'adoba: beef casserole.

Costelles a la brasa amb allioli: flame-roast lamb cutlets with garlic mayonnaise.

Costelles de cabrit rostides: roast goat kid cutlets.

Cuixa de xai al forn: roast leg of lamb.

Estofat de bou: beef stew with sausages, potatoes, herbs and sometimes a little chocolate.

Barcelona's cheese and honey market *(see p135)* in the Plaça del Pi

Estofat de quaresma: a filling Lenten vegetable stew.

Freginat: calf's liver with onions.

Fricandó: braised veal with wild mushrooms.

Llom de porc: pork chops.

Oca amb peres: goose with pears – traditional village festival fare.

Niu: a huge fish and meat stew from Palafrugell, Costa Brava, with pigeon, cuttlefish, cod tripe, pig's trotters, egg and garlic mayonnaise.

Peus de porc a la llauna: pig's trotters in a spicy sauce.

Pollastre amb samfaina: chicken with *samfaina (see p26).*

Pota i tripa: lamb's trotters and tripe.

Tripa a la catalana: tripe in *sofregit (see p26)* and wine with pine nuts and almonds.

Xai amb pèsols: lamb with peas.

CAÇA (GAME)

Although the hunting season is from October to February, some game is available all year round, especially rabbit.

Becada amb coc: woodcock in a bread roll.

Civet de llebre: jugged hare.

Conill a la brasa amb allioli: rabbit with garlic mayonnaise.

Conill amb cargols: rabbit with snails.

Conill amb xocolata: rabbit with garlic, liver, almonds, fried bread, chocolate and old wine.

Aubergines (eggplant) and peppers, used in abundance

Estofat de porc senglar amb bolets: wild boar casserole with wild mushrooms.

Guatlles amb salsa de magrana: quail in pomegranate sauce.

Perdiu: partridge.

Perdius amb farcellets de col: partridge with cabbage dumplings.

VERDURES (VEGETABLES)

Albergínies: aubergines (eggplant).

Bledes: chard.

Bolets: mushrooms.

Calçots: leek-sized green onions, roasted on an open fire and dipped in a spicy tomato sauce. A spring-time speciality of the Tarragona region.

Carbassó arrebossat: battered courgettes (zucchini).

Carxofes: artichokes.

Julivert: parsley.

Mongetes tendres i patates: French beans and potatoes.

Pastanagues: carrots.

Pebrots: red peppers.

POSTRES (DESSERTS)

Although *pastisseria* (pastries) and *dolços* (sweets) are very popular in Catalonia, desserts in restaurants are generally uneventful. The choice may be simply ice cream or fruit: apple *(poma)*, peach *(pressec)*, banana *(plàtan)*, orange *(taronja)*, grapes *(raïm)*.

Crema catalana: rich egg custard *(see p27).*

Figues amb aniset: figs in anise.

Flam: crème caramel.

Formatge: cheese. There is little local cheese.

Gelat: ice cream.

Mató: fresh goat's cheese, eaten with honey, sugar or jam.

Menjar blanc: an almond blancmange.

Peres amb vi negre: pears in red wine.

Postre de músic: a bowl of mixed nuts and dried fruit, once given as a reward to itinerant musicians.

Recuit: curdled sheep's (or cow's) milk in a small pot.

Mel i mató – a traditional dessert of soft cheese served with honey

Choosing a Restaurant

THE RESTAURANTS in this guide have been selected across a wide range of price categories for their good value, exceptional food and interesting location. The chart below lists restaurants in Barcelona by area; those in the *Further Afield* section are listed under their respective districts; and restaurants in the rest of Catalonia are arranged by town.

	CREDIT CARDS	TAPAS BAR	FIXED-PRICE MENU	GOOD WINE LIST	OUTDOOR TABLES

OLD TOWN

AGUT. Map 5 A3.   ℗
Carrer d'En Gignàs 16. 93 315 17 09.
Painters used to exchange their artwork for a hearty Catalan meal here. Specialities include aubergine (eggplant) terrine and Girona steaks. ● *Sun D, Mon.* ▤

	MC V		■	●	

CAL PEP. Map 5 B3.   ℗
Plaça de les Olles 8. 93 310 79 61.
According to some seafood fanatics, Pep's *peixet fregit* (fried fish) is the best in the world. Other recommended dishes include clams with ham, fried baby squid, and crayfish with onion. ● *Mon L, public hols, Easter.* ▤

	AE DC MC V	●			

EGIPTE. Map 5 A2.   ℗
La Rambla 79. 93 317 74 80.
This popular, lively place with a good-value menu serves Mediterranean specialities and salt cod prepared in ten different ways. ▤

	AE DC MC V		■	●	

PLA DE LA GARSA. Map 5 B2.   ℗
Carrer dels Assaonadors 13. 93 315 24 13.
This pretty restaurant, once the stables of a medieval palace, offers an exceptional-value lunch menu. Wide choice of quality pâtés and cheeses at night, and an interesting range of red wines. ● *Sun L & 24 Dec D, 25–26 Dec L.* ▤

	AE MC V		■	●	

LES QUINZE NITS. Map 5 A3.   ℗
Plaça Reial 6. 93 317 30 75.
Conveniently located, this attractive restaurant draws a young crowd and offers good Catalan dishes at reasonable prices. ▤ ♿

	AE DC MC V		■	●	

ROMESCO. Map 2 F3.   ℗
Carrer de Sant Pau 28. 93 318 93 81.
A popular spot just off La Rambla with home-style cooking, a lively atmosphere and unbeatable prices. The house speciality is *frijoles* (a Cuban dish of rice, black beans, fried banana and eggs). ● *Sun & Aug.*

		●	■		

LA VERONICA. Map 5 A3.   ℗
Carrer d'Avinyó 30. 93 412 11 22.
Functional but fun, this trendy pizzeria has been instrumental in the renaissance of this interesting district. Delicious *pizzes* (pizzas) which change according to season. Hot soups in winter, chilled soups in summer. Lively terrace day and night. ● *Mon L, Tue L.*

	MC V				■

AGUA. Map 6 D4.   ℗℗
Passeig Marítim de la Barceloneta 30. 93 225 12 72.
The latest trendy place to eat paellas, this designer restaurant on the beach offers a wide range of Mediterranean food and an appealing terrace. ▤ ♿

	AE MC V	●			■

AMAYA. Map 5 A1.   ℗℗
La Rambla 20-24. 93 302 10 37.
This classic, popular Basque-Catalan restaurant offers a good selection of tapas at the bar and half-portions of many dishes that appear on the encyclopedic menu. Fantastic wine list. ▤

	AE DC MC V	●	■	●	

CAFÈ DE L'ACADÈMIA. Map 5 B3.   ℗℗
Carrer de Lledó 1. 93 315 00 26.
This attractive restaurant gives a new interpretation to traditional Catalan cooking. Modern details and paintings combine well with ancient stone walls. Umbrellas shade candle-lit tables in the square. ● *Sat, Sun & public hols.* ▤

	AE DC MC V		■		■

CAN CULLERETES. Map 5 A2.   ℗℗
Carrer d'En Quintana 5. 93 317 30 22.
The city's oldest restaurant, established in 1786, serves traditional Catalan dishes such as *peix variat* (a seafood medley). ● *Sun D, Mon & 3 weeks Jul.* ▤

	MC V		■	●	

Price categories for a three-course evening meal for one, including a half-bottle of house wine, tax and service: Ⓟ under 3,000 ptas ⓅⓅ 3,000–4,500 ptas ⓅⓅⓅ 4,500–6,000 ptas ⓅⓅⓅⓅ over 6,000 ptas	**TAPAS BAR** In addition to the main dining room, there is a bar serving tapas and *racions* (larger portions). **FIXED-PRICE MENU** A good-value, fixed-price menu is offered at lunch or dinner, or both, usually with three courses. **GOOD WINE LIST** Denotes a wide range of good wines, or a more specialized selection of local wines. **OUTDOOR TABLES** Facilities for eating outdoors – on a terrace or in a garden or courtyard – often with a good view.	CREDIT CARDS	TAPAS BAR	FIXED-PRICE MENU	GOOD WINE LIST	OUTDOOR TABLES

CAN MAJÓ. Map 5 B5.   ⓅⓅ
Carrer de l'Almirall Aixada 23. ☎ 93 221 54 55.
This renowned seafood restaurant in Barceloneta serves great rice dishes such as a peeled shellfish paella and *suquet* (a delicious fish and potato stew). Extensive wine list. ● *Mon.* ▤

| | AE DC MC V | | ■ | ● | |

LOS CARACOLES. Map 5 A3.   ⓅⓅ
Carrer dels Escudellers 14 ☎ 93 302 31 85.
This bustling restaurant, just off La Rambla, serves straightforward dishes such as paella, suckling lamb, and chicken roasted on a spit. ▤

| | AE DC MC V | ● | | ● | |

ESTEVET. Map 2 F1.   ⓅⓅ
Carrer de Valldonzella 46. ☎ 93 302 41 86.
A traditional, welcoming restaurant decorated with the original tiles and paintings from appreciative customers. The ebullient owner will guide you with the starters. Try the roast shoulder of young goat. ● *Sun & 2 weeks in Aug.* ▤

| | AE DC MC V | | ■ | ● | |

FONDA SENYOR PARELLADA. Map 5 B3.   ⓅⓅ
Carrer de l'Argenteria 37. ☎ 93 310 50 94.
With wooden benches and old chandeliers, this atmospheric restaurant is a great choice for authentic Catalan cuisine. ● *Sun, public hols.* ▤

| | AE DC MC V | | | ● | |

REIAL CLUB MARÍTIM DE BARCELONA. Map 5 A4.   ⓅⓅ
Moll d'Espanya. ☎ 93 221 62 56.
A classic nautical club restaurant with spectacular views of the port. The elaborate cuisine includes dishes such as aubergine (eggplant) terrine with goat's cheese, and gilthead with apples and a cider sauce. ▤ ● *Sun D.*

| | DC MC V | | | ● | ■ |

EL SALÓN. Map 5 B3.   ⓅⓅ
Carrer de l'Hostal d'En Sol 6, 8, ☎ 93 315 21 59.
A refreshingly different restaurant-cum-bar with a great atmosphere and situated in a little street just off Plaça de Traginers. Its eclectic, ever-changing menu is mostly Mediterranean with a dash of Oriental charm. ● *Sun & public hols.* ▤

| | MC V | | | | |

CASA LEOPOLDO. Map 2 F3.   ⓅⓅⓅ
Carrer de Sant Rafael 24. ☎ 93 441 30 14.
This delightful restaurant, set in old stables and a carriage house, has been in the same family since 1929 and the menu, featuring good-quality regional dishes, has altered little since then. Good service. ● *Aug.* ▤

| | AE DC MC V | | ■ | ● | |

SET PORTES. Map 5 B3.   ⓅⓅⓅ
Passeig de Isabel II 14. ☎ 93 319 29 50.
This lavishly decorated restaurant is reminiscent of an elegant Parisian café. It serves 11 types of paella, and delicious home-made cannelloni. ▤

| | AE DC MC V | | | ● | |

CARBALLEIRA. Map 5 B3.   ⓅⓅⓅ
Carrer de la Reina Cristina 3. ☎ 93 310 10 06.
The first Galician seafood restaurant in Barcelona, and one of the best. For a superior lunchtime tapa at the bar, try the *arròs a la banda* – rice cooked in fish stock and served with *allioli* (garlic mayonnaise). ● *Sun D, Mon.* ▤

| | AE DC MC V | ● | | | |

TALAIA. Map 6 E5.   ⓅⓅⓅⓅ
Anexo Torre Mapfre, Carrer de la Marina 16. ☎ 93 221 90 90.
This stunning, sleek restaurant overlooking the Port Olímpic marina offers wonderful food. You can order half portions (*pica-pica*) of most dishes. ▤ ♿

| | AE DC MC V | | ■ | ● | |

EIXAMPLE

BILBAO. Map 3 B2.   ⓅⓅ
Carrer del Perill 33. ☎ 93 458 96 24.
A classic, bustling restaurant where little has changed since it opened in the early 1950s. Traditional seasonal Catalan home cooking. The wine list includes more than 30 types of *cava (see pp28–9).* ● *Sun, Aug & public hols.* ▤ ♿

| | | | ■ | ● | |

For key to symbols see back flap

Price categories for a three-course evening meal for one, including a half-bottle of house wine, tax and service:

Ⓟ under 3,000 ptas
ⓅⓅ 3,000–4,500 ptas
ⓅⓅⓅ 4,500–6,000 ptas
ⓅⓅⓅⓅ over 6,000 ptas

TAPAS BAR
In addition to the main dining room, there is a bar serving tapas and *racions* (larger portions).

FIXED-PRICE MENU
A good-value, fixed-price menu is offered at lunch or dinner, or both, usually with three courses.

GOOD WINE LIST
Denotes a wide range of good wines, or a more specialized selection of local wines.

OUTDOOR TABLES
Facilities for eating outdoors – on a terrace or in a garden or courtyard – often with a good view.

	CREDIT CARDS	TAPAS BAR	FIXED-PRICE MENU	GOOD WINE LIST	OUTDOOR TABLES
ROIG ROBÍ. Map 3 A2. ⓅⓅⓅ Carrer de Sèneca 20. 93 218 92 22, 93 127 97 38. Small, intimate restaurant offering authentic Catalan cuisine, with a lovely interior courtyard for summer. The terrines, fresh salads and any of the rice or seafood dishes are excellent. ● *Sat L & Sun.* 目	AE DC MC V		■	●	■
EL TRAGALUZ. Map 3 A3. ⓅⓅⓅ Passatge de la Concepció 5. 93 487 06 21. Two different dining concepts are offered here: the ground floor is a sushi bar, while the first has contemporary Mediterranean cuisine. The restaurant's logo is by graphic designer Javier Mariscal *(see p17)*. ● *Sat L, Sun & Aug.* 目	AE DC MC V	●	■	●	■

FURTHER AFIELD

	CREDIT CARDS	TAPAS BAR	FIXED-PRICE MENU	GOOD WINE LIST	OUTDOOR TABLES
EIXAMPLE ESQUERRA: *Chicoa.* ⓅⓅ Carrer d'Aribau 73. 93 453 11 23. A haven for lovers of salt cod, with more than ten different preparations of the celebrated *bacallà* on offer. As well as other seafood and meat dishes, there is a good Penedès rosé house wine. ● *Sun & Aug.* 目	AE MC V			●	
EIXAMPLE ESQUERRA: *Jaume de Provença.* ⓅⓅⓅ Carrer de Provença 88. 93 430 00 29. The chef's original and creative Catalan cuisine has established his restaurant as among the city's finest. Despite the business-like decor the food is excellent and the service attentive. ● *Sun D, Mon & Aug.* 目	AE DC MC V		■	●	
GRÀCIA: *Envalira.* **Map 3 B1.** ⓅⓅ Plaça del Sol 13. 93 218 58 13. Some would claim this family-run restaurant is the only place to sample Catalonia's famous rice dishes. The most unusual is *arròs a la milanesa.* They also serve individual paellas – a rarity. ● *Sun D, Mon, Aug, Easter & Christmas.* 目	AE MC			●	
GRÀCIA: *Giardinetto Notte.* **Map 3 B1.** ⓅⓅⓅ Carrer Granada del Penedès 22. 93 218 75 36. Mediterranean and Italian dishes are served in this romantic setting. Try the home-made pasta with a bottle of Catalan wine. ● *Sat L, Sun & Aug.* 目	AE DC MC V		■	●	
GRÀCIA: *Botafumeiro.* **Map 3 A2.** ⓅⓅⓅⓅ Carrer Gran de Gràcia 81. 93 218 42 30. Fine-quality seafood and Galician specialities are served in this stylish restaurant. Mouthwatering desserts and an extensive wine list. ● *Aug.* 目 ♿	AE DC MC V	●		●	
GRÀCIA: *Ot.* **Map 3 C2.** ⓅⓅⓅ Carrer de Torres 25. 93 284 77 52. Very small (eight tables). The customer has no choice here but is guaranteed a gourmet experience, thanks to the creative cooking of its two New Generation Catalan chefs. Advance booking essential. ● *Sat L, Sun, Aug & public hols.* 目	MC V		■	●	
PEDRALBES: *Neichel.* ⓅⓅⓅⓅ Beltrán i Rózpide 16. 93 203 84 08. European haute cuisine with Catalan touches is served in one of the city's most prestigious establishments. It has an excellent selection of cheeses and over 300 wine labels. ● *Sat L, Sun & 1–7 Jan, Easter, Aug.* 目	AE DC MC V		■	●	
POBLENOU: *Els Pescadors.* ⓅⓅⓅ Plaça de Prim 1. 93 225 20 18. Once a fisherman's tavern, this restaurant serves fish fresh from the quayside, excellent *a la llauna* (baked), especially *llobarro* (sea bass) or *dorada* (bream). Good game in season. ● *24–26 Dec, 31 Dec–1 Jan.* 目	AE DC MC V			●	■
SANT GERVASI: *La Balsa.* ⓅⓅⓅⓅ Carrer de la Infanta Isabel 4. 93 211 50 48. As well as exquisite Catalan cuisine, including an excellent goose liver starter, there are great views of Barcelona from the terrace of this restaurant. ● *Sun & Mon L.* 目	AE DC MC			●	■

SANTS: *Peixerot.* ⓅⓅⓅ
Torre Catalunya, Carrer de Tarragona 177. ☏ 93 424 69 69.
First-class seafood predominates on the menu of this comfortable, modern restaurant. Great rice dishes and shellfish. ● *Sun D.* ▤
AE DC MC V

TIBIDABO: *El Asador de Aranda.* ⓅⓅⓅ
Avinguda del Tibidabo 31. ☏ 93 417 01 15.
At the foot of Tibidabo, in a striking Modernista house, this very Castilian restaurant is a carnivore's dream: lamb roasted in a wood-burning oven is the speciality. Excellent wine list. ▤ *Sun D, public hols D.* ▤ ♿
AE DC MC V

TIBIDABO: *La Venta.* ⓅⓅⓅ
Plaça Doctor Andreu. ☏ 93 212 64 55.
An attractive restaurant at the foot of Tibidabo. Its glass-covered terraces, with views of the city, are open in summer and provide a bright, greenhouse setting in winter. Catalan-French cuisine. ● *Sun.* ▤
AE DC MC V

CATALONIA

ALTAFULLA: *Faristol.* ⓅⓅ
Carrer de Sant Martí 5 (Tarragona). ☏ 977 65 00 77.
Wine was once made in this delightful, 18th-century house, now decorated with antiques. Try the superb chocolate mousse. ● *Oct–May: Mon–Thu*
MC V

ANDORRA LA VELLA: *Borda Estevet.* ⓅⓅ
Carretera de la Comella 2 (Andorra). ☏ (00–376) 86 40 26.
This old country house, decorated in rustic style, is still used for the traditional practice of drying the tobacco grown nearby. Ask for the meat *a la llosa* (brought to you on a hot slate). ▤ ● *1 Jan.*
AE MC V

ARENYS DE MAR: *Hispania.* ⓅⓅⓅⓅ
Carrer Real 54, Carretera NII (Barcelona). ☏ 93 791 04 57.
Authentic Catalan cuisine which has won accolades from near and far. The classic clam *suquet*, similar to a fricassee, and the *crema catalana* (a rich caramel custard) are both delicious. ● *Sun D, Tue, Easter & Oct.* ▤
AE DC MC V

ARTIES: *Casa Irene.* ⓅⓅⓅ
Hotel Valartíes, Carrer Major 3 (Lleida). ☏ 973 64 43 64.
Located in a picturesque village, this restaurant offers wonderful, French-influenced food and three *menús de desgustació.* ● *Mon, Tue L & Nov.* ▤
AE DC MC V

BEGUR: *La Pizzeta.* Ⓟ
Ventura i Sabater 2 (Girona). ☏ 972 62 38 84.
It is essential to book in this popular alternative pizzeria in an elegant village house. It also serves unusual salads, pasta and grilled meat. Ideal for families. Interesting wines. ● *Tue, Oct–Easter.* ♿
AE MC V

BERGA: *Sala.* ⓅⓅ
Passeig de la Pau 27 (Barcelona). ☏ 93 821 11 85.
Classic Catalan dishes are offered here, many of which feature mushrooms. Game is available in season. ● *Sun D, Mon.* ▤
AE DC MC V

BOLVIR DE CERDANYA: *Torre del Remei.* ⓅⓅⓅⓅ
Camí Reial (Girona). ☏ 972 14 01 82.
This stunning palace surrounded by gardens has been impeccably restored and now houses an elegant restaurant and hotel. The chef will delight you with his gourmet dishes and superb wine selection. ▤
AE DC MC V

CALAFELL: *Giorgio.* ⓅⓅ
Carrer Ángel Guimerá 4 (Tarragona). ☏ 977 69 11 59.
Delicious home-made Italian food, served on a terrace overlooking the sea. The lasagne is legendary. ● *Mon–Thu.*
AE DC MC V

CAMBRILS: *Joan Gatell-Casa Gatell.* ⓅⓅⓅⓅ
Passeig Miramar 26, Cambrils Port (Tarragona). ☏ 977 36 00 57.
This restaurant is known for its seafood. The rice dishes, shellfish and lobster casserole are all first class. ● *Sun D, Mon & mid-Dec–mid-Jan.* ▤
AE DC MC V

CASTELL-PLATJA D'ARO: *Joan Piqué.* ⓅⓅⓅ
Barri de Crota 3 (Girona). ☏ 972 81 79 25.
A lovely, 14th-century *masia* (farmhouse) serving the innovative cuisine of the Empordà region, such as frogs' legs in pesto sauce. ● *Tue & Oct–Easter.* ▤
AE DC MC V

Price categories for a three-course evening meal for one, including a half-bottle of house wine, tax and service:

- ℗ under 3,000 ptas
- ℗℗ 3,000–4,500 ptas
- ℗℗℗ 4,500–6,000 ptas
- ℗℗℗℗ over 6,000 ptas

TAPAS BAR
In addition to the main dining room, there is a bar serving tapas and *racions* (larger portions).

FIXED-PRICE MENU
A good-value, fixed-price menu is offered at lunch or dinner, or both, usually with three courses.

GOOD WINE LIST
Denotes a wide range of good wines, or a more specialized selection of local wines.

OUTDOOR TABLES
Facilities for eating outdoors – on a terrace or in a garden or courtyard – often with a good view.

	CREDIT CARDS	TAPAS BAR	FIXED-PRICE MENU	GOOD WINE LIST	OUTDOOR TABLES
FALSET: *El Cairat.* ℗℗ Carrer Nou 3 (Tarragona). 977 83 04 81. One of the best restaurants in the Priorat wine-growing region. Creatively adapted local dishes include salt cod with aubergines (eggplant) and meatballs with wild mushrooms. Excellent local wines. ● *Sun D, Mon & Nov.*	AE MC V			●	
FIGUERES: *Ampurdán.* ℗℗℗ Hotel Ampurdán, Carretera NII (Girona). 972 50 05 62. Gourmets congregate here to enjoy Josep Mercader's legendary cuisine. The fresh broad beans (fava beans) with mint and the salt cod with a garlic mousseline are both exquisite. Delightful terrace for dining in summer.	AE DC MC V		■	●	■
LA FLORESTA: *Casa Blava.* ℗ Avinguda de Montserrat 26 (Barcelona). 93 674 93 51. Paellas are cooked here on open log fires. Also grilled meats and *calçots* in season (large spring onions grilled and served with a delicious sauce). Garden for children. Very close to Barcelona. ● *Wed & eve except Fri & Sat.*	AE DC MC V	●	■		■
GIRONA: *Cal Ros.* ℗℗ Cort Reial 4. 972 21 73 79. Typical Catalan food and other regional specialities are available at very reasonable prices in this old, but charming, establishment. ● *Sun D, Mon.*	MC V			●	■
GIRONA: *El Celler de Can Roca.* ℗℗℗ Carretera Taialá 40. 972 22 21 57. The capital's best restaurant, where Juan Roca creates imaginative dishes, such as lamb stuffed with sweetbreads and cinnamon. ● *Sun & Mon.*	AE DC MC V		■	●	
LLEIDA: *Forn del Nastasi.* ℗℗℗ Carrer Salmeron 10. 973 23 45 10. Excellent regional cuisine including chargrilled vegetables *(escalivada)* and snails *a la llauna* (oven-baked). ● *Sun D, Mon & 1st two weeks in Aug.*	AE DC MC V		■	●	
LLORET DE MAR: *El Trull.* ℗℗℗ Ronda Europa, Cala Canyellas (Girona). 972 36 49 28. Rustic dining room serving grilled lobster which you can choose from the aquarium. The *arrosat* (noodles with seafood) are also good.	AE DC MC V		■	●	■
MARTINET: *Boix.* ℗℗℗ Carretera N260 (Lleida). 973 51 50 50. A famous Catalan restaurant, located on the banks of the Riu Segre, serving roast leg of lamb so tender you can eat it with a spoon.	AE DC MC V		■	●	■
MONT-RAS: *La Cuina de Can Pipes.* ℗℗℗℗ Barri Canyellas (Girona). 972 30 48 87. This elegant, 18th-century farmhouse serves exquisitely delicate regional dishes. Try the *tournedo de foie.* ● *Jan & Feb, 1 Sep–14 Jul: Sun D–Wed L.*	MC V			●	
PERALADA: *Castell de Peralada.* ℗℗℗ Casino Castell de Peralada (Girona). 972 53 81 25. Dine in the incomparable medieval setting of this castle and try any of the dishes of the Empordà region and the castle's own house wine.	AE DC MC V		■	●	■
PERATALLADA: *Bonay.* ℗℗ Plaça de les Voltes 13 (Girona). 972 63 40 34. A timeless restaurant in an attractive village in the Empordà region. The succulent dishes include oca amb naps (goose with turnips). ● *Mon, Nov.*	MC V		■		■
PORRERA: *Lo Teatret.* ℗ Carrer del Onze de Setembre 4 (Tarragona). 977 82 81 61. This restaurant in the former village theatre serves traditional dishes with a modern touch: enjoy salt cod, herring, lamb or wild-mushroom cannelloni. Priorat wines – difficult to find in other parts of Catalonia. ● *Mon.*	MC V		■	●	■

Reus: *El Pa Torrat.* ⓅⓅ
Avinguda Reus 24, Castellvell del Camp (Tarragona). 977 85 52 12.
Home cooking with dishes such as roast rabbit with *allioli* (garlic mayonnaise)
and stuffed *calamars* (squid). ● *Sun D, Mon D; last two weeks Aug & Dec.*
AE DC MC V

Roses: *El Bulli.* ⓅⓅⓅⓅ
Cala Montjoi (Girona). 972 15 04 57.
Considered by many to be one of Spain's best restaurants and perhaps one of
Europe's most beautiful. Expensive, but worth it. ● *mid Oct–mid Mar.*
AE DC MC V

Sant Carles de la Ràpita: *Miami Can Pons.* ⓅⓅ
Avinguda Constitució nr. 37 (Tarragona). 977 74 05 51.
Good-quality Catalan cooking is served here by the Pons family. The *suquet*
and the *crema catalana* are just two of the specialities. ● *7-31 Jan.*
AE DC MC V

Sant Celoni: *El Racó de Can Fabes.* ⓅⓅⓅⓅ
Carrer de Sant Joan 6 (Barcelona). 93 867 28 51.
Santi Santamaría is considered one of Spain's best chefs and this delightful country
restaurant is a gastronomic paradise. The ever-changing seasonal menu
combines many types of fresh regional produce. ● *Sun D & Mon.*
AE DC MC V

Sant Feliu de Guíxols: *Can Toni.* ⓅⓅ
Carrer Garrofers 54 (Girona). 972 32 10 26.
Enjoy the traditional cooking of the Empordà region here. Many dishes include
mushrooms when in season (September–March). ● *Tue (in low season).*
MC V

Sant Sadurní d'Anoia: *El Mirador de les Caves.* ⓅⓅⓅ
Carretera Sant Sadurní-Ordal, Subirats (Barcelona). 93 899 31 78.
The duck with a foie gras and truffle sauce is one of the superb dishes served
here. ● *Sun D & Mon D, Aug 8-23.*
AE DC MC V

La Seu d'Urgell: *El Castell.* ⓅⓅⓅⓅ
Carretera N260 (Lleida). 973 35 07 04.
At the foot of La Seu d'Urgell castle, surrounded by beautiful countryside, lies
this idyllic hotel-restaurant serving modern Catalan cuisine. The wine list will
delight the most sophisticated wine lovers.
AE DC MC V

Sitges: *Al Fresco.* ⓅⓅ
Pau Barrabeitg 4 (Barcelona). 93 894 06 00.
Mediterranean and Oriental cuisines are expertly combined here. Superb desserts.
● *Mon & Tue in winter, Mon in summer & Dec–mid-Jan.*
AE DC MC V

Sitges: *El Velero* ⓅⓅⓅ
Passeig de la Ribera 38 (Barcelona). 93 894 20 51.
A seaside restaurant whose imaginative creations include sole fillets on a bed
of mushrooms topped with crab sauce, and lobster with a chickpea sauce.
● *Sun D & Mon (in winter)*
AE DC MC V

Tarragona: *El Merlot.* ⓅⓅⓅ
Carrer Caballers 6. 977 22 06 52.
Situated in the old part of town, this restaurant serves Mediterranean cuisine,
with specialities including dishes of game in season and home-made desserts.
● *Sun, Mon L.*
MC V

Tavertet: *Can Miquel.* Ⓟ
Les Fonts (Barcelona). 93 856 50 83.
Family-run restaurant serving hearty mountain dishes such as *estofat de porc
senglar* (wild boar stew) and *ànec amb peres* (duck with pears). ● *Mon & Tue.*
DC MC V

Valls: *Masia Bou.* ⓅⓅ
Carretera Lleida (Tarragona). 977 60 04 27.
Many interesting dishes are on offer, but the speciality is *calçotadas* (onions
charred over embers, served with *romesco* sauce – *see p26*). ● *Tue in summer.*
AE DC MC V

Vic: *Ca L'U.* ⓅⓅ
Plaça Santa Teresa 4 (Barcelona). 93 886 35 04.
Archetypal market-town restaurant serving wholesome stews and game. Famed
for its sole with prawns. Saturday market-day breakfasts, such as pigs' trotters
and bean stews, are not for the faint-hearted. ● *Sun D & Mon.*
DC MC V

Vic: *Floriac.* ⓅⓅ
Carretera Manresa-Vic, Klu 39, 5, Collsuspina (Barcelona). 93 743 02 25.
16th-century *masia* (farmhouse) serving quality regional cuisine and excellent
game dishes when available. Check winter opening. ● *2 weeks Feb, 2 weeks Jul.*
AE DC MC V

Cafés and Bars

THIS SECTION LISTS the best and most colourful cafés and bars in Barcelona, including both the traditional and the new and fashionable. Most cafés serve a small selection of alcoholic drinks as well as soft drinks, and most bars offer coffee, so customers will nearly always find something to their liking in any estabishment.

	CAFÉ	BAR	TAPAS SERVED	REGIONAL OR THEMED	NIGHTCLUB	OUTDOOR TABLES	LIVE MUSIC
OLD TOWN							
AL LIMÓN NEGRO: Map 5 A3 Carrer dels Escudellers Blancs 3. 【 93 318 97 70. One of the latest trendy places to hang out. Good food that changes every six months with the chef. ◑ 6pm–3am.		●	■				
BAR RA: Map 2 F2 Plaça de la Garduña 1. 【 93 301 41 63. A trendy, small, Post-Modern bar just behind La Boqueria market serving deliciously varied food. Good value lunch menu. ◑ 8am–2am.		●	■			●	
BOADAS: Map 5 A1 Carrer dels Tallers 1. 【 93 318 88 26. Barcelona's oldest and most atmospheric cocktail bar is run under the eagle eye of Maria Dolors Boadas, daughter of the Cuban-Catalan founder. Slick waiters mix heady potions – try a *mojito* (white rum with lemon juice, mint leaves and lots of ice). ◑ noon–2am Mon–Sat.		●					
BODEGA LA PALMA: Map 5 B3 Carrer de la Palma de Sant Just 7. 【 93 315 06 56. A well restored *bodega* (wine cellar), where wine from enormous barrels is served in ceramic pitchers. Excellent *truites* and *pa amb tomàquet (see p124)*. Bustling at breakfast time. ◑ 8am–3:30pm & 7–10pm Mon–Sat. ◉ Aug.		●	■				
CAFÉ MARÈS: Map 5 B2 Plaça de Sant Iu Nr 6. 【 93 310 30 14. A delightful summer café in the patio of the Museu Frederic Marès. A peaceful spot by the cathedral. ◑ Mar– end Sep: 10am–10pm Tue–Sun.	■						
CAFÉ ZURICH: Map 5 A1 Plaça de Catalunya. 【 93 317 91 53. Reopened in 1998 as a replica of the legendary café demolished to build El Triangle commercial centre, this born-again Zurich is rapidly reclaiming its status as a landmark and meeting place. ◑ May–Oct: 8am–1am; Nov–Apr: 8am–11pm.	■					●	
CASTELLS: Map 5 A1 Plaça Bonsuccés 1. 【 93 302 10 54. A friendly, bustling, local bar that has been in the same family since the 19th century. Fresh, home-made tapas. Busy on nights when Barça has won a match. ◑ 8am–2am Mon–Sat. ◉ Jul.		●	■				
GRANJA M VIADER: Map 5 A1 Carrer d'En Xuclà 4–6. 【 93 318 34 86. The oldest *granja* (milk bar) in Barcelona, where the famous Cacaolat (chocolate drink) was invented. *Suizos* (hot chocolate topped with cream), *ensaimadas* (yeast cakes) and *crema catalana (see p27)* are among its fattening delights. ◑ 9am–1:45pm & 5–8:45pm.	■						
IRATI: Map 5 A2 Carrer del Cardenal Casañas, nr 15–17. 【 93 302 30 84. One of the first in a new wave of bars in Barcelona, serving genuine Basque *pinchos* (tapas). Join the crush at the bar, take your pick, sip Basque Txakoli wine and count up the sticks to pay. Great fun. ◑ noon–midnight. ◉ Sun pm, Mon, Aug & Christmas.		●	■	●			
JAMBOREE: Map 5 A3 Plaça Reial 17. 【 93 301 75 64. Once a convent, this establishment is now one of the best jazz clubs in town, with a busy programme of national and international musicians. Disco from 1am. ◑ 10:30pm–5am.		●			■		■

TAPAS
Tapas are small snacks that may be either hot or cold and are charged for individually, allowing customers to choose as many or few as they like. A *ració* is a larger portion.

REGIONAL OR THEMED
Barcelona has many bars themed either on different regions of Spain or on other countries.

NIGHTCLUB
Most nightclubs and discos are open until 5 or 6am and charge entry fees.

OUTDOOR TABLES
In Barcelona, outdoor tables are usually on the pavement in a street or square, but cafés and bars at the Port Olímpic, Maremágnum and Port Vell often have terraces with sea views.

LIVE MUSIC
This is played regularly, each venue indicated having its own schedule.

	Café	Bar	Tapas Served	Regional or Themed	Nightclub	Outdoor Tables	Live Music
LA JARRA: Map 5 A3 Carrer de la Mercè 9. ☎ 93 315 17 59. Frequented for its *jamón canario* (ham cooked on the bone served with steamed potatoes) rather than its decor, this is an essential stop on a street full of tapas bars. ☐ 11am–2am. ● Wed & mid-Aug–mid-Sep.		●	■				
KASPARO: Map 5 A1 Plaça de Vicenç Martorell 4. ☎ 93 302 20 72. Interesting sandwiches and snacks are served all day long at this popular bar. Sit in the sun or enjoy the shade under the arches of this quiet square just behind Plaça Catalunya. ☐ 9am–midnight (11pm in winter). ● Jan.		●	■			●	
PASTIS: Map 2 F4 Carrer de Santa Mónica 4. ☎ 93 318 79 80. An atmospheric French bar that forms part of the history of this once rather seedy end of La Rambla. It offers *pastis* and timeless French music. Live on Sundays. ☐ 7:30pm–3:30am (2:30am Sat & Sun).		●		●			■
EL VASO DE ORO: Map 5 C4 Carrer de Balboa 6 ☎ 93 319 30 98. More a Madrileño concept than Catalan, this classic *cervesería* (beer-cellar) hidden behind the waterfront in Barceloneta serves draught beer in three sizes and delicious seafood tapas. The crush at the bar contributes to the atmosphere. ☐ 8am–midnight. ● 6 Sep–6 Oct.		●	■				
EL XAMPANYET: Map 5 B3 Carrer de Montcada 22. ☎ 93 319 70 03. Famous for its *xampanyet* (sparkling wine) and anchovies, this is the perfect spot in which to relax after visiting the Picasso Museum a few doors away. One of the prettiest bars around, it is decorated with original ceramic tiles. ☐ noon–4pm & 6:30–11pm. ● Sun eve, Mon & Aug.		●	■				

EIXAMPLE

	Café	Bar	Tapas Served	Regional or Themed	Nightclub	Outdoor Tables	Live Music
LA BODEGUETA: Map 3 A3 Rambla de Catalunya 100 ☎ 93 215 48 94. A smoky wine bar full of character and atmosphere – something of an oasis in the middle of the elegant Eixample district. ☐ 8am–1.30am.			●	■			
BRACAFÉ: Map 3 B5 Carrer de Casp 2. ☎ 93 302 30 82. Seriously good coffee in a classic, bustling café. Opened in 1932, its stylish interior has remained intact. Enjoy people-watching from the attractive covered terrace. ☐ 7am–11pm Mon–Sat, 9am–11pm Sun.	■					●	

FURTHER AFIELD

	Café	Bar	Tapas Served	Regional or Themed	Nightclub	Outdoor Tables	Live Music
ANTILLA BARCELONA Carrer de Arago 141-143. ☎ 93 451 21 51. This nightclub specializes in the sensual slide of salsa sounds, even offering classes to those who are not naturally funky. ☐ 10:30pm–5am.					■		■
KITTY O'SHEA'S Carrer de la Nau Santa Maria 5–7. ☎ 93 280 36 75. The first of Barcelona's various Irish pubs. The unpromising surroundings belie the authentic decor and atmosphere within. Delicious Irish beef and Sunday brunch. Charming staff. ☐ 11am–2am.		●		●			
SOL SOLER: Map 3 B1 Plaça del Sol 21. ☎ 93 217 44 40. On Gràcia's most popular square, this is a tapas bar with a difference: the tapas are tasty and unusual and the decor attractive, with marble tables, ceramic tiles and large mirrors. ☐ 7pm–2:30am.		●	■			●	

SHOPPING IN BARCELONA

A CITY WITH impeccable style, Barcelona is where you'll find the best in Catalan, Spanish and international design. For those in search of fashion, a good place to begin a tour of Barcelona is on the streets around the Passeig de Gràcia, which make up the most important shopping area, and where crowds browse among the well-known fashion and design stores. In this area there are also many

A Modernista shop window

interesting old stores such as bakeries, herbalists and pharmacies – some displaying beautiful Modernista frontages. For those who enjoy the hustle and bustle of small crowded streets, the Barri Gòtic, in the heart of the city, has something for everyone. Particularly interesting are the antiques dealers and the stores specializing in traditional crafts such as carnival masks, ceramics and handmade espadrilles.

Some of the beautifully displayed confectionery at Escribà

FOOD AND DRINK

B ARCELONA'S pastry shops are sights in themselves and, with its displays of chocolate sculptures, no *pastisseria* is more enticing or spectacular than **Escribà**. Other food stores also have a great deal of character, none more so than **Colmado Quílez** in the Eixample. This wonderful old place stocks a huge range of hams, cheeses and preserves, in addition to a comprehensive selection of Spanish and foreign wines and spirits.

DEPARTMENT STORES AND 'GALERIES'

T HE BRANCH of **El Corte Inglés**, Spain's largest department store chain, on Plaça Catalunya is a Barcelona landmark and a handy place to find everything under one roof, including plug adaptors and services like key-cutting. Other branches are located around the city. Barcelona's hypermarkets also sell a wide

range of goods. As they are on the outskirts of the city – south along the Gran Via towards the airport, and on the Avinguda Meridiana to the north – a car is the best way to reach them.

The *galeries* (fashion malls), built mostly during the affluent 1980s, are hugely popular. Both branches of **Bulevard Rosa**, on the Passeig de Gràcia and the Avinguda Diagonal, have hundreds of stores selling clothes and accessories. Also on the Avinguda Diagonal is **L'Illa**, a large, lively shopping mall containing chain stores as well as specialist retailers.

FASHION

I NTERNATIONAL fashion labels are found alongside clothes by young designers on and around the Passeig de Gràcia. **Adolfo Domínguez** stocks classically styled clothes for men and women; **Armand Basi** sells quality leisure and sportswear; and discount designer fashion is available at

Contribuciones. Many stores offer traditional, fine-quality tailoring skills and **Calzados E Solé**, which is situated in the Old Town, specializes in classic handmade shoes and boots.

SPECIALITY STORES

A WALK AROUND Barcelona can reveal a wonderful choice of stores selling traditional craft items and handmade goods that in most places have now been largely replaced by the production line. **La Caixa de Fang** has a good variety of Catalan and Spanish ceramics, among them traditional Catalan cooking pots and colourful tiles. **L'Estanc** has everything for the smoker, including the best Havana cigars. **La Manual Alpargatera** is an old shoe store that specializes in Catalan-style espadrilles. These are handmade on the premises and come in all colours. The city's oldest store, **Cereria Subirà** *(see pp52–3)*, sells candles in every imaginable form.

Menswear department in Adolfo Domínguez

DESIGN, ART AND ANTIQUES

IF YOU ARE interested in modern design, or just looking for gifts, you should pay a visit to **Vinçon**, the city's famous design emporium. Situated on the Passeig de Gràcia, it has everything for the home, including beautiful fabrics and furniture. A must is **BD-Ediciones de Diseño**, which has the feel of an art gallery. Housed in a building designed by Domènech i Montaner, the store has furniture based on designs by Gaudí and Charles Rennie Mackintosh, and sells wonderful contemporary furniture and accessories.

Most of the commercial art and print galleries are found on Carrer Consell de Cent, in

Mouthwatering fruit stalls in La Boqueria market

the Eixample, while the Barri Gòtic especially the Carrer de la Palla and Carrer del Pi – is the best place to browse around small but fascinating antiques shops. As well as fine furniture and old dolls, **L'Arca de l'Avia** sells antique silks and lace, all of which are set out in pretty displays.

BOOKS AND NEWSPAPERS

MOST CITY CENTRE newsstands sell English-language newspapers, but the best stocks of foreign papers and magazines are at FNAC at **L'Illa** and at **Crisol**, which also sells books, videos, CDs and photographic equipment.

The stylishly sparse display of furniture at Vinçon

MARKETS

NO-ONE SHOULD miss the chance to look around **La Boqueria** on La Rambla, one of the most spectacular food markets in Europe. Antiques are sold in the Plaça Nova on Thursdays, and cheese, honey and sweets in the Plaça del Pi on the first and third Friday, Saturday and Sunday of each month. On Sunday mornings coin, stamp and book stalls are set up in the Plaça Reial, and a craft market is held near the Sagrada Família. The city's traditional flea market, **Encants Vells** *(see p89)*, takes place on Mondays, Wednesdays, Fridays and Saturdays.

DIRECTORY

FOOD AND DRINK

Colmado Quílez
Rambla de Catalunya 63.
Map 3 A4.
[93 215 23 56.

Escribà Pastisseries
La Rambla 83. **Map** 2 F4.
[93 301 60 27.

Gran Via de les Corts
Catalanes 546. **Map** 2 E1.
[93 454 75 35.

DEPARTMENT STORES AND 'GALERIES'

Bulevard Rosa
Passeig de Gràcia 55.
Map 3 A4.
[93 309 06 50.

El Corte Inglés
Pl Catalunya 14. **Map** 5 B1.
[93 302 12 12.

L'Illa
Avinguda Diagonal 557.
[93 444 00 00.

FASHION

Adolfo Domínguez
P de Gràcia 89. **Map** 3 A3.
[93 215 13 39.

Armand Basi
Pl de Gràcia 49.
Map 3 A3.
[93 215 14 21.

Calzados E Solé
Carrer Ample 7.
Map 5 A3.
[93 301 69 84

Contribuciones
Riera de Sant Miquel 30.
Map 3 A2.
[93 218 71 40.

SPECIALITY STORES

La Caixa de Fang
C/ Freneria 1. **Map** 5 B2.
[93 315 17 04.

Cereria Subirà
Bajada Llibreteria 7.
Map 5 B2. [93 315 26 06.

L'Estanc
Via Laietana 4. **Map** 5 B3.
[93 310 10 34.

La Manual Alpargatera
C/ d'Avinyó 7. **Map** 5 A3.
[93 301 01 72.

DESIGN, ART AND ANTIQUES

L'Arca de l'Avia
Carrer dels Banys Nous 20.
Map 5 A2.
[93 302 15 98.

BD-Ediciones de Diseño
Carrer de Mallorca 291.
Map 3 B4.
[93 458 69 09.

Vinçon
P de Gràcia 96. **Map** 3 B3.
[93 215 60 50.

BOOKS AND NEWSPAPERS

Crisol
C/ Consell de Cent 341.
Map 3 A4.
[93 215 31 21.

MARKETS

La Boqueria
La Rambla 100. **Map** 5 A2.

Encants Vells
Plaça de les Glòries
Catalanes. **Map** 4 F5.

ENTERTAINMENT IN BARCELONA

FEW CITIES CAN MATCH the vitality of Barcelona, and nowhere is this more evident than in its live arts scene. The stunning Palau de la Música Catalana and the new Auditori de Barcelona have keen and critical audiences. They host some of the world's greatest classical musicians, including Montserrat Caballé and Josep (José) Carreras, both of whom are *barcelonins*.

Busker in the Barri Gòtic

Equally dynamic are the many exciting contemporary theatre and dance companies performing year round at indoor and outdoor venues. Modern music fans are well provided for at numerous rock, live jazz and salsa clubs, not to mention the buskers on La Rambla or in the squares of the Barri Gòtic. A tradition of old Barcelona that continues to thrive is its brash, glittering dance halls.

The magnificent interior of the Palau de la Música Catalana

ENTERTAINMENT GUIDES

THE MOST COMPLETE guide to what's going on each week in Barcelona is the *Guía del Ocio*, out every Thursday. It includes a cinema listings section. The Friday *El País* and *La Vanguardia* also have entertainments supplements.

SEASONS AND TICKETS

THEATRE AND concert seasons for the main venues run from September to June, with limited programmes at other times. In general, the city's varied menu of entertainments reflects its rich multi-cultural artistic heritage. In summer the city hosts the Festival del Grec *(see p31)*, a showcase of international music, theatre and dance, held at open-air venues. There is also a wide variety of concerts to choose from during the Festa de la Mercè *(see p32)* in September. The simplest way to get theatre and concert tickets is to buy

them at the box office of the relevant venue, although tickets for many theatres can also be bought from branches of the Caixa de Catalunya or La Caixa savings banks. Tickets for the Grec *(see p31)* festival are sold at tourist offices.

CLASSICAL MUSIC

BARCELONA's Modernista **Palau de la Música Catalana** *(see p61)* is one of the world's most beautiful concert halls, with its stunning interior decor and world-renowned acoustic. Also inspiring is the **Auditori de Barcelona**, opened in 1999 to give the city two modern halls for large-scale and chamber concerts. Its reputation was boulstered when it became the home of the Orquestra Simfònica de Barcelona.

Musical life suffered a setback when the Liceu opera house burned down in 1994. Fortunately, the city had enough credit in the bank of operatic excellence to ensure that its reputation remained un-

diminished. Restoration was completed in 1999, and the Liceu is now back in operation at full-octave level.

THEATRE AND DANCE

WORTH SEEING are Catalan contemporary theatre groups such as Els Comedians or La Cubana whose original style combines a thrilling mélange of theatre, music, mime and elements from traditional Mediterranean fiestas.

The **Mercat de les Flors** *(see p79)*, a converted former flower market in Montjuïc, is an exciting theatre presenting high-quality productions of classic and modern plays in Catalan. The new **Teatre Nacional de Catalunya** *(see p89)*, next to the Auditori de Barcelona, is another fine showcase for Catalan drama.

Although classical ballet has suffered from a lack of venues since the loss of the Liceu, there are many contemporary dance companies and regular performances are staged at the Mercat de les Flors in Montjuïc.

Outrageous stage show at one of Barcelona's many clubs

Auditorium of the Teatre Nacional de Catalunya

CAFÉS, BARS AND CLUBS

AMONG BARCELONA'S most famous modern sights are the hi-tech designer bars built in the prosperous 1980s, for example the **Mirablau**, which looks over the city. The **Torres de Ávila**, in the Poble Espanyol *(see p81)*, is the height of post-Modernism. **Otto Zutz** and the less chic but still fun **Apolo** both have live music. **La Paloma** is a fine dance hall complete with a 1904 interior where the *paso doble* rules.

Two of the best-known champagne and cocktail bars are in the old city: **Boadas** *(see p132)* and **El Xampanyet**. The **Bar Velódromo** is a friendly Art Deco café. The cafés on the secluded Plaça del Sol in the Gràcia district are an ideal place for a quiet drink.

ROCK, JAZZ AND WORLD MUSIC

BIG NAMES like David Byrne and Paul McCartney have performed at **Zeleste**. In summer, festivals and open-air concerts are held around the city. Jazz venues include the **Harlem Jazz Club** and **Jamboree**, and salsa fans will enjoy a quick slink down to **Antilla Barcelona**.

AMUSEMENT PARK

IN SUMMER, Barcelona's giant amusement park on the summit of **Tibidabo** *(see p88)* is open till the early hours at weekends, but also busy on other days. A visit is even more enjoyable if you travel there by tram, funicular or cable car.

SPORTS

THE UNDOUBTED kings of sport in Catalonia are **FC Barcelona**, known as Barça. They have the largest football stadium in Europe, Camp Nou, and a fanatical following *(see p87)*. Barcelona also has a high-ranking basketball team.

Packed house at the gigantic Camp Nou stadium

DIRECTORY			
CLASSICAL MUSIC	Map 4 F5. [93 306 57 00.	**La Paloma** Carrer del Tigre 27. **Map** 2 F1. [93 301 68 97.	**Harlem** **Jazz Club** Carrer de la Comtessa de Sobradiel 8. [93 310 07 55.
Auditori de **Barcelona** Carrer de Lepant 150. **Map** 6 E1. [93 317 10 96.	**CAFÉS, BARS** **AND CLUBS**		
	Apolo Carrer Nou de la Rambla 113. **Map** 2 E3. [93 441 40 01.	**Torres de Ávila** Poble Espanyol, Avinguda del Marquès de Comillas. **Map** 1 A1. [93 424 93 09.	**Zeleste** Carrer dels Almogàvers 122. **Map** 6 F2. [93 309 12 04.
Palau de la Música **Catalana** Carrer de Sant Francesc de Paula 2. **Map** 5 B1. [93 268 10 00.			
	Bar Velódromo Carrer de Muntaner 213. [93 430 51 98.	**El Xampanyet** Carrer Montcada 22. **Map** 5 B2. [93 319 70 03.	**AMUSEMENT** **PARK**
THEATRE AND **DANCE**	**Boadas** Carrer dels Tallers 1. **Map** 5 A1. [93 318 95 92.	**ROCK, JAZZ AND** **WORLD MUSIC**	**Tibidabo** [93 211 79 42.
Mercat de les Flors Carrer de Lleida 59. **Map** 1 B3. [93 426 18 75.	**Mirablau** Plaça Doctor Andreu. [93 418 58 79.	**Antilla Barcelona** Carrer de Aragó 141–143. [93 451 21 51.	**SPORTS**
Teatre Nacional **de Catalunya** Plaça de les Arts.	**Otto Zutz** Carrer de Lincoln 15. **Map** 3 A1. [93 238 07 22.	**Jamboree** Plaça Reial 17. **Map** 5 A3. [93 301 75 64.	**FC Barcelona** Camp Nou, Avinguda Aristides Maillol. [93 496 36 00.

Sports and Outdoor Activities

Fʀᴏᴍ ᴛʜᴇ ᴍᴏᴜɴᴛᴀɪɴꜱ to the sea, Catalonia provides all manner of terrain for enjoying the outdoor life. The hot summer months can be filled with water activities, from fishing to white-water rafting, while skiers head for the hills with the first snowfalls of winter. Nature lovers will find spectacular wildlife habitats, while Barcelona city offers beaches and numerous sports facilities.

City Facilities

Bᴀʀᴄᴇʟᴏɴᴀ ʜᴀꜱ ᴀʀᴏᴜɴᴅ 30 municipal pools *(piscines municipales)*, including the **Piscines Bernat Picornell** next to the **Estadi Olímpic** and **Palau Sant Jordi** sports stadia on Montjuïc. The pools were the venue for the 1992 Olympic swimming events. The Estadi Olímpic is an athletics stadium and is often used for concerts. The Palau Sant Jordi is used for indoor sports, as well as musical and recreational activities. Tennis fans are well provided for and the **Centre Municipal de Tennis Vall d'Hebron** caters for younger players too. Ice-skating can be fun and the **Pista de Gel del FC Barcelona** offers skate rental and runs an ice hockey school. Golf courses within easy reach of Barcelona are **Golf Sant Cugat** and **Golf El Prat**. There are several riding stables, and the **Escola Hípica** at Sant Cugat allows day outings over the Collserola hills. Cycle shops hire by the hour, half day and full day. **Un Cotxe Menys** organizes cycle tours around Barcelona.

Airborne Activities

Cᴀᴛᴀʟᴏɴɪᴀ ʜᴀꜱ several small airports where planes can be hired and parachute jumps made. Two well-known flying clubs are **Aeroclub** in Sabadell and **Grup Aeri** in La Selva (Girona province). Paragliding is popular from any high spot and **Free Evolució** offers all kinds of adventure sports, including bungee jumping and ballooning, as an exciting alternative way to see the sights.

Bird-watching

Bɪʀᴅ ʟɪꜰᴇ in Catalonia is a huge attraction for dedicated bird-watchers. Northern European visitors in particular will be thrilled by the sight of hoopoes, bee-eaters, golden orioles and pratincoles. Two major wetland areas, where migratory birds include flamingoes, are **Delta de l'Ebre** *(see p111)*, south of Tarragona, with a visitor centre in Deltebre, and **Aiguamolls de l'Empordà** around Sant Pere Pescador in the Bay of Roses. Both are easy to get to, and their visitor centres supply binoculars and guide services.

Griffon vulture

The best times to visit are early morning and evening. The Pyrenees are home to many raptors, including short-toed, golden and Bonelli eagles, and Egyptian, griffon and bearded vultures. The **Parc Natural del Cadí-Moixeró** *(see p96)*, in the foothills of the Pyrenees, has a visitor centre in Bagà. Look out for alpine choughs, wallcreepers and peregrine falcons, as well as black wood-peckers in the wooded areas.

An angler's paradise – fishing for trout amid spectacular scenery

Field Sports

Sᴇᴀ ꜰɪꜱʜɪɴɢ is free, but a permit *(un permís)* is required for river fishing. Permits can usually be obtained through local tourist offices.

The Noguera Pallaresa and Segre are fine trout fishing rivers and the season runs from mid-March to the end of August. The game-hunting season is generally from October to March, but it can vary. Short leases and permits can be obtained from the **Medi Natural** in Barcelona or from a local hunting association *(associació de caça)*. Travel agents specializing in hunting and fishing breaks will also readily organize licences.

Hiking

Aʟʟ ᴛʜᴇ ɴᴀᴛɪᴏɴᴀʟ ᴘᴀʀᴋꜱ and reserves publish maps and walking suggestions. Good areas close to Barcelona are the Collserola hills and the chestnut woods of Montseny. Long-distance GR *(Gran Recorrido)* footpaths criss-cross Catalonia and the walking

Paragliding above the Vall d'Aran in the eastern Pyrenees

Shooting the rapids on the white waters of the Noguera Pallaresa

possibilities in the **Parc Nacional d'Aigüestortes** (see p95) and the Pyrenees are particularly good, with mountain refuges (see p115) for serious hikers. Walkers can obtain advice and information from the **Centre Excursionista de Catalunya** (see p53). The **Llibreria Quera**, in Carrer de Petritxol in Barcelona's Barri Gòtic, is the best bookshop for maps and guidebooks.

All the usual rules apply to those setting off to explore the wilderness – check weather forecasts, wear appropriate clothing, take adequate provisions and let someone know where you are going.

WATER SPORTS

THERE ARE AROUND 40 marinas along Catalonia's 580 km (360 miles) of coast, and a very wide range of watersports and activities is available. In Barcelona itself, the **Centre Municipal de Vela Port Olímpic** gives sailing lessons and has a variety of craft. The Costa Brava has long been a

good spot for scuba diving. The best place is around the protected Illes Medes (see p103), from the resort of L'Estartit. There are also diving schools around Cadaqués and Cap Begur, notably at Calella de Palafrugell, launching point for the Illes Ullastres.

The town of Sort on the Riu Noguera Pallaresa is a centre for exciting water sports such as white-water rafting, canoeing, kayaking and cave diving. Bookings for these and other adventure activities can be made through **Guies del Pirineu** or **Super Esport**.

WINTER SPORTS

THE PYRENEES offer great winter skiing just two or three hours' drive from Barcelona and at weekends the resorts fill up with city crowds. There are some 20 ski areas. La Molina is good for beginners and Baqueira-Beret (see p95) is where Spain's royal family skis. Puigcerdà (see p96) in the Cerdanya is a good base for downhill and nordic skiing within reach of 15 ski stations in Catalonia, Andorra and France. The **Associació Catalana d'Estacions d'Esquí i Activitats de Muntanya** (ACEM) supplies resort details, while **Teletiempo**, a weather hotline, provides information on current weather conditions. In Barcelona, a dry ski slope has been installed beside the Piscines Bernat Picornell on Montjuïc.

Skiing at one of the many ski stations in the Pyrenees within easy reach of Barcelona

DIRECTORY

Aeroclub de Sabadell
93 710 19 52.

Aiguamolls de l'Empordà
972 45 42 22.

Associació Catalana d'Estacions d'Esquí i Activitats de Muntanya (ACEM)
93 416 01 94.

Centre Excursionista de Catalunya
93 315 23 11.

Centre Municipal de Tennis Vall d'Hebron
93 427 65 00.

Centre Municipal de Vela Port Olímpic
93 221 14 99.

Un Cotxe Menys
93 268 21 05.

Delta de l'Ebre
977 48 96 79.

Escola Hípica
93 589 89 89.

Estadi Olímpic/ Palau Sant Jordi
93 426 20 89.

Free Evolució
93 454 91 41.

Golf El Prat
93 379 02 78.

Golf Sant Cugat
93 674 39 08.

Grup Aeri
972 47 42 32.

Guies del Pirineu
93 415 58 38.

Llibreria Quera
93 318 07 43.

Medi Natural
93 304 67 00.

Parc Nacional d'Aigüestortes
973 62 40 36.

Parc Natural del Cadí-Moixeró
93 824 41 51.

Piscines Bernat Picornell
93 423 40 41.

Pista de Gel del FC Barcelona
93 496 36 30.

Super Esport
93 280 31 50.

Teletiempo
906 36 53 08.

SURVIVAL
GUIDE

PRACTICAL INFORMATION

CATALONIA has an excellent tourist infrastructure and Barcelona is particularly well organized for visitors. There are tourist offices in every town and all offer help in finding accommodation, restaurants and activities in their area. Larger offices usually have a wealth of leaflets in several languages. August is Spain's main vacation month.

Sign for a tourist office

Many businesses close for the whole month and roads are very busy at the beginning and end of this period. At any time of year, try to find out in advance if your visit will coincide with local *festes* (fiestas). Although these are attractions, they often entail widespread closures. It is a good idea to plan leisurely lunches, as most of Catalonia stops from 2pm to 4pm.

Sign to a town hall

A "closed" sign

LANGUAGE

THOUGH CATALAN is the language spoken by native Catalans, Catalonia is a bilingual country where people also speak *castellano* (Spanish). If you respond in Spanish to a question or greeting made in Catalan, the speaker will automatically switch to Spanish. All official signs and documents are in both languages. However, as Barcelona in particular regards itself as truly cosmopolitan, most tourist literature is also in English and French.

MANNERS

CATALANS GREET and say goodbye to strangers at bus stops, in lifts, in shops and in other public places. They shake hands when introduced and whenever they meet. Women usually kiss on both cheeks when they meet, and friends and family members of both sexes may kiss or embrace briefly.

VISAS AND PASSPORTS

VISAS ARE NOT required for tourists who are citizens of specified countries including the EU, Austria, Finland, Iceland, Liechtenstein, Norway, Sweden, the USA, Canada and

New Zealand. Spanish embassies will supply a list of the other countries in the non-visa category. Tourists from these countries may stay 90 days within a continuous 180-day period. The *Oficina d'estrangers de Barcelona* in the city (a local government office) deals with visa extensions. Proof of employment, study schedules, or sufficient funds for living are needed for a long stay. Tourists from certain other countries, including Australia, must first obtain an entry visa.

No parking sign

TAX-FREE GOODS AND CUSTOMS INFORMATION

NON-EU RESIDENTS can reclaim *IVA* (VAT) on single items worth over 15,000 pesetas bought in shops displaying a "Tax-free for Tourists" sign. (Food, drink, cars, motorbikes, tobacco and medicines are exempt.) You pay the full price and ask the sales assistant for a *formulari* (tax exemption form), which you ask customs to stamp as you leave Spain (this must be within six months of the purchase). You receive the refund by mail or on your credit card account. Banco Exterior branches at Barcelona airport will give refunds on completed *formularis*.

TOURIST INFORMATION

BARCELONA HAS three main *oficines de turisme* providing information on the city, its attractions, transport and

places to stay and eat, all run by **Turisme de Barcelona**.

A fourth office, in the Passeig de Gràcia, run by **Turisme de Catalunya**, a department of the Generalitat (Catalonia's government), provides information on the rest of the region. Other major towns have tourist offices providing information published by the Generalitat and the province's local administration *(patronat)*.

There is a Spanish National Tourist Office in the following English-speaking cities: New York, Chicago, Miami, Los Angeles, London and Toronto.

In Barcelona during the summer, pairs of young information officers, known as Red Jackets and generally English-speaking, provide tourist information in the streets of the Barri Gòtic, La Rambla and the Passeig de Gràcia.

Turisme de Catalunya's Barcelona office

OPENING HOURS

MOST MUSEUMS and monuments close on Mondays. On other days they generally open from 10am to 2pm and, in some cases, reopen from 4 or 5pm to 8pm. Churches may only be opened for services. In smaller towns it is common for churches, castles and other sights to be kept locked. The

◁ **Boats in Barcelona's Port Olímpic with the hill of Montjuïc in the background**

Students enjoy reduced admission fees to many museums and galleries

key *(la clau)*, available to visitors on request, will be with a caretaker, kept at the town hall *(ajuntament)*, or perhaps with the owners of the local bar. Admission is charged for most museums and monuments. On Sundays, museum admission is often free.

FACILITIES FOR THE DISABLED

CATALONIA'S association for the disabled, the Federació ECOM *(see p115)*, has hotel lists and travel advice for the whole region. Spain's national association, COCEMFE, has a tour company, **Servi-COCEMFE**, that publishes guide books to facilities in Spain and will help plan vacations.

COCEMFE sign for disabled access

Tourist offices and the social services departments of town halls supply information on local facilities. A travel agency, **Viajes 2000**, specializes in vacations for disabled people.

SPANISH TIME

SPAIN IS ONE HOUR ahead of Greenwich Mean Time (GMT) in winter *(l'hivern)* and two hours ahead in summer *(l'estiu)*, and uses the 24-hour clock. *La matinada* is the small hours, *el matí* (morning) lasts until about 1pm, while *migdia* (midday) is from 1 to 4pm. *La tarda* is the afternoon and evening. *La nit* is the night.

STUDENT INFORMATION

HOLDERS OF THE International Student Identity Card (ISIC) are entitled to benefits, such as discounts on travel and reduced entrance charges to museums and galleries. Information is available from all national student organizations and, in Barcelona, from **Viatgeteca**, which sells the international student card and youth hostel cards. **Unlimited Youth Student Travel** specializes in student travel.

ELECTRICAL ADAPTORS

SPAIN'S ELECTRICITY supply is 220 volts, but the 125-volt system still operates in some old buildings. Plugs for both have two round pins. A three-tier standard travel converter enables you to use appliances from abroad on both supplies. Heating appliances should be used only on 220 volts.

CONVERSION CHART

Imperial to metric
1 inch = 2.54 centimetres
1 foot = 30 centimetres
1 mile = 1.6 kilometres
1 ounce = 28 grams
1 pound = 454 grams
1 pint = 0.6 litre
1 gallon = 4.6 litres

Metric to imperial
1 millimetre = 0.04 inch
1 centimetre = 0.4 inch
1 metre = 3 feet 3 inches
1 kilometre = 0.6 mile
1 gram = 0.04 ounce
1 kilogram = 2.2 pounds
1 litre = 1.8 pints

DIRECTORY

CONSULATES

Australia
Gran Via de Carles III 98, 9°,
08028 Barcelona.
[93 330 94 96.

Canada
Passeig de Gràcia 77, 3°,
08008 Barcelona.
[93 215 07 04.

Ireland
Gran Via de Carles III 94, 10°-2ª
08028 Barcelona.
[93 491 50 21.

United Kingdom
Avinguda Diagonal 477,
08036 Barcelona.
[93 419 90 44.

United States
Passeig de la Reina Elisenda 23,
08034 Barcelona.
[93 280 22 27.

TOURIST OFFICES

Turisme de Barcelona
Plaça de Catalunya 17, subterrani,
08002 Barcelona.
[906 30 12 82.

Ajuntament, Plaça Sant Jaume 1,
08002 Barcelona.
[906 30 12 82.

Estació Sants, Pl Països Catalans,
08014 Barcelona.
[906 30 12 82.

Turisme de Catalunya
Palau Robert, Pg de Gràcia 107,
08008 Barcelona.
[93 238 40 00

DISABLED

Servi-COCEMFE
Calle Eugenio Salazar 2,
28002 Madrid.
[91 413 80 01.

Viajes 2000
Paseo de la Castellana 228-230,
28046 Madrid.
[91 323 10 29.

YOUTH/STUDENT

Unlimited Youth Student Travel & Viatgeteca
Carrer Rocafort 116-122,
08015 Barcelona.
[93 483 83 78.

Personal Security and Health

I N CATALONIA, as in most parts of western Europe, rural areas are quite safe, while towns and cities warrant more care. Keep cards and money in a belt, don't leave valuables in your car and avoid poorly lit areas at night. If you feel ill, there will always be a local *farmàcia* (pharmacy) open. In Spain, pharmacists prescribe as well as advise. Report lost documents to your consulate *(see p143)* and to the *Policia Nacional* at the local *comissaria* (police station). Emergency numbers are listed opposite.

Front of a high-street *farmàcia* (pharmacy) in Catalonia

IN AN EMERGENCY

T HE NEW NATIONAL telephone number throughout Spain for all emergency services is 112. After dialling, ask for *policia* (police), *bombers* (fire brigade) or *ambulància* (ambulance). Local numbers for the individual emergency services (opposite) still also apply. Outside Barcelona, the largely voluntary *Creu Roja* (Red Cross) often responds to 112 (or other) emergency calls for ambulances.

Ambulances take admissions to hospital *urgències* (accident and emergency) departments.

Creu Roja

Red Cross ambulance sign

URGÈNCIES

Accident and Emergency sign

MEDICAL TREATMENT

A NY EU NATIONAL who falls ill in Spain is entitled to social security cover. To claim medical treatment, UK citizens must obtain Form E111 from the Department of Health, a post office or GP surgery prior to travelling. This form must be given to anyone who treats you, so take several copies. It is normally contained within the booklet *Health Advice for Travellers*, which explains the health care you are entitled to, and where and how to claim. Not all treatments are covered by Form E111, so it is a good idea to arrange private medical insurance as well.

For private medical care in Spain ask at a tourist office, or at your consulate or hotel for the name and number of a doctor – if necessary, one who speaks English. Visitors from the US should make sure their insurance covers medical care abroad. If payment is needed at the time of treatment, ask for an itemized bill. Some insurance companies will ask for an official translation. Extra private cover may be needed for emergency hospital care.

PHARMACIES

F OR NON-EMERGENCIES, a *farmacèutic* (pharmacist) can advise and, at times, prescribe without a doctor's consultation. The *farmàcia* sign is an illuminated green or red cross. The addresses of those open at night or at weekends are listed in all pharmacy windows or may be found in local newspapers.

PERSONAL SECURITY

V IOLENT CRIME is rare but it is wise to take sensible precautions when out and about. Always be vigilant with handbags, wallets and cameras, especially in crowds, and take a taxi to your lodgings at night.

In Barcelona, pickpockets are more active at Plaça de Catalunya, Carrer Ferran, the cathedral, Sagrada Família and Sants station. Take extra care on La Rambla where muggings have been on the increase.

POLICE IN CATALONIA

U NTIL RECENTLY police services in Catalonia were organized into three forces as in the rest of Spain. This system still operates in some parts of Catalonia: the *Guàrdia Civil* (paramilitary Civil Guard), in olive-green, polices mainly borders, airports and rural areas; the *Policia Nacional*, in blue, deals with major crime in

Policia Nacional

Mosso d'Esquadra

Guàrdia Urbana

larger towns and national security, as well as immigration, work permits and residence documents; and the *Guàrdia Urbana*, also in blue, deals with traffic regulation and the policing of local communities.

The *Guàrdia Civil* and the *Policia Nacional* are gradually being replaced by an autonomous Catalan police force, the *Mossos d'Esquadra*. It is hoped that by 2004 the *Mossos* will have assumed all their predecessors' duties throughout the region. Girona province has almost achieved this, but in the city of Barcelona the *Mossos* still play a largely ceremonial role.

The current model of police car for the *Guàrdia Urbana*

A patrol car of the *Policia Nacional*

Fire engine showing the Barcelona fire service emergency number

LEGAL ASSISTANCE

SOME HOLIDAY (vacation) insurance policies cover legal costs and provide a helpline you can call.

If you are arrested, you have the right to telephone your consulate (*see p143*), which should have a list of bilingual lawyers. The *Col·legi d'Advocats* (Lawyers' Association) can guide you on getting legal advice or representation.

If you need an interpreter, ask your consulate or look in the *Pàgines Grogues* (Yellow Pages) telephone directory under *Traductors* (Translators) or *Intèrprets* (Interpreters). *Traductors oficials* or *jurats* are qualified to translate legal or official documents.

PERSONAL PROPERTY

HOLIDAY insurance is there to protect you financially in the event of the loss or theft of your property, but it is best to take preventative

An ambulance displaying the Barcelona 061 emergency number

measures – making use of hotel safes and avoiding carrying large sums of money.

Report a loss or theft straight away to the *Policia Nacional* at the local *comisaría*, as many insurance companies give you only 24 hours. You must make a *denúncia* (written statement) to the police and get a copy for your insurers.

Your consulate can replace a missing passport, but cannot provide financial assistance.

PUBLIC CONVENIENCES

PUBLIC CONVENIENCES are rare in Catalonia. Most people simply walk into a bar, café, department store or hotel and ask for *els serveis* or *el wàter* (in Catalan), or *los servicios* or *los aseos* (in Spanish). On motorways (highways), there are toilets at service stations. Women may have to ask for *la clau* (the key). Always carry toilet tissue with you, as it is often not provided.

OUTDOOR HAZARDS

CATALONIA'S HOT summers, combined with wind and bone-dry vegetation, are ideal for forest fires. To avoid the risk, extinguish cigarettes in car ashtrays and take empty bottles away with you.

If climbing or hill-walking go properly equipped and let someone know your route. Do not enter a *vedat de caça* (hunting reserve) or *camí particular* (private driveway).

DIRECTORY

EMERGENCY SERVICES

Police (*Policia*)
Fire Brigade (*Bombers*)
Ambulance (*Ambulància*)
[112 (national number).

Police (local numbers)
[091 – Policia Nacional
092 – Guàrdia Urbana (Barcelona, Lleida, Girona, Tarragona).
Fire Brigade (local numbers)
[080 (Barcelona), 085 (Lleida, Girona, Tarragona).

Ambulance (local numbers)
[061 (Barcelona), 091 (Lleida, Girona, Tarragona).

Banking and Local Currency

Y OU MAY ENTER SPAIN with an unlimited amount of
money, but if you intend to export more than one
million pesetas, you should declare it. Traveller's cheques
may be exchanged at banks, bureaux de change (canvi
in Catalan, cambio in Spanish), some hotels and some
shops. Banks generally offer the best exchange rates.
The cheapest exchange rate may be offered on your
credit or direct debit card, which may be used in cash
dispensers displaying the appropriate sign.

24-hour cash dispenser

BANKING HOURS

A S A RULE of thumb, banks
throughout Catalonia are
open from 8am to 2pm on
weekdays. Some open until
1pm on Saturdays, but most
remain closed on Saturdays in
August. Branches of some of
the larger banks in the centre
of Barcelona are beginning to
extend their weekday opening hours, but this is not yet
a widespread practice.

Bureau de change

CHANGING MONEY

M OST BANKS have a foreign
exchange desk signed
Canvi/Cambio or Moneda
estrangera/extranjera. Always
take your passport as ID to
effect any transaction.
    You can draw up to 50,000
pesetas on major credit cards
at a bank. Several US and UK
banks have branches in Barcelona, including **Bank of
America** and **Barclays**. If
you bank with them, you
can cash a cheque there.
    A bureau de change,
indicated by the sign
Canvi/ Cambio, or the sign
"Change", will invariably
charge higher rates of commission than a bank, but will
often remain open after hours.

Caixes d'estalvi/Cajas de
ahorro (savings banks) also
exchange money. They open
from 8:30am to 2pm on weekdays, and on Thursdays also
from 4:30pm to 7:45pm. They
have a highly visible profile,
actively supporting the arts
and good public works.

CHEQUES AND CARDS

T RAVELLER'S CHEQUES can be
purchased at American
Express (AmEx), Thomas Cook
or your bank. All are accepted
in Spain. If you exchange Am-
Ex cheques at an AmEx office,
commission is not charged.
You can purchase cheques in
pesetas from any bank. Euro-
cheques may also be used to
change money at a bank but
will be phased out before
European monetary union.
    The most widely accepted
card in Spain is the **VISA** card.
MasterCard (Access)/Euro-
card and **American Express**
are also useful currency. The
major banks will allow cash
withdrawals on credit cards.
    When you pay with a card,
cashiers will usually pass it
through a reading machine.
Sometimes, however, you will
be asked to punch your PIN
into a small keypad attached
to the machine.

Credit card reader with PIN keypad

CASH DISPENSERS

I F YOUR CARD is linked to
your home bank account,
you can use it with your PIN
to withdraw money from cash
dispensers, which are widespread. Nearly all take VISA
or MasterCard (Access) cards.
    When you enter your PIN,
instructions are displayed in
Catalan, Spanish, English,
French and German. Many
dispensers are inside buildings
these days, and to gain access
customers must run their cards
through a door-entry system.
    Cards with Cirrus and
Maestro logos can also be
widely used to withdraw
money from cash machines.

CURRENCY

THE CURRENCY of Spain is the peseta (plural pesetas), usually abbreviated to "pta", or "ptas". In Catalan it is known as the pesseta (plural pessetes) and abbreviated to "pta" and "ptes". It is common to speak of *duros* (the same in both languages) in popular speech: 1 *duro* is 5 pesetas, *cinc/cinco* (5) *duros* are equal to 25 pesetas and *mil* (1,000) *duros* is 5,000 pesetas.

Since January 1997 only coins minted after 1986 have been in use. All older ones were phased out to avoid confusion as so many designs were in circulation. The almost worthless 1-peseta coin is still in circulation despite proposals to withdraw it. It is little used and shop assistants giving change will often round the figure up or down to the nearest 5 pesetas.

The seven other denominations of coin now in use are easy to distinguish by shape and colour, but the designs will change periodically.

New coins are not sold in special commemorative packs, but are put straight into circulation and so stay around for a relatively long time – a useful tip for collectors. Coins commemorating the 1994 World Cup, for example, were still in circulation after the 1998 World Cup.

Spanish coins cannot be sold back to banks outside Spain.

1,000 pesetas

2,000 pesetas

Bank Notes
Spanish bank notes are in four denominations. The 1,000-peseta note (two designs, both in green) is the smallest, followed by the 2,000-peseta note (pink), the 5,000-peseta note (ochre with brown and purple) and the 10,000-peseta note (blue).

5,000 pesetas

10,000 pesetas

Coins
Spanish coins, shown here at actual size, are in denominations of 5 ptas, 10 ptas, 25 ptas, 50 ptas, 100 ptas, 200 ptas and 500 ptas. The 500-pta, 100-pta, 25-pta and 5-pta coins are all a dull gold. The 200-pta, 50-pta and 10-pta coins are all silver coloured.

5 pesetas

10 pesetas

25 pesetas

50 pesetas

100 pesetas

200 pesetas

500 pesetas

Communications

Standard issue postage stamp

Pᴜʙʟɪᴄ ᴛᴇʟᴇᴘʜᴏɴᴇꜱ, run by the Spanish telecommunications company Telefón-ica, are easy to find and operate with a card or coins, but international calls have a high charge. The postal service, Correos, is identified by a crown insignia in red or white on a yellow background. Registered mail and telegrams can be sent from all Correos offices. These also sell stamps, but it is more usual, and quicker, to buy them from *estancs* (tobac-conists). There are no public phones in Correos offices.

Logo of the Spanish telecom system

Uꜱɪɴɢ ᴀ Cᴏɪɴ ᴀɴᴅ Cᴀʀᴅ Tᴇʟᴇᴘʜᴏɴᴇ

1 Lift the receiver, and wait for the dialling tone and for the display to show *Inserte monedas o tarjeta.*

2 Insert either coins *(monedas)* or a card *(tarjeta).*

3 Key in the number firmly, but not too fast – Spanish phones prefer you to pause between digits.

4 As you press the digits, the number you are dialling will appear on the display. You will also be able to see how much money or how many units are left and when to insert more coins.

5 When your call is finished, replace the receiver. The phonecard will then re-emerge automatically or any excess coins will be returned.

Telefónica

A 1,000-peseta phonecard

Denominations of pesetas accepted in coin-operated telephones

Tᴇʟᴇᴘʜᴏɴɪɴɢ

Aꜱ ᴡᴇʟʟ ᴀꜱ ᴘᴜʙʟɪᴄ telephone boxes *(cabines)*, bars often have payphones. Both types take 5-, 25- and 100-peseta coins. There is a high minimum connection charge, especially for international calls, so ensure that you have plenty of change ready. Phone-cards are more convenient and can be bought at *estancs* and newsstands. Some phones are equipped with electronic multi-lingual instruction displays.

Calls can also be made from *locutoris* (public telephone offices) and paid for after-wards. The cheapest offices are run by Telefónica. Private ones, often located in shops, are much pricier.

The charges for international calls are divided into four bands: EU countries; non-EU European countries and North-west Africa; North and South America; and the rest of the world. With the exception of local calls, using the telephone system can be expensive, especially if calling from a hotel, which may add a sur-charge. A call from a *cabina*

Uꜱᴇꜰᴜʟ Sᴘᴀɴɪꜱʜ Dɪᴀʟʟɪɴɢ Cᴏᴅᴇꜱ

- When calling within a city, within a province, or to call another province, dial the entire number. The province is indicated by the initial digits: Barcelona numbers start with 93, Lleida 973, Girona 972 and Tarragona 977.
- To make an international call, dial 00, followed by the country code, the area code and the number.
- Country codes are: UK 44; Eire 353; France 33; US and Canada 1; Australia 61; New Zealand 64. It may be necessary to omit the initial digit of the destination's area code.
- For operator/directory service, dial 1003.

- For international directory enquiries, dial 1008 for EU countries and 1005 for the rest of the world.
- To make a reversed-charge (collect) call within the EU, dial 900 99 00 followed by the country code; to the US or Canada, dial 900 99 00 followed by 11 or 15 res-pectively. Numbers for other countries are in the A-K telephone directory under *Comunicaciones Internacionales.*
- To report technical faults, dial 1002.
- The speaking clock is on 093, the weather on 906 36 53 08, wake-up calls on 096.

or a *locutori* costs 35 per cent more than a call made from a private telephone.

Reversed-charge (collect) calls made to EU countries may be dialled directly, but most others must be made through the operator.

Spain abolished provincial area codes in 1998, so the full number, including the initial 9, must always be dialled.

POSTAL SERVICE

CORREOS, Spain's postal service, is rather slow. It is better to send any urgent or important post by *urgente* (express) or *certificado* (registered) mail, or to use a private courier service.

Post can be registered and telegrams sent from all Correos offices. However, it is more convenient to buy stamps for postcards and letters from an *estanc* (tobacconist's).

Postal rates fall into four price bands: the EU, the rest of Europe, the US, and the rest of the world. Parcels must be weighed and stamped by Correos and must be securely tied with string, or a charge may be made at the counter to have them sealed by a clerk.

Main Correos offices open from 8am to 9pm from Monday to Friday and from 9am to 7pm on Saturday. Branches in the suburbs and in villages open from 9am to 2pm from Monday to Friday and from 9am to 1pm on Saturday.

Catalan mailbox

ADDRESSES

IN CATALAN ADDRESSES the street name is written first, followed by the building number, the floor number, and the number or letter of the apartment. For example, C/ Mir 7, 5^e-A means apartment A on floor 5 of building number 7 in Carrer Mir. Carrer is often shortened to C/. Floor designations are: *Baixos* (ground floor), *Entresol*, *Principal*, 1^r, 2^n and so on, meaning that 2^n is in fact the 4th level above the ground.

Some of Catalonia's daily papers

Some newer buildings use the less complicated designation of *Baixos* followed 1^r, 2^n and so on upwards. Postcodes (zip codes) have five digits; the first two are the province number.

TELEVISION AND RADIO

CATALANS HAVE a choice of watching TV3 in Catalan run by the regional government, or TVE1 and TVE2, Spain's two state television channels. There is one independent Catalan channel, Canal 33, which has a high cultural content, and three Spanish independent stations: Tele 5, Antena 3, and Canal+ (Canal Plus). Some Canal+ programmes are only viewable with a station decoder. Most foreign films on television (and in cinemas) are dubbed. Subtitled films are listed as *V.O. (versión original)*.

Satellite channels such as CNN, Cinemanía and Eurosport and many other European channels can be received in Catalonia.

The main radio stations are Catalunya Ràdio, and COM Ràdio, the Spanish state Radio Nacional de España, and the independent stations Radio 2, broadcasting classical music, and Ser, a Spanish general-interest station.

Catalan magazines

NEWSPAPERS AND MAGAZINES

SOME NEWSAGENTS and kiosks in Barcelona city centre stock periodicals in English. Newspapers in English available on the day of publication are the *International Herald Tribune*, the *Financial Times* and the *Guardian International*. Others can be found a day after publication. *The European* newspaper and popular weekly news magazines such as *Time*, *Newsweek* and *The Economist* are readily available.

The main Catalan-language newspapers are *Avui* and *El Periódico* (the latter also having a Spanish edition). *La Vanguardia*, in Spanish, is published in Barcelona and is widely respected. The other Spanish newspapers with large circulations are *El País*, *El Mundo* and *ABC. El Mundo*, aimed at young people, tends to have a lot of news features; *El País* and *ABC* are very strong on international news.

Barcelona's best weekly listings magazine for arts, leisure events and eating out is *Guía del Ocio*, published in Spanish. Lifestyle and sports magazines are also popular.

A newsstand on La Rambla in Barcelona

TRAVEL INFORMATION

CATALONIA's three main airports – El Prat, Girona and Reus – receive international flights from all over the globe. While Barcelona's El Prat handles mainly scheduled services, Girona and Reus deal with package holiday flights. Rail networks and toll highways radiate from Barcelona to serve the region's major towns. Barcelona has a well-developed ringroad *(ronda)* system, and a tunnel through the Collserola Hills brings the inland highways right into the city. Both its Metro and suburban train links are excellent but, as much of Catalonia is mountainous, buses or a car are the only way to see many rural sights.

Spain's national airline

Duty-free shopping at Barcelona's El Prat airport

ARRIVING BY AIR

BARCELONA IS SERVED by many international airlines. The Spanish national carrier, **Iberia**, offers daily scheduled flights to Barcelona from all west European capitals. It also offers connections with eastern Europe, but the only direct flight is from Moscow. Direct flights from several other east European capitals are, however, offered by other airlines.

British Airways is currently the only UK airline offering scheduled flights to Barcelona, with daily flights from London Heathrow and London Gatwick and four flights a week from Birmingham. Iberia and **Debonair** both offer a direct service from Manchester.

Delta Air Lines and **TWA** each offer direct flights to Barcelona from the US. Iberia operates a comprehensive service from both the US and Canada, offering regular flights from Montreal via Madrid. No airlines operate direct flights between Spain and Australasia.

Catalonia's other two international airports handle charter flights: Girona serves the Costa Brava, and Reus, near Tarragona, the Costa Daurada.

For passengers arriving from Madrid or other Spanish cities, most of Spain's domestic flights are operated by Iberia, its associated airlines **Aviaco** and **Air Nostrum**, and **Air Europa**, **Pan-Air** and **Spanair**.

The most frequent shuttle service between Madrid and Barcelona is Iberia's Pont Aeri (Puente Aéreo). It flies every quarter of an hour at peak times and passengers can buy tickets just 15 minutes in advance using a self-ticketing machine. If a flight is full, those passengers still waiting are offered a seat on the next one. The flight takes 50 minutes. Other services between Madrid and Barcelona are less frequent but, on the whole, their prices tend to be lower.

Pont Aeri
Puente Aéreo

Sign for the shuttle service linking Barcelona and Madrid

The major international car rental companies *(see p155)* have desks at all three terminals of El Prat airport. Girona airport also has some of the main rental companies on site

(see p155)

DIRECTORY			
AIRPORT INFORMATION	**Canada** [(800) 772 4642.	**Delta Air Lines** [93 412 43 33 (Spain). [(800) 221 1212 (US).	**Costa Cruises** [93 487 56 85 (Spain). [020 7323 3333 (UK).
Barcelona El Prat [93 298 38 38.	**UK** [0990 341 341. **US** [(800) 772 4642.	**Pan-Air** [91 329 23 01 (Spain).	**Grimaldi Group** [93 443 98 98 (Spain).
Girona [972 18 66 00.	**OTHER AIRLINES**	**Spanair** [902 13 14 15 (Spain).	**Thomson Cruises** [0990 502 562 (UK).
Reus [977 77 98 00.	**Air Europa** [902 401 501 (Spain).	**TWA** [93 215 84 86 (Spain). [(800) 892 8466 (US).	**TRAVEL TO THE BALEARIC ISLANDS**
IBERIA, AVIACO, AIR NOSTRUM	**British Airways** [902 11 13 33 (Spain). [0345 222111 (UK).	**SEA TRAVEL**	**Buquebus** [902 414 242 (Spain).
International and domestic flights [902 400 500 (Spain).	**Debonair** [902 14 62 00 (Spain). [0541 500300 (UK).	**Atlas Cruises and Tours** [(800) 942 3301 (US).	**Trasmediterránea** [902 45 46 45 (Spain). [020 7491 4968 (UK).

EL PRAT AIRPORT, BARCELONA

Barcelona's airport is 12 km (7 miles) from the city centre. Terminal A handles international arrivals and foreign airlines' departures. Terminals B and C are for departures on Spanish airlines and arrivals from European Union countries. Trains to the Plaça de Catalunya in the city centre leave every 30 minutes. For inter-city rail services get off at Sants mainline station. There is also a shuttle bus, the Aerobus, running every 15 minutes, which will take you to Plaça de Catalunya.

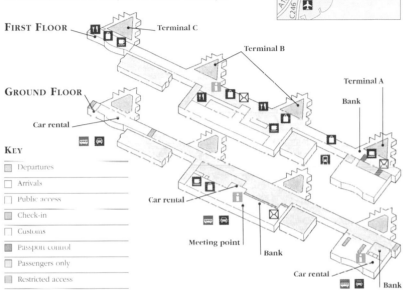

FIRST FLOOR — Terminal C

Terminal B

Terminal A

GROUND FLOOR

Bank

Car rental

KEY

- Departures
- Arrivals
- Public access
- Check-in
- Customs
- Passport control
- Passengers only
- Restricted access

Car rental

Meeting point

Bank

Car rental

Bank

---

and cars can be delivered to Reus from nearby Tarragona. There will also be local firms offering tempting deals, but read the small print carefully.

AIR FARES

AIR FARES to Barcelona and the coastal resorts vary through the year, depending on demand. They are generally highest during the summer months. Special deals, particularly for weekend city breaks in Barcelona, are often available in the winter and may include a number of nights at a hotel. Christmas and Easter flights are almost always booked up well in advance.

Charter flights from the UK to Girona and Reus can be very cheap, but tend to be less reliable, and often fly at unsociable hours.

Flying between Barcelona and other cities in Spain is an expensive way to travel compared with other options.

SEA TRAVEL

IN 1998 THE **Grimaldi Group** established a new scheduled ferry service between Genoa and Barcelona. US travel company **Atlas Cruises and Tours** offers transatlantic cruises between the US and Barcelona, as well as cruises around the Mediterranean. **Costa Cruises** offers Mediterranean cruises starting in Barcelona, while **Thomson Cruises**, in the UK, has cruises calling at Barcelona, but starting out from Mallorca.

TRAVEL TO THE BALEARIC ISLANDS

BARCELONA IS THE main city on the Spanish mainland from which to reach the Balearic Islands. Flights are run by Iberia, Air Europa and Spanair; a passenger hydrofoil (a kind of catamaran) service, which takes three hours, by **Buquebus**; and car ferry crossings, which take about eight hours, by **Trasmediterránea**. It is wise to book in advance, especially in summer.

Trasmediterránea car ferry to the Balearic Islands in Barcelona harbour

Travelling by Train and Metro

Metro and FGC rail services sign

THERE ARE TWO PROVIDERS of rail services in Catalonia. The Spanish national **RENFE** *(Red Nacional de Ferrocarriles Españoles)* operates Spain's inter-city services including first-class Talgo trains and some of Barcelona's commuter services *(rodalies)*. The Catalan government's **FGC** *(Ferrocarrils de la Generalitat de Catalunya)* runs some suburban trains in Barcelona and a number of special-interest services in Catalonia's provinces. Barcelona also has the Metro, an efficient city-wide network of underground (subway) trains.

Escalator down to a platform *(andana)* at Sants mainline station in Barcelona

ARRIVING BY TRAIN

THERE ARE DIRECT international train services to Barcelona from several European cities including Paris, Montpellier, Geneva, Zurich and Milan. Long train journeys can be made more bearable by booking a sleeping compartment on an overnight train. This option is only available on direct services. All trains entering the eastern side of Spain from France go through Port Bou/Cerbère or La Tour de Carol on the Franco-Spanish border. Travelling to Barcelona from departure points not offering a direct service may mean picking up a connection here. Most international trains arrive at Sants, Estació de França or Passeig de Gràcia mainline stations, all located in the centre of Barcelona.

Services to Barcelona from other cities in Spain are fast and frequent. From Madrid, Seville, Málaga, A Coruña or Vigo there is a service called **Auto-Express** which allows you to take your car with you.

Logo of the Spanish national rail service

EXPLORING CATALONIA BY TRAIN

CATALONIA HAS a network of regional trains *(regionals)* covering the whole of Catalunya and run by RENFE. There are three types – the *Catalunya Exprés* linking the main towns with few stops in between, and the *Regional* and *Delta* trains which take longer and stop frequently. A high-speed Euromed service from Barcelona to Tarragona (continuing south to Castelló, València and Alacant/Alicante) leaves from Sants station.

FGC *(Ferrocarrils de la Generalitat de Catalunya)* is a network of suburban trains run by the Catalan government in and around Barcelona. FGC also runs some other special services, such as Spain's only rack railway (cog railroad) from Ribes de Freser *(see inside back cover)* to Núria in the Pyrenees. It also runs the cable cars and funiculars at the Monastery of Montserrat *(see pp104–5)* and at Vallvidrera, as well as several historic steam trains and an electric train for tourists and enthusiasts. Details are available at the FGC station at Plaça de Catalunya or by calling the FGC number listed above.

(see inside back cover) ... *(see pp104–5)*

DIRECTORY

PUBLIC TRANSPORT

Information
[010.

RENFE Information and Credit Card Bookings
[93 490 02 02 (national).

[93 490 11 22 (international).

Auto-Express
[93 490 02 02.

Bige Tickets
Young People's Tourist Office,
Carrer de Calàbria, 147.
[93 483 83 83.

FGC Information
[93 205 15 15.

TMB Information
[93 298 70 00.

BUYING TRAIN TICKETS

TICKETS FOR TALGO, inter-city and international trains and for other *llarg recorregut* (long-distance) travel by train may be bought at any of the major RENFE railway stations from the *taquilla* (ticket office). They are also sold by travel agents, plus a booking fee. Reservations for national and international journeys can be made by phone using a credit card number, not less than 24 hours in advance.

Tickets for local and regional services are purchased from station booking offices. In larger stations they can be bought from machines. Tickets for *rodalies* (local services) cannot be reserved. A one-way journey is *anada* and a round trip is *anada i tornada*.

Ticket machine for *regionals* trains

Ticket machine for *rodalies* trains

Automatic ticket barriers at one of Barcelona's Metro stations

TRAIN FARES

RENFE OFFERS a ten per cent discount on specified days to encourage people to travel. They are called *dies blaus* (blue days) and are shown in blue on timetables. Fares for rail travel depend on the speed and quality of the service. Tickets for Talgo trains are more expensive than local and regional trains. RENFE offers discounts to children and people over 60, groups of ten and through travel cards on local, regional and long-distance trains. Tourists of any nationality, normally resident outside Spain, are eligible for a tourist railcard, available at RENFE stations, which allows unlimited travel on the RENFE network.

Interrail tickets for those under 26 and Eurodomino tickets for those over 26 are available to people from EU member states and ten other European countries. The Eurail pass, Euro pass and Eurail youth pass are for people from outside Europe. All of these tickets, which offer substantial discounts on rail travel, can be purchased at Barcelona's Sants and Estació de França stations. Bige tickets, available through the **Young People's Tourist Office**, are for people under 26, of any nationality, and carry a discount of up to 40 per cent on journeys from any point in Spain to Europe. To purchase one of these cards, you will need proof of your age and identity.

THE BARCELONA METRO

THERE ARE FIVE underground Metro lines in Barcelona, identified by number and colour. Platform signs distinguish between trains and their direction by displaying the last station on

Metro interchange sign showing where to change to another line

the line. In the street it is easy to spot a Metro station – look for a sign bearing a red "M" on a white diamond background. The Metro is usually the quickest way to get around the city, especially as some tickets are now valid for the Metro and some FGC lines. A RENFE or FGC sign at a Metro station

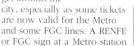

A one way (single) Metro ticket for Barcelona's subway

indicates a RENFE or FGC connection. Metro trains run from 5am to 11pm from Monday to Thursday, from 6am to midnight on Sunday, from 5am to 2am on Friday, Saturday and the day before a public holiday, and from 6am to 11pm on a weekday public holiday.

BARCELONA TICKETS AND TRAVELCARDS

VISITORS TO BARCELONA will find a comprehensive range of tickets and money-saving travelcards available to suit their itineraries and length of stay. Some cover train, bus and Metro. Combined tickets now allow travellers to hop from Metro to FGC train lines without leaving the station to pay again. Tickets are as follows: *T-dia* and *T-mes* tickets are for unlimited daily and monthly travel respectively; the *T-1* ticket, for ten single journeys, can be used on Metro, bus and FGC; the *T 2*, also for ten trips, is for combining journeys on Metro, bus and FGC in one trip; the *T-50/30* is for 50 journeys within 30 days on Metro and FGC. Details of special tourist travel cards available are described on the inside back cover of this guide.

USING A METRO TICKET MACHINE

Credit cards accepted by the machine are listed here.

3b. Insert credit card.

3c. Insert banknote(s).

4 Collect your ticket and any change due.

Logo of **Transports Metropolitans Urbans (TMB)**, which integrates all services.

1 Select language: Catalan/Spanish, English, French.

2 Select ticket: *senzill* (single trip), *T-2* (10 trips), *T-50/30* (50 trips in 30 days), then quantity required.

3a. Insert coins: the coins accepted are listed alongside.

Easy-reach language and ticket-type buttons for wheelchair users.

Venda de Bitllets

Travelling by Car and Bus

Barcelona road signs

DRIVING CONDITIONS in Catalonia vary enormously, from the dense road network and heavy traffic in and around Barcelona to almost empty country roads in the provinces, where villages, and in particular petrol (gas) stations, can be far apart. Toll highways (auto-pistes) are fast and free-flowing, but the ordinary main roads along the coast are usually very busy at all times of day. For tourists without private cars, joining an organized bus tour is a good way to visit well-known, but rather more remote, places of interest.

Canvi de sentit (slip or access road) 300 m (330 yd) ahead

ARRIVING BY CAR

MANY PEOPLE drive to Spain via the French motorways (highways). The most direct routes across the Pyrenees are the motorways through Hendaye in the west and Port Bou in the east. The most scenic routes snake over the top: the three main passes into Catalonia come down into the Vall d'Aran, Andorra, and Puigcerdà in the Cerdanya. From the UK, car ferries run from Plymouth to Santander and from Portsmouth to Bilbao in northern Spain.

Logo of the leading Spanish car-rental company

CAR RENTAL

INTERNATIONAL car rental companies, such as **Hertz**, **Avis** and **Europcar**, as well as some Spanish ones, such as **National ATESA**, operate all over Catalonia. You are likely to get better deals with international companies if you arrange a car from home. A hire car is un cotxe de lloguer. Catalonia's three main airports (see p150) have car rental desks. However, those at Girona and Reus have irregular opening hours, so if you need a car there, it is best to book in advance and they will meet your requirements. Avis offers deals in chauffeur-driven cars from major cities.

TAKING YOUR OWN CAR

A GREEN CARD and a bail bond from a motor insurance company are needed to extend your comprehensive cover to Spain. In the UK, the RAC, AA and Europ Assistance have sound rescue and recovery policies with European cover.

Vehicle registration, insurance documents and your driver's licence must be carried at all times. Non-EU citizens should obtain an international driver's licence; in the US, these are available through the AAA. You may also be asked for a passport or national identity card as extra identification.

A country of origin sticker must be displayed on the rear of foreign vehicles. All drivers must carry a red warning triangle, spare light bulbs and a first-aid kit. Failure to do so will incur on-the-spot fines.

DRIVING IN CATALONIA

AT JUNCTIONS give way to the right unless directed otherwise. Left turns across the flow of traffic are indicated by a canvi de sentit sign. Speed

limits for cars without trailers are as follows: 120 km/h (75 mph) on autopistes (toll motorways/highways); 100 km/h (62 mph) on autovies (non-toll motorways); 90 km/h (56 mph) on carreteres nacionals (main roads) and carreteres comarcals (secondary roads); 60 km/h (37 mph) in urban areas. There are on-the-spot speeding fines of up to 75,000 pesetas. The blood alcohol legal limit is 40 mg per millilitre – tests are frequently given and drivers over the limit are fined.

Front and rear seat belts must be worn. Ordinary leaded fuel (benzina), unleaded fuel (benzina sense plom) and diesel (gas oil) are all available everywhere and sold by the litre.

Speed limit 60 km/h (37 mph)

AUTOPISTES

ON TOLL MOTORWAYS (auto-pistes) long-distance tolls are calculated per kilometre. Over some stretches near cities a fixed toll is charged. There are three channels at the peatge (toll booths/plaza): Automàtic has machines for credit cards or the right coins; in Manual

A filling station run by a leading chain with branches throughout Spain

an attendant takes your ticket and money; for *Telepago* you need an electronic chip on your windscreen (windshield). *Autopistes* have emergency telephones every 2 km (1.25 miles) and service stations every 40 km (25 miles).

TAXIS

BARCELONA'S TAXIS are yellow and black, and display a green light when they are free. Most taxis are metered and show a minimum fee at the start of a journey. Rates increase after 10pm and at weekends, although the minimum fee stays the same. In unmetered taxis, such as those in villages, it is best to negotiate a price for the trip before setting off. Supplements are charged for going to and from the airport and for suitcases. **Radio Taxis** have cars adapted for disabled people, but they need to be booked a day ahead. They also have some cars that will take up to seven people.

One of Barcelona's taxis

PARKING

CENTRAL Barcelona has a pay-and-display system, with charges in force from 9am to 2pm and 4pm to 8pm Monday to Friday and all day Saturday. You can park in blue spaces for about 250 pesetas per hour. Tickets are valid for two hours but can be renewed. At underground car parks (parking lots), *lliure* means there is space, *complet* means full. Most are attended, but in automatic ones, you pay before returning to your car. Do not park where the pavement edge is yellow or where there is a private exit (*gual*). Signs saying "1–15" or "16–30" mean you can park on those dates in the month on the side of the street where the sign is placed.

Barcelona bus stop

Granollers bus station in Barcelona province

LONG-DISTANCE BUSES

SPAIN'S LARGEST inter-city bus company, **Autocares Julià**, is an agent for **Eurolines**. This runs regular services from all over Europe to Sants bus station in Barcelona. Buses from towns and cities in Spain arrive at Estació del Nord.

Julià Tours and **Pullmantur** offer tours of Barcelona. A number of companies run day trips or longer tours to places of interest in Catalonia. **Turisme de Catalunya** (see p143) in Barcelona has details of trips to all parts of Catalonia; in other towns, local tourist offices will know about tours in their provinces.

BUSES IN BARCELONA

AN EXCELLENT way to sightsee is by *Bus Turístic*. It runs from April through to December on two routes from Plaça de Catalunya. A ticket, bought on board, is valid for both routes and lets you get on and off or change routes as you please. The main city buses are white and red. You can buy a single ticket on the bus, or a *T-1* or *T-2* ten-trip ticket at Metro stations, valid for bus, Metro and FGC (see p153). Other combined tickets are described on the inside back cover. The *Nitbus* runs nightly from 10pm to 4am; the *TombBus* covers the big shopping streets from Plaça de Catalunya to Plaça Pius XII; and the *Aerobus* is an excellent service between Plaça de Catalunya and El Prat airport.

DIRECTORY

CAR RENTAL

National ATESA
📞 93 298 34 33 (Barcelona airport).
📞 902 100 101 toll-free in Spain.

Avis
📞 902 135 531 toll free in Spain.

Europcar
📞 93 298 33 00 (Barcelona airport).

Hertz
📞 902 102 405.

TOUR BUS OPERATORS

Autocares Julià
📞 93 402 69 00.

Eurolines
📞 020 7730 8235 in UK.
📞 93 490 40 00 in Barcelona.

Julià Tours
📞 93 317 04 34.

Pullmantur
📞 93 317 12 97.

BUS STATIONS

Estació del Nord
Carrer d'Alí Bei 80.
📞 93 265 65 08.

Estació de Sants
Carrer de Viriat.
📞 93 490 02 02.

TAXIS

Radio Taxis
📞 93 433 10 20/357 77 55.
📞 93 300 11 00/358 11 11 (taxis for the disabled).

BARCELONA STREET FINDER

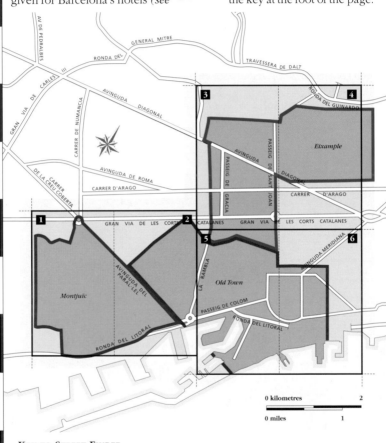

T HE MAP REFERENCES given with the sights, shops and entertainment venues described in the Barcelona section of the guide refer to the street maps on the following pages. Map references are also given for Barcelona's hotels (see pp116–21), restaurants (see pp126–31) and cafés and bars (see pp132–3). The schematic map below shows the areas of the city covered by the Street Finder. The symbols for sights, features and services are listed in the key at the foot of the page.

KEY TO STREET FINDER

▪ Major sight	⛴ Golondrina boarding point	✝ Church
▪ Place of interest	🚡 Cable car	✉ Post office
▪ Other building	🚡 Funicular station	═ Railway line (railroad)
⇌ Main train station	🚕 Taxi rank	← One-way street
Ø Local (FGC) train station	P Parking	▬ Pedestrianized street
◈ Metro station	i Tourist information	
▬ Main bus stop	✚ Hospital with A&E unit	**SCALE OF MAP PAGES**
▭ Bus station	🚓 Police station	0 metres 250
		0 yards 250

Street Finder Index

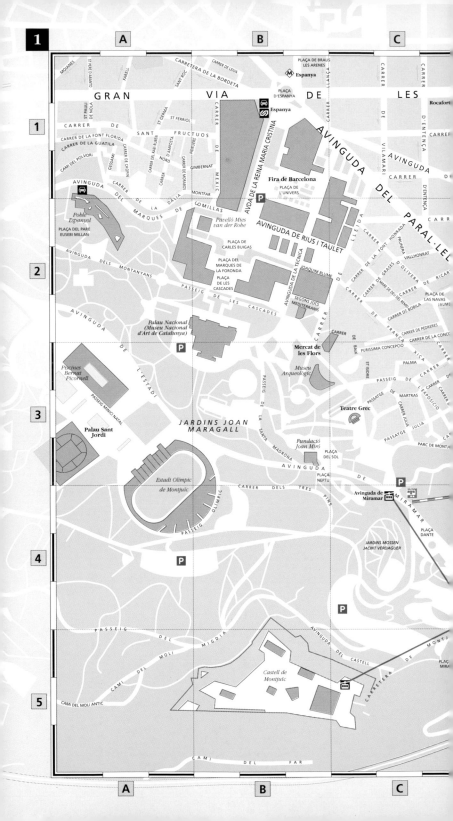

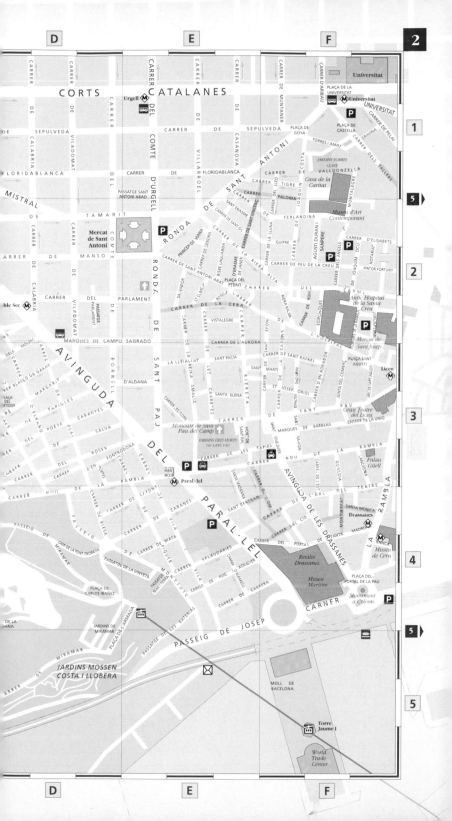

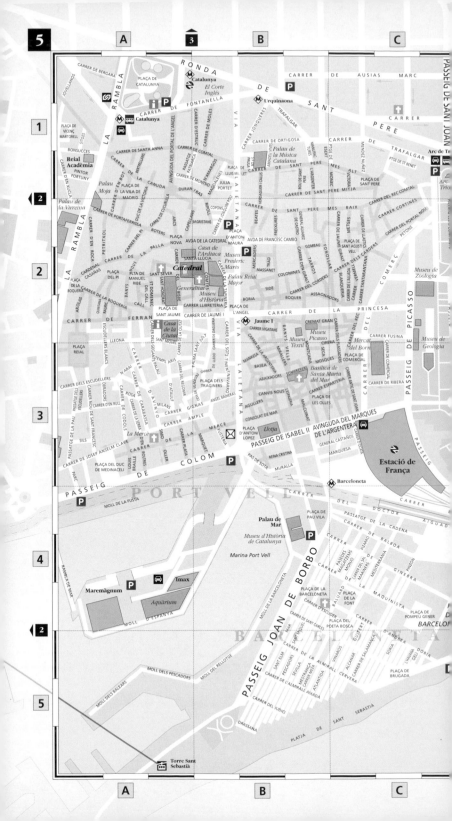

CARRER DE AUSIAS MARC
Auditori
de Barcelona
Teatre Nacional
de Catalunya
CARRER DE BOLIVIA

CARRER DE RIBES CARRER DE ALI-BEI CARRER DE TANGER

ALI-BEI
CARRER DE ROGER
Estació
del Nord
CARRER DE VILANOVA
CARRER DE LA MERIDIANA
CARRER DE SANCHO DE AVILA

PARC DE L'ESTACIO
DEL NORD

CARRER DELS ALMOGAVERS
CARRER DE SARDENYA
CARRER DELS ALMOGAVERS

Marina

CARRER DE BUENAVENTURA MUÑOZ
CARRER DE NAPOLS
AVINGUDA DE LA MARINA
CARRER DE JOAN
DE PALLARS

ASSEIG DE PUJADES
PERE IV
CARRER DE PUJADES
2

Bogatell
CARRER DE ZAMORA

ARC DE LA
CIUTADELLA
CARRER DE WELLINGTON
CARRER DE LLULL
CARRER DE CARRER DE LLULL

Museu d'Art
Modern
Universitat
Pompeu
Fabra
CARRER DE FRANCESC
CARRER DE RAMON
CARRER DEL PAMPLONA
TURRO
CARRER D'ALABA

Parlament de
Catalunya
CARRER DE
CARRER DE
DR
TRUFTA
CARRER DE FREDERIC

PARC
ZOOLOGIC
CARRER DE VILLENA
PARC
CARLES I
CARRER DE MOSSOS
CARRER DEL JOAN
CARRER DE BOGATELL
D'ICARIA

CIRCUMVAL·LACIO
Ciutadella-
Vila Olímpica
CARRER D'ARANDA
AVINGUDA DE LA MARINA
VILA
OLIMPICA

AIGUADER
CARRER DE SALVADOR ESPRIU
4

PLAÇA DEL
DOCTOR PONT I FREIXAS
PL. DELS
VOLUNTARIS
OLIMPICS
PARC DEL PORT OLIMPIC
PASSEIG MARITIM DE NOVA ICARIA

Hospital Nra
Sra del Mar
PASSEIG MARITIM DEL PORT OLIMPIC

PASSEIG MARITIM DE LA BARCELONETA
PLATJA DE LA BARCELONETA
MOLL DE LA MARINA
Port Olimpic
MOLL DE GREGAL
5

MOLL DE XALOC
Centre
Municipal
de Vela

Mar Mediterrani

General Index

Acknowledgments

DORLING KINDERSLEY would like to thank the following people whose contributions and assistance have made the preparation of this book possible.

MAIN CONTRIBUTOR

ROGER WILLIAMS contributed to the *Eyewitness Travel Guide to Spain* and has written Barcelona and Catalonia titles for Insight Guides. He was also the main contributor to the *Eyewitness Travel Guide to Provence. Lunch with Elizabeth David*, set around the Mediterranean, is his latest novel.

ADDITIONAL CONTRIBUTORS

Mary Jane Aladren, Pepita Arias, Emma Dent Coad, Rebecca Doulton, Josefina Fernández, Nick Rider, David Stone, Judy Thomson, Clara Villanueva.

DESIGN AND EDITORIAL ASSISTANCE

Special thanks are due to Amaia Allende, Queralt Amella Miró (Catalan Tourist Board), Gillian Andrews, Imma Espuñes i Amorós, Alrica Green, Elly King, Barbara Minton, Alícia Ribas Sos.

PROOFREADER

Stewart J Wild.

INDEXER

Hilary Bird

SPECIAL PHOTOGRAPHY

Max Alexander, D. Murray/J. Selmes, Dave King, Clive Streeter.

PHOTOGRAPHY PERMISSIONS

© Obispado de VIC; © Cabildo de la Catedral de Girona; Teatre Nacional de Catalunya (Barcelona); Institut Mpal. del Paisatge Urba i la Qualitat de Vida, Ajuntament de Barcelona.

Dorling Kindersley would like to thank all the cathedrals, churches, museums, restaurants, hotels, shops, galleries and other sights too numerous to thank individually.

PICTURE CREDITS

KEY: t=top; tl=top left; tlc=top left centre; tc=top centre; trc=top right centre; tr=top right; cla=centre left above; ca=centre above; cra=centre right above; cl=centre left; c=centre; cr=centre right; clb=centre left below; cb=centre below; crb=centre right below; bl=bottom left; b=bottom; bc=bottom centre; bcl=bottom centre left; br=bottom right; bcr=bottom centre right; d=detail.

Works of art have been reproduced with the permission of the following copyright holders:

Dona i Ocell Joan Miró © ADAGP, Paris & DACS, London 1999; *Morning* George Kolbe © DACS 1999, IOC/Olympic Museum Collections; Tapestry of the Foundation Joan Miró 1975 © ADAGP, Paris & DACS London; *Rainy Taxi* © Salvador Dalí - Foundation Gala - Salvador Dalí/DACS 1999.

The publisher would like to thank the following individuals, companies and picture libraries for their kind permission to reproduce their photographs:

ACE PHOTO LIBRARY: Mauritius 17t; AISA, Barcelona: 12b, 16b, 21bl, *San Jorge* Jaume Huguet 24c, 36, 37c, 40cb, 42c, 42bl, 144bc; AQUILA PHOTOGRAPHICS. Adrian Hoskins 94bla; 94bl; James Pearce 19b; NATIONAL ATESA: 154cr.

MIKE BUSSELLE: 91b, 93b, 94t.

CODORNIU: 29t, 29c; BRUCE COLEMAN COLLECTION: Erich Crichton 18tr; José Luis González Grande 19tr; Norbert Schwirtz 19tl; Colin Varwdell 19 cra; COCEMFE: 134c; COVER, Madrid: Pepe Franco 134c; Matias Nieto 139b.

EYE UBIQUITOUS: James Davies 104br. FREIXENET: 28c, 29b; FUNDACION COLLECTION THYSSEN-BORNEMISZA: *Madonna of Humility* Fra Angelico 87t;

FUNDACIO JOAN MIRO, Barcelona: *Flama en l'espai i dona nua* Joan Miró 1932 © ADAGP, Paris and DACS, London 1999 80t.

GODO PHOTO: 111t, José Luis Dorada 107t.

ROBERT HARDING PICTURE LIBRARY: 23tr, 57ca, 68ca, 80b, 81b.

THE ILLUSTRATED LONDON NEWS PICTURE LIBRARY: 43t; INDEX, Barcelona: CJJ.17b, 40t, 43c; IMAGE BANK: 22b, 69b; Andrea Pistolesi 84; IMAGES COLOUR LIBRARY: 22c, 151b; AGE Fotostock 76, 95b, 100–101, 135t, 135c, 138cr; NICK INMAN: 18b.

LIFE FILE PHOTOGRAPHIC: Xabier Catalan 23c; Emma Lee 23cra.

ORONOZ, Madrid: 37b, 38t, 38c, 41bl, 42t.

NATURAL SCIENCE PHOTOS: C Dani & I Jeske 138c; NATURPRESS, Madrid: 15b; Oriol Alamany 30c, 33b; Walter Kvaternik 33c, 44–45, 145b.

MAS SALVANERA: Ramón Ruscalleda 115t; MARY EVANS PICTURE LIBRARY: 45 (inset); JOHN MILLER: 90; MUSEU NACIONAL D'ART DE CATALUNYA: J. Calveras J. Sagrista 82-83; *La Compañia de Santa Barbara* 1891 Ramon Marti Alsina 41t, *El Tombant del Loing* Alfred Sisley 63t; MUSEU PICASSO: *Auto Retrato* Pablo Ruiz Picasso © DACS 1999 60bl, *Las Meninas* Pablo Ruiz Picasso 1957 © DACS 1999 61b.

PICTURES COLOUR LIBRARY: 70–71; PRISMA,Barcelona: 4t, *Paralelo Año 1930* Roger Bosch 8–9, 9 (inset), 16t, *Procesión en Santa María del Mar* Carbo Cases 24t, *Jardines de Aranjuez* 1907 Rusiñol y Prats 24b, *Esperando la Sopa* 1899 Isidro Monell y Monturiol 25t, *La Catedral de los Pobres* Mir Trinxet 25c, *Litografía* Tàpiés © ADAGP, Paris & DACS, London 1999 25b, 34–35, 41cb, 42 cra, 113 (inset), 134b, 137c, 141 (inset), 150ca, 155t; Carles Aymerich 20bl, 32c; A. Bofill 17c; Barbara Call 15t; Jordi Cami 30b; Albert Heras 2–3, 32b; Kuwenal 39t, 39c; Mateu 31c.

RAIMAT: 28cb; RED-HEAD: 50; REX FEATURES: 99cb; ELLEN ROONEY:1.

M ANGELES SÁNCHEZ: 31b; SCIENCE PHOTO LIBRARY: Geospace 10; SPECTRUM COLOUR LIBRARY: 22tr; STOCKPHOTOS, Madrid: 138b; Campillo 139t.

JACKET: all special photography except ELLEN ROONEY: front tl, t; ROBERT HARDING PICTURE LIBRARY: front cl; NATURPRESS: W. Kvaternik R. Olivas spine b.

FRONT END PAPER: clockwise John Miller; Image Bank Andrea Pistolesi; Red-Head; Images Colour Library/ AGE Fotostock.

English-Catalan Phrase Book

IN AN EMERGENCY

Help!	Auxili!	ow-**gzee**-lee
Stop!	Pareu!	**pah**-reh-oo
Call a doctor!	Telefoneu un metge!	teh-leh-fon-**eh**-oo oon **meh**-djuh
Call an ambulance!	Telefoneu una ambulància!	teh-leh-fon-**eh**-oo oo-nah ahm-boo-**lahn**-see-ah
Call the police!	Telefoneu la policia!	teh-leh-fon-**eh**-oo lah poh-lee-**see**-ah
Call the fire brigade!	Telefoneu els bombers!	teh-leh-fon-**eh**-oo uhlz boom-**behs**
Where is the nearest telephone?	On és el telèfon més proper?	on-ehs uhl tuh-leh-fon mehs proo-**peh**
Where is the nearest hospital?	On és l'hospital més proper?	on-ehs loos-pee-tahl mehs proo-**peh**

COMMUNICATION ESSENTIALS

Yes	Sí	see
No	No	noh
Please	Si us plau	sees plah-oo
Thank you	Gràcies	**grah**-see-uhs
Excuse me	Perdoni	puhr-**thoh**-nee
Hello	Hola	**oh**-lah
Goodbye	Adéu	ah-they-oo
Good night	Bona nit	**bo**-nah neet
Morning	El matí	uhl muh tee
Afternoon	La tarda	lah **tahr** thuh
Evening	El vespre	uhl **vehs**-pruh
Yesterday	Ahir	ah-**re**
Today	Avui	uh-voo-**ee**
Tomorrow	Demà	duh-**mah**
Here	Aquí	uh-**kee**
There	Allà	uh-**lyah**
What?	Què?	keh
When?	Quan?	kwahn
Why?	Per què?	puhr keh
Where?	On?	ohn

USEFUL PHRASES

How are you?	Com està?	kom uhs-**tah**
Very well, thank you.	Molt bé, gràcies.	mol beh **grah**-see-uhs
Pleased to meet you.	Molt de gust.	mol duh **goost**
See you soon.	Fins aviat.	feenz uhv-**yat**
That's fine.	Està bé.	uhs-**tah** beh
Where is/are . . .?	On és/són?	ohn ehs/**sohn**
How far is it to . . .?	Quants metres/ kilòmetres hi ha d'aquí a . . .?	kwahnz meh-truhs/kee-**loh**-muh-truhs yah dah-**kee** uh
Which way to . . .?	Per on es va a . . .?	puhr on uhs **bah** ah
Do you speak English?	Parla anglès?	**par**-luh an-**glehs**
I don't understand	No l'entenc.	noh luhn-**teng**
Could you speak more slowly, please?	Pot parlar més a poc a poc, si us plau?	pot par-**lah** mehs pok uh pok sees plah-oo
I'm sorry.	Ho sento.	oo **sehn**-too

USEFUL WORDS

big	gran	gran
small	petit	puh-**teet**
hot	calent	kah-**len**
cold	fred	fred
good	bo	boh
bad	dolent	doo-**len**
enough	bastant	bahs-**tan**
well	bé	beh
open	obert	oo-**behr**
closed	tancat	tan-**kat**
left	esquerra	uhs-**kehr**-ruh
right	dreta	**dreh**-tuh
straight on	recte	**rehk**-tuh
near	a prop	uh **prop**
far	lluny	**lyoon**yuh
up/over	a dalt	uh **dahl**
down/under	a baix	uh bah-**eeshh**
early	aviat	uhv-**yat**
late	tard	tahrt
entrance	entrada	uhn-**trah**-thuh
exit	sortida	soor-**tee**-tuh
toilet	lavabos/ serveis	luh-**vah**-boos sehr-**beh**-ees

| more | més | mess |
| less | menys | men**yees** |

SHOPPING

How much does this cost?	Quant costa això?	kwahn kost ehs-**shoh**
I would like . . .	M'agradaria . . .	muh-grad-uh-**ree**-ah
Do you have?	Tenen?	**tehn**-un
I'm just looking, thank you	Només estic mirant, gràcies.	noo-mess ehs-**teek** mee-**rahn** grah-see-uhs
Do you take credit cards?	Accepten targes de crèdit?	ak-**sehp**-tuhn tahr-**zhuhs** duh **kreh**-deet
What time do you open?	A quina hora obren?	ah **keen**-uh oh-ruh **oh**-bruhn
What time do you close?	A quina hora tanquen?	ah **keen**-uh oh-ruh **tan**-kuhn
This one.	Aquest	ah-**ket**
That one.	Aquell	ah-**kehl**
expensive	car	kahr
cheap	bé de preu/ barat	beh thuh **preh**-oo/bah-rat
size (clothes)	talla/mida	**tah**-lyah **mee**-thuh
size (shoes)	número	noo-mehr-oo
white	blanc	blang
black	negre	neh-gruh
red	vermell	vuhr-**mel**
yellow	groc	grok
green	verd	behrt
blue	blau	blah-oo
antique store	antiquari/botiga d'antiguitats	an-tee-**kwah**-ree/boo-tee-gah/dan-tee-ghee-**tats**
bakery	el forn	uhl forn
bank	el banc	uhl bang
book store	la llibreria	lah lyee-bruh-**ree**-ah
butcher's	la carnisseria	lah kahr-nee-suh-**ree**-uh
pastry shop	la pastisseria	lah pahs-tee-suh-**ree** uh
chemist's	la farmàcia	lah fuhr-**mah**-see-ah
fishmonger's	la peixateria	lah peh-shuh-tuh-**ree**-ah
greengrocer's	la fruiteria	lah froo-ee-tuh-**ree**-uh
grocer's	la botiga de queviures	lah boo-**tee**-guh duh keh-vee-**oo**-ruhs
hairdresser's	la perruqueria	lah peh-roo-kuh-**ree** uh
market	el mercat	uhl muhr-**kat**
newsagent's	el quiosc de premsa	uhl kee-**ohsk** duh **prem**-suh
post office	l'oficina de correus	loo-fee-**see**-nuh duh koo-**reh**-oos
shoe store	la sabateria	lah sah-bah-tuh-**ree**-uh
supermarket	el supermercat	uhl soo-puhr-muhr-**kat**
tobacconist's	l'estanc	luhs-**tang**
travel agency	l'agència de viatges	la **jen**-see-uh duh vee-**ad**-juhs

SIGHTSEEING

art gallery	la galeria d' art	lah gah-luh-**ree** yuh dart
cathedral	la catedral	lah kuh-tuh-**thrahl**
church	l'església	luhz-**gleh**-zee-uh
garden	el jardí	uhl zhahr-**dee**
library	la biblioteca	lah beb-blee-oo-**teh**-kuh
museum	el museu	uhl moo-**seh**-oo
tourist information office	l'oficina de turisme	loo-fee-**see**-nuh thuh too-**reez**-muh
town hall	l'ajuntament	luh-djoon-tuh-**men**
closed for holiday	tancat per vacances	tan-**kat** puhr bah-**kan**-suhs
bus station	l'estació d'autobusos	luhs-tah-see-**oh** dow-toh-**boo**-zoos
railway station	l'estació de tren	luhs-tah-see-**oh** thuh tren

STAYING IN A HOTEL

| Do you have a vacant room? | ¿Tenen una habitació lliure? | teh-nuhn oo-nuh ah-bee-tuh-see-**oh** **lyuh**-ruh |

double room with	habitació doble amb	ah-bee-tuh-see-oh doh-bluh am
double bed	llit de matrimoni	lyeet duh mah-tree-moh-nee
twin room	habitació amb dos llits/ amb llits individuals	ah-bee-tuh-see-oh am dohs lyeets/ am lyeets in-thee-vee-thoo-ahls
single room	habitació individual	ah-bee-tuh-see-oh een-dee-vee-thoo-ahl
room with a bath	habitació amb bany	ah-bee-tuh-see-oh am bahnyuh
shower	dutxa	doo-chuh
porter	el grum	uhl groom
key	la clau	lah klah-oo
I have a reservation	Tinc una habitació reservada	ting oo-nuh ah-bee-tuh-see-oh reh-sehr-vah-thah

EATING OUT

Have you got a table for...	Tenen taula per...?	teh-nuhn tow-luh puhr
I would like to reserve a table.	Voldria reservar una taula.	vool-dree-uh reh-sehr-vahr oo-nuh tow-luh
The bill please.	El compte, si us plau.	uhl kohm-tuh sees plah-oo
I am a vegetarian	Sóc vegetarià/ vegetariana	sok buh-zhuh-tuh-ree-ah buh-zhuh-tuh-ree-ah-nah
waitress	cambrera	kam-breh-ruh
waiter	cambrer	kam-breh
menu	la carta	lah kahr-tuh
fixed-price menu	menú del dia	muh-noo thuhl dee-uh
wine list	la carta de vins	lah kahr-tuh thuh veens
glass of water	un got d'aigua	oon got dah-ee-gwah
glass of wine	una copa de vi	oo-nuh ko-pah thuh vee
bottle	una ampolla	oo-nuh am-pol-yuh
knife	un ganivet	oon gun-ee-veht
fork	una forquilla	oo-nuh foor-keel-yuh
spoon	una cullera	oo-nuh kool-yeh-ruh
breakfast	l'esmorzar	les-moor-sah
lunch	el dinar	uhl dee-nah
dinner	el sopar	uhl soo-pah
main course	el primer plat	uhl pree-meh plat
starters	els entrants	uhlz ehn-tranz
dish of the day	el plat del dia	uhl plat duhl dee-uh
coffee	el cafè	uhl kah-feh
rare	poc fet	pok fet
medium	al punt	ahl poon
well done	molt fet	mol fet

MENU DECODER (see also pp26–7 & 124–5)

l'aigua mineral	lah-ee-gwuh mee-nuh-rahl	mineral water
sense gas/amb gas	sen-zuh gas/am gas	still/sparkling
al forn	ahl forn	baked
l'all	lahlyuh	garlic
l'arròs	lahr-roz	rice
les botifarres	lahs boo-tee-fah-rahs	sausages
la carn	lah karn	meat
la ceba	lah seh-buh	onion
la cervesa	lah-sehr-ve-sah	beer
l'embotit	lum-boo-teet	cold meat
el filet	uhl fee-let	sirloin
el formatge	uhl for-mah-djuh	cheese
fregit	freh-zheet	fried
la fruita	lah froo-ee-tah	fruit
els fruits secs	uhlz froo-eets seks	nuts
les gambes	lahs gam-bus	prawns
el gelat	uhl djuh-lat	ice cream
la llagosta	lah lyah-gos-tah	lobster
la llet	lah lyet	milk
la llimona	lah lyee-moh-nah	lemon
la llimonada	lah lyee-moh-nah-thuh	lemonade
la mantega	lah mahn-teh-gah	butter
el marisc	uhl muh-reesk	seafood
la menestra	lah muh-nehs-truh	vegetable stew
l'oli	loll-ee	oil
les olives	luhs oo-lee-vuhs	olives
l'ou	loh-oo	egg

el pa	uhl pah	bread
el pastís	uhl pahs-tees	pie/cake
les patates	lahs pah-tah-tuhs	potatoes
el pebre	uhl peh-bruh	pepper
el peix	uhl pehsh	fish
el pernil salat serrà	uhl puhr-neel suh-lat sehr-rah	cured ham
el plàtan	uhl plah-tun	banana
el pollastre	uhl poo-lyah-struh	chicken
la poma	la poh-mah	apple
el porc	uhl pohr	pork
les postres	lahs pohs-truhs	dessert
rostit	rohs-teet	roast
la sal	lah sahl	salt
la salsa	lah sahl-suh	sauce
les salsitxes	lahs sahl-see-chuhs	sausages
sec	sehk	dry
la sopa	lah soh-puh	soup
el sucre	uhl-soo-kruh	sugar
la taronja	lah tuh-rohn-djuh	orange
el te	uhl teh	tea
les torrades	lahs too-rah-thuhs	toast
la vedella	lah veh-theh-lyuh	beef
el vi blanc	uhl bee blang	white wine
el vi negre	uhl bee neh-gruh	red wine
el vi rosat	uhl bee roo-zaht	rosé wine
el vinagre	uhl bee-nah-gruh	vinegar
el xai/el be	uhl shahee/uhl beh	lamb
el xerès	uhl shuh-rehs	sherry
la xocolata	lah shoo-koo-lah-tuh	chocolate
el xoriç	uhl shoo-rees	red sausage

NUMBERS

Number	Catalan	Pronunciation
0	zero	seh-roo
1	un (masc)	oon
	una (fem)	oon-uh
2	dos (masc)	dohs
	dues (fem)	doo-uhs
3	tres	trehs
4	quatre	kwa-truh
5	cinc	seeng
6	sis	sees
7	set	set
8	vuit	voo-eet
9	nou	noh-oo
10	deu	deh-oo
11	onze	on-zuh
12	doce	doh-dzuh
13	tretze	treh-dzuh
14	catorze	kah-tohr-dzuh
15	quinze	keen-zuh
16	setze	set-zuh
17	disset	dee-set
18	divuit	dee-voo-eet
19	dinou	dee-noh-oo
20	vint	been
21	vint-i-un	been-tee-oon
22	vint-i-dos	been-tee-dohs
30	trenta	tren-tah
31	trenta-un	tren-tah oon
40	quaranta	kwuh-ran-tuh
50	cinquanta	seen-kwahn-tah
60	seixanta	seh-ee-shan-tah
70	setanta	seh-tan-tah
80	vuitanta	voo-ee-tan-tah
90	noranta	noh-ran-tah
100	cent	sen
101	cent un	sent oon
102	cent dos	sen dohs
200	dos-cents (masc)	dohs-sens
	dues-centes (fem)	doo-uhs sen-tuhs
300	tres-cents	trehs-senz
400	quatre-cents	kwah-truh-senz
500	cinc-cents	seeng-senz
600	sis-cents	sees-senz
700	set-cents	set-senz
800	vuit-cents	voo-eet-senz
900	nou-cents	noh-oo-cenz
1,000	mil	meel
1,001	mil un	meel oon

TIME

one minute	un minut	oon mee-noot
one hour	una hora	oo-nuh oh-ruh
half an hour	mitja hora	mee-djuh oh-ruh
Monday	dilluns	dee-lyoonz
Tuesday	dimarts	dee-marts
Wednesday	dimecres	dee-meh-kruhs
Thursday	dijous	dee-zhoh-oos
Friday	divendres	dee-ven-druhs
Saturday	dissabte	dee-sab-tuh
Sunday	diumenge	dee-oo-men-juh

DORLING KINDERSLEY *TRAVEL GUIDES*

TITLES AVAILABLE

THE GUIDES THAT SHOW YOU WHAT OTHERS ONLY TELL YOU

COUNTRY GUIDES

AUSTRALIA • CANADA • FRANCE • GREAT BRITAIN
GREECE: ATHENS & THE MAINLAND • THE GREEK ISLANDS
IRELAND • ITALY • MEXICO • PORTUGAL • SCOTLAND
SOUTH AFRICA • SPAIN • THAILAND

REGIONAL GUIDES

BARCELONA & CATALONIA • CALIFORNIA
FLORENCE & TUSCANY • FLORIDA • HAWAII
JERUSALEM & THE HOLY LAND • LOIRE VALLEY
MILAN & THE LAKES • NAPLES WITH POMPEII & THE
AMALFI COAST • PROVENCE & THE COTE D'AZUR • SARDINIA
SEVILLE & ANDALUSIA • SICILY • VENICE & THE VENETO
GREAT PLACES TO STAY IN EUROPE

CITY GUIDES

AMSTERDAM • BERLIN • BUDAPEST • DUBLIN • ISTANBUL
LISBON • LONDON • MADRID • MOSCOW • NEW YORK
PARIS • PRAGUE • ROME • SAN FRANCISCO
ST PETERSBURG • SYDNEY • VIENNA • WARSAW

TRAVEL PLANNERS

AUSTRALIA • FRANCE • FLORIDA
GREAT BRITAIN & IRELAND • ITALY • SPAIN

DK TRAVEL GUIDES CITY MAPS

LONDON • NEW YORK • PARIS • ROME
SAN FRANCISCO • SYDNEY

DK TRAVEL GUIDES PHRASE BOOKS

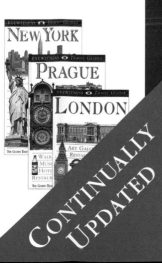

CONTINUALLY UPDATED

Rail Transport Maps

The main map shows the whole of Barcelona's Metro system, which has 111 stations on five lines. It also shows the city's FGC suburban lines, funiculars and tram *(see pp152–3)*. Public transport in Barcelona is modern and efficient, and the drive for a more integrated system is progressing rapidly – combined tickets now allow interchange between different modes of transport. A special ticket for tourists is the *Barcelona Card*, available in one-day, two-day or three-day values, which offers unlimited travel on Metro and bus, and discounts at leading sights and museums. The inset map shows Catalonia's mainline rail network, which is run by RENFE, the Spanish state system. The stations selected for inclusion here are those closest to sights described in this guide.

KEY

▬ Metro Line 1	▬ RENFE airport-rail connection
▬ Metro Line 2	✚ Funicular
▬ Metro Line 3	═ Tramvia Blau (Blue Tram)
▬ Metro Line 4	○ Interchange station
▬ Metro Line 5	⮑ RENFE mainline train station
▬ FGC train service (Ferrocarrils de la Generalitat de Catalunya)	

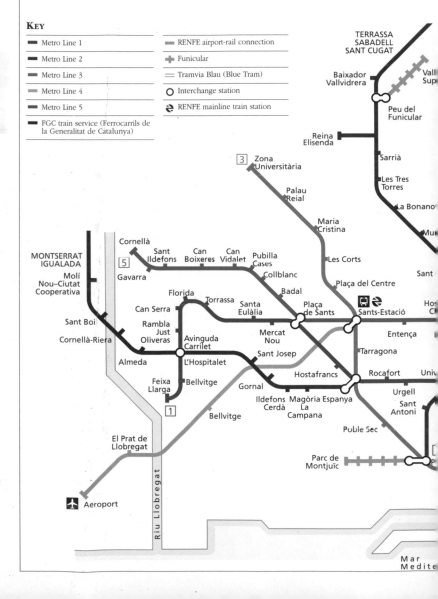